*f*P

THE RULE OF THREE

Surviving and Thriving
in Competitive Markets

JAGDISH SHETH
AND RAJENDRA SISODIA

THE FREE PRESS

New York   London   Toronto   Sydney   Singapore

THE FREE PRESS
A Division of Simon & Schuster, Inc.
1230 Avenue of the Americas
New York, NY 10020

THE FREE PRESS and colophon are trademarks
of Simon & Schuster, Inc.

For information regarding special discounts for bulk purchases, please contact
Simon & Schuster Special Sales at 1-800-456-6798 or business@simonand
schuster.com

Book design by Susan Hood

Manufactured in the United States of America

10 9 8 7 6 5 4 3 2 1

Library of Congress Cataloging-in-Publication Data

Sheth, Jagdish
The rule of three : surviving and thriving in competitive markets /
Jagdish Sheth and Rajendra Sisodia.
p. cm.
Includes bibliographical references (p.) and index.
1. Competition.   2. Efficiency, Industrial.   I. Sisodia, Rajendra.   II. Title.

HD41 .S542 2001
658—dc21   2001050118

ISBN 0-7432-0560-X

To Tom Peters, James Bryan Quinn, and Bill Davidson, who encouraged me to write this book.

Jag Sheth

To my children, Alok, Priya, and Maya (my personal Rule of Three), and my wife, Shailini, for the many evenings and weekends that this book took me away from them.

Raj Sisodia

Contents

THE
RULE OF
THREE

Introduction

The Rule of Three:
What It Is and How It Works

The skies are open for business, and the U.S. airline industry is in the midst of a major reshuffling. AMR, the parent company of American Airlines, recently acquired Trans World Airlines, which had filed for bankruptcy. Delta Airlines is rumored to be in acquisition talks with Continental, the fifth largest U.S. airline. At this writing, the UAL Corporation, parent of United Airlines, was attempting to acquire most of the assets of US Airways, subject to approval by the Justice Department.

Such events indicate that the industry is moving in the direction of a consolidated structure that supports three major "generalists"— American, United, and Delta—while leaving room for smaller, more narrowly focused "specialists." Carriers such as Southwest, Jet Blue, and Midwest Express continue to do well in their niches. A number of mid-sized airlines, however, seem stuck in a no-man's land between the big generalists and the specialists: Northwest, Continental, and US Airways. Their size and the breadth of their service are not enough to protect them from the powerful forces of competition.

Big companies also are not protected either from competitive market forces or from acquiring hands. On the contrary, they are just as vulnerable—in many cases, even more so—than small firms, and sometimes they must scale back. General Motors, the world's largest producer of cars and trucks, has had such traumatic operational difficulties that recently GM executives announced that the long-standing Oldsmobile line would be discontinued after 2001. Although they wield enormous power, these giants of industry cannot rely on their size, their alliances, or their command of the market to protect them from aggressive competitors and changes in their industries. "The bigger they come, the harder they fall" runs the old adage. That rule applies to dinosaurs in any era, both in nature and in the business world. For over 150 years we've known that natural selection processes favor those species and individuals who are the most efficient, healthy, and fit. According to what we call the Rule of Three, "natural" competitive market structures evolve by an analogous selection process that favors the strongest, most efficient companies. Chapter 1 describes the typical pattern of market evolution in which four forces come together to promote efficiency: industry consolidation, government intervention, the establishment of de facto standards (either for products or processes), and shared infrastructure.

Natural Market Structures

Simply put, the Rule of Three states that naturally occurring competitive forces—if allowed to operate without excessive government intervention—will create a consistent structure across nearly all mature markets. In one group, three major players compete against each other in multiple ways: they offer a wide range of related products and services, and they serve most major market segments. The Big 3 are familiar enough in the automobile industry: General Motors, Ford, and DaimlerChrysler. But there are plenty of other examples: ExxonMobil, Texaco, and Chevron among petroleum producers; Philips, SCS-Thomson, and Siemens in the European semiconductor market; TRW, Equifax, and TransUnion among credit bureaus; Gerber, Beech-Nut, and Heinz in the production of baby foods; Merck, Johnson & Johnson, and Bristol-Myers Squibb among the pharmaceuticals. These are the "full-line generalists" that form the core, the inner circle, of the market in which they participate. Why competitive markets favor three major players—not two or four or more—is an important question we take up in chapter 2.

As a market matures, the Big 3 become better defined and better able to solidify their positions. Anyone who wants to participate in that market has to play by the rules the big boys set. Because it is extremely difficult to go toe-to-toe against a full-line generalist, smaller players begin to carve out those areas in which they can effectively specialize. Usually they choose one of two paths: either they become *product specialists* such as Cambridge Soundworks and Carver Corporation in high-end stereo tuners, amplifiers, and audio equipment, Leather World in trendy clothing, or Comedy Central and CNN in the vast television network industry now ruled by NBC, ABC, and CBS (with the Fox Network close behind); or they define themselves as *market specialists* targeting a specific demographic group or geographical region. The Limited, for example, serves the apparel and fashion needs of young, educated, moderately affluent professional women. The WB network focuses on teens and their voracious need for entertainment.

In some cases a company becomes a *super-nicher,* specializing in both a product category and a market segment. Foot Locker is a product specialist focused on athletic shoes, but it serves several demographic markets, including children (Kids Foot Locker) and women (Lady Foot Locker). Southwest Airlines began as a company offering "no-frills" air service to a particular geographical area; while it has extended that service to other regions, it has maintained the consistency of its service.

As markets grow and mature, there is yet a third group of participants. Neither fish nor fowl, they are often too large and diverse to be considered specialists, yet not large enough to compete successfully against the Big 3. That is, they cannot match the #1, #2, and #3 players in achieving economies of scale and scope. Nor are they as effective at meeting specific customer requirements as the specialists. Therefore, they have neither the scale nor the loyalty advantage. Accordingly they may compete on price and try to reduce costs by cutting product quality and service, but their return on assets (ROA) remains very low, if not negative. Even worse, they are caught in a "ditch" between the Big 3 on the right side and the product or market specialists on the left side (see diagram). The Big 3 usually control between 70 and 90 percent of the market, whereas each product or market specialist, by appealing to a small group with specialized needs, controls between 1 and 5 percent of the market. Those companies caught in the ditch typically capture only between 5 and 10 percent of a given market, and find themselves unable to compete effectively against either the Big 3 or the specialists.

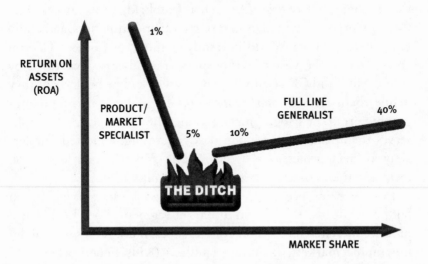

The Rule of Three and the "Ditch"

Financial performance and market share do not usually have a linear relationship; that is, performance does not necessarily improve with market share gains, nor deteriorate with market share decreases. In virtually every industry with three big players, the pattern is distinctly nonlinear. The Big 3 usually do well; that is, they may have low margins but excellent returns on assets. The ditch, however, remains a major trap for the mid-sized companies—those that are smaller than the Big 3 but bigger than the niche players—whose financial performances are usually the worst of all. Once you move beyond the ditch and go further down the scale of market share, financial performance starts to improve as niche players reap the profits of high margins.

In the diagram, note that the slope of the relationship between market share and return on assets is steeply negative for specialists, but shallow and positive for generalists. These slopes indicate that the financial performance of specialists deteriorates rapidly with undisciplined growth in market share, whereas generalists achieve a slow and steady improvement in performance as they gain market share. For generalists, however, performance improvements slow considerably as they expand beyond 40 percent market share and may even deteriorate, as we discuss in chapter 3.

US Airways, for example, grew out of the mergers that Allegheny Airlines struck with several regional specialists including Mohawk (New York and New England), Lake Central (Indiana and Ohio), Pacific Southwest (California), and Piedmont (Mid-Atlantic and South), each of which served the needs of a well-defined geographical area. When US Air tried to become a full-line generalist, the company ran up against American, United, and Delta, and it lost money, falling into the ditch between the far-flying generalists and the specialists. Unable to mount a real challenge to the Big 3, US Airways corporate executives have explored merging with other airlines, including United. The company will soon become just another topic in books on aviation history. The predicament of such ditch-dwellers is the topic of chapter 4.

In nearly all markets, the various players comprising the Big 3, the specialists, and the ditch-dwellers share a number of important characteristics. Our analysis of literally hundreds of markets, both local and global, provides evidence from which we can observe the maturation of these industries and draw inferences about the nature of competition and the fundamental "laws" that govern competitive markets. Bloated, inefficient companies may rule for a while, but they don't last long. The pattern in competitive markets indicates that only the most efficient rise to the top.

Even mature markets, however, can suffer radical disruption when technology or regulation changes or when the entry of a new player succeeds in altering the rules of competition. In 1987, the Big 3 in coffee—General Foods, Procter & Gamble, and Nestlé—controlled about 90 percent of the U.S. market. But Starbucks appeared on the scene, creating a market for upscale coffee that dramatically challenged the Big 3 and the commodity-like nature of their offerings. All three had produced canned, ground coffees that were made from the inexpensive beans of the robusta coffee plant of West

Africa. Competition between the leaders was based strictly on price, since the tastes of their products were virtually indistinguishable. In chapter 8 we examine this industry disruption in greater detail and chronicle the toppling of incumbent leaders as external forces destabilize competitive markets.

In observing both the forest and the trees, we have studied the elements that characterize companies holding similar positions within their respective industries. For instance, most #1 companies should and do behave differently than #2 companies. Most #3 companies exhibit significant differences in strategy and outlook that distinguish them from their two major competitors. Ditch-dwellers also share certain characteristics, and only a limited number of alternatives, some decidedly unpleasant, are available to them as they try to extricate themselves: they can go bankrupt; they can attempt to get out on their own by becoming product or market specialists; they can merge with another ditch-dweller in hopes that their combined resources will enable them to challenge one of the Big 3; or they can choose to be acquired by one of the major players.

Specialists, in contrast, are well advised to stay in that position unless they can detect inherent weaknesses in one of the Big 3 and choose a compatible partner from the ditch with which to merge. In chapters 6 and 7, we present strategies appropriate to each of these market positions and examine the implications for industries such as pharmaceuticals and airlines that are becoming global in scope.

Balancing Efficiency and Competitive Intensity

Without outside intervention and government controls, competitive markets evolve in ways that ultimately reward the most efficient companies. Efficiency is the first rule of the game.

Markets can evolve in such a way that either they are nearly free of competition, as in the case of a monopoly, or they become so intensely competitive that no one makes any money. Contrary to popular perception, markets can have *too much* competition: customers get confused by the sheer volume of choice, so much so that they don't buy anything; and competing companies duel it out by lowering prices or cutting back on quality such that their returns are severely compromised.

Whether in an athletic contest, a global market, or a simple struggle for existence, there are two primary forces that exert pressure on all players: (1) the *demand for efficiency* and (2) the *need for relief from excessive competitiveness.* In the business world, as in the natural world, these forces can exert both a push and a pull effect on everyone. Some markets become so intensely competitive that nearly all participants are strangled. A natural response is to give in to this push by seeking release from the competition even though it may mean lower profits. In other cases when competitors raise the efficiency bar, one can feel pulled to compete more fiercely, to move that much faster just to keep pace or to try to break out of the pack. As a result, profits go to making the business more efficient, sleeker, faster, and more attractive to customers or would-be suitors.

The effects of this relentless drive for efficiency filter down to each of the company's stakeholders. Squeezed for greater productivity but often inadequately rewarded for their contributions, employees become increasingly disgruntled. Customers, the supposed beneficiaries of cutthroat competition, also feel the negative impact of hyperintense competition. While prices may fall, service usually takes a tumble as well: how often do you find unhappy employees offering customers great personal service? Nostalgic for the way it *used* to be, before competition reached this fever pitch, customers come to feel as if they have been forgotten in the process. As the company spends more of its profits on operations, new initiatives, and the latest technology, shareholders grow increasingly dissatisfied with quarterly announcements of lowered expectations and falling market capitalization.

When the drive for efficiency runs headlong into the wastefulness of hypercompetition, most markets respond with a logical solution. The initial players, whose numbers are large in an infant market, experience a shakeout, often several in succession. Three dominant players eventually emerge, with any number of specialists and niche players off to the side. As we will see in later chapters, this structure offers the best possible balance between efficiency and competitive intensity since the specialists enjoy their high margins and loyal customers while the Big 3 rely on volume to drive up their returns on assets.

Specialists and full-line generalists exist side by side in any market. Think of their relationship as analogous to that of the stores in a large shopping mall. Anchoring the structure are the major department stores, which offer a full line of products and services and get most of the mall traffic. Along the corridors or spokes of the mall are the specialty shops, which cater to a well-defined audience (market specialists such as The Gap, Banana Republic, Victoria's Secret) or which sell only specific items (product specialists such as Hallmark, Swatch, Kay Jewelers). In the Rule of Three, this hypothetical market (the mall) is anchored by three full-line generalists with a number of product and market specialists occupying largely noncompetitive positions.

Prognostications and Promises

Economists have long assumed that markets are either oligopolistic, in which a handful of large firms divide up the spoils, or monopolistic, with many smaller firms coexisting in specialized niches. The reality in most markets is clearly different. While they may start out approximating monopolistic competition, they end up in a pattern that includes *both* types of players. With startling regularity, we have found that the number of dominant players in each industry is confined to three. Any other number, greater or smaller, is usually a temporary aberration.

The Rule of Three is most common in the United States. We see it in markets for beer, soft drinks, aircraft manufacturing (until recently, as we discuss later), long-distance telephone communications, and many others. Appendix 2 describes many of these in detail.

The banking industry in the United States has long been highly fragmented. In 1995, according to the U.S. Small Business Administration, there were over 10,000 banking organizations—a number that declined only slightly by 1999 to just under 8,700. Large banks have been merging at a furious pace, while new, more specialized banks are entering the market at the same time that many midsized banks are exiting. This industry is undergoing a process of consolidation. While the Big 3 have yet to emerge, Citicorp's merger with the Travelers Group and NationsBank's acquisition of Bank of America make those two entities early favorites. A third survivor may be the recent combination of Wells Fargo & Company and

Norwest Corporation, although Bank One and First Union are certainly still in the running. There is a long way to go before the banking industry completes this process.

Evidence is mounting that the phenomenon of the Rule of Three is occurring in European and Asian markets with greater frequency than before, especially in the wake of globalization. In the Japanese elevator and escalator industry, for example, Toshiba, Hitachi, and Mitsubishi control almost 90 percent of the Japanese market. Those three major players provide 30-minute service response anywhere in Japan on any day under any circumstances. As that industry globalizes, however, we predict that Otis will present a serious challenge to their domination.

In the United Kingdom, Thomson, Airtours, and Owners Abroad dominate the market for prepackaged vacations. Among British grocery retailers, the Big 3 are Sainsbury, Tesco, and Argyll, which also happens to be the owner of the U.S. chain Safeway. In book manufacturing, the lion's share of the market goes to Coral, Ladbrokes, and William Hill. In the cement industry, the Big 3 are Blue Circle, Rugby Portland, and Castle, each one scrambling for a higher share of a dwindling market.

The financial performance of the Big 3 improves with market share—but only up to a point. Beyond approximately a 40 percent share of the market, the Big 3 begin to experience diseconomies of scale and come under the watchful eye of regulators and antitrust litigation. If, on the one hand, the market leader holds a market share between 50 and 70 percent, a third full-line generalist has little room and will either fall into the ditch or be forced to become a specialist. Boeing and Airbus, for example, pushed McDonnell Douglas into the ditch and eventually led to Boeing's acquisition of the company in 1997. If, on the other, the market leader—say, IBM in the heyday of mainframes—commands 70 percent or more of the market, there is practically no room for either a second or a third full-line generalist. Such dominance, however, rarely lasts, and newcomers will gradually gain a foothold to challenge even the most powerful company. These precedents are surely not lost on Microsoft, although the signs are increasing that the software maker is no longer as dominant as it once was, with Linux controlling a greater share of the market for operating systems.

Inferences about the Rule of Three receive substantial support from researchers who have found distinct evidence of "natural market structures" characterized by a progression of market shares among industry leaders, as well as a "stuck-in-the-middle" competitive position in which companies are too small to succeed as generalists but too big to succeed as specialists.[1] Nowhere in this literature, however, did we find an overarching theory of market evolution that accurately describes the patterns we had seen. This book seeks to fill that gap.

An understanding of the Rule of Three will greatly benefit anyone involved in business, including CEOs and managers who are concerned with their company's market performance and strategies for competing. Managers need to learn and appreciate business context. In particular, they must understand how their industry is structured, what stage of evolution it has entered, and how that evolution is likely to continue. With this perspective they can better cultivate their innate strengths, formulate reasonable strategies to leverage their position within the industry, and maximize their chances of success.

We believe that the degrees of managerial freedom are limited, that managers are not completely free to choose which markets they want to compete in and which competitors to target. Although some may view themselves as "masters of their universe," there are forces beyond their control that are constantly changing the structure of their industries. Thus, they need to rely on the best managerial judgment and tools for strategic analysis they can muster. The Rule of Three will prove valuable, not only in helping them to see both the forest and the trees, but also in sharpening their foresight and preparing them to deal with future turns in their competitive markets. The framework presented in this book, we believe, will be invaluable in helping them understand and meet both immediate and long-term challenges.

Based on a company's relative position within its industry, and the stage of that industry's evolution, there are smart choices and foolhardy ones. Ignoring the market structure presented by the Rule of Three can cause business managers and entrepreneurs to engage in "unnatural" acts of marketplace behavior, which are doomed to failure. Observing the laws of competitive markets, however, will help them set objectives that their companies can reasonably hope to meet while they set strategies that will help them get out and stay out of the ditch. In chapter 1, we lay out the laws that are fundamental to competition and the relative stability of industries and markets.

1

Four Mechanisms for Increasing Efficiency

In 1966, the U.S. Supreme Court refused to allow two supermarkets in Los Angeles to merge. The Vons Grocery Company and Shopping Bag Food Stores, had they been allowed to combine, would have controlled a whopping 7.5 percent of the market. Over 3,800 single-store grocers would still have been doing business in the city. In spite of these statistics, the Court ruled against the merger, citing "the threatening trend toward concentration."[1]

Much has changed in the public's perception of merger activity in the four decades since the Supreme Court's ruling in the Los Angeles supermarket case. Over time, the view that market efficiencies matter and that consumer welfare is actually enhanced by a measure of industry concentration has slowly gained acceptance, although there still are loud complaints from consumer groups that this or that merger will result in higher prices. In truth, markets remain highly competitive even after such concentration, and industries that have experienced consolidation have seen prices remain stable or actually fall. To be sure, profits are generally higher in concentrated industries, but the prices consumers pay may actually decline. This evidence suggests that efficiency gains are a prime driver of greater profitability and market evolution.

For that evolution to be sustainable, markets need both growth and efficiency. Growth comes primarily from understanding and shaping customer demand, whereas efficiency is a function of operations. Through the cyclical pursuit of these objectives, markets become organized and reorganized over time.

Once its basic viability has been established, a start-up industry enjoys high growth but has low efficiency. No matter what criterion is used to measure efficiency—revenue per customer, revenue relative to assets deployed, revenue per employee, for instance—the start-up costs are high. The first shakeout occurs during the industry's initial growth phase to make it more efficient without sacrificing growth. Subsequent attempts to make the industry more efficient come from four key sources or events: the creation of standards, the development of an industry-wide cost structure as well as a shared infrastructure, government intervention, and industry consolidation through shakeouts. These four drivers force the industry as well as the players in it to become more and more efficient in order to stay competitive. As we will see in this chapter, they can occur at any time and in any order, sometimes independently, sometimes closely dependent on each other. Their primary effect, however, is to promote efficiency and fair competition within an industry such that no one company becomes a monopoly.

In subsequent shakeouts, the industry is reorganized for growth, typically through market expansion, including globalization. Driven primarily by investor demands, companies at this stage are concerned with growth of all kinds: revenue growth, cash flow growth, earnings growth, growth in the number of customers and revenue per customer, and growth in market capitalization. To continue to attract investment capital and growth, the industry needs to make productive use of all inputs, including capital, labor, and management talent.

The Creation of Standards

Market inefficiency can hasten the creation of de facto standards. Henry Ford paved the way for one such standard when he devised the highly efficient assembly-line manufacturing process for the Model T. Bill Gates was fortunate indeed when Microsoft received the nod from IBM and others to make the MS-DOS operating system the standard for personal computers. Once that standard was set, even Big Blue, known primarily for its hardware, could not wrest away control with its proprietary OS/2 system.

When standards play a major role and remain largely proprietary, there may not be room for three separate platforms. Typically at most two platforms can survive in the broad market: VHS & Beta for video recorders, VHS-C and 8mm for camcorders, PAL and NTSC for television broadcasts, CDMA and GSM for wireless telephony, PC and Mac for personal computing. Eventually, one platform becomes dominant, if not universal. Thus, 8mm has a big lead over VHS-C, PCs have triumphed over the Mac, and VHS has overwhelmed Beta. The other platform, if it survives, is relegated to a niche market.

The simultaneous existence of two or more standards, as in the case of NTSC and PAL, can be attributed in large part to protectionist ideologies and government regulation. Thanks to a double standard in the worldwide electric industry, tourists must contend with shifting between 110 volts and 220 volts, not to mention remembering to pack a variety of prongs and socket styles; in Europe alone there are some 20 different types of electrical plugs currently in use. To the delight of those tourists, these types of essentially meaningless and highly inefficient differences will start to go away as the electric industry adopts universal standards and the world at large becomes more driven by market economies. The cost of converting to a new single standard, however, is estimated to be $125 billion![2]

Already we can see the power of a fully adopted worldwide standard in the World Wide Web. The extraordinarily rapid diffusion of this technology across the globe has resulted in large measure because of that single standard. Emerging industries today are highly cognizant of this fact, and organizations that set industry standards now occupy an influential place in the world economy. The impact of evolving standards is illustrated by the stories of the evolution of the VCR industry and the development in Europe of the Group Special Mobile (GSM) network.

The VCR Industry[3]

Based in Redwood City, California, the Ampex Corporation invented video tape recorder (VTR) technology in 1956. It sold machines to professionals initially for $75,000, but it was never successful in creating a product for ordinary consumers. However, it was successful in licensing its technology to Sony, which turned it into a competitive advantage.

Sony first introduced videocassette recorders (VCR) to the mass market in 1971, but even its "U-Matic" machines and cassettes were too big and expensive. Accordingly, Sony made modifications and repositioned the machines for industrial users. Next, Sony approached JVC and Matsushita—two of its biggest competitors—about establishing a standard (based on a new Sony technology) that would reduce the size of both machines and cassettes. JVC and Matsushita would accept only the U-Matic format, and JVC refused to cooperate or compromise on technology for smaller machines.

In 1971, JVC established a video home system (VHS) project team and charged it with the mission to develop a viable VCR for consumers, not just one that was technologically possible, but something consumers would prefer. Experimenting with ten different ways of building a home VCR, Sony settled by mid-1974 on the Betamax prototype. It set up a new plant to produce 10,000 units a month, but designed the machine to record for only one hour, reasoning that customers would use it to record television programs for later viewing. Later, when Sony asked Matsushita and JVC to adopt the Beta format, both refused, citing the one-hour recording limit as a major drawback. JVC's VHS format, then in development, would deliver up to three hours. After the Betamax was launched, Hitachi tried unsuccessfully to license Betamax technology from Sony, which basically had decided to go it alone.

Meanwhile, JVC formed an alliance of companies around the VHS standard before it shipped any products. The group included Matsushita, Hitachi, Mitsubishi, Sharp, Sanyo, and Toshiba. The standards war was on, and not even the intervention of Japan's Ministry of International Trade and Industry (MITI) in 1976 could succeed in resolving the dispute.

After JVC's launch in October 1976, Sony recruited Sanyo and Toshiba to join the Beta group. The split between the two formats continued for another ten years. Sony did well at first, in part because of its wide distribution. In 1976 and 1977, its market share was over 50 percent, but the company lost ground quickly. By late 1978,

Matsushita with 35.8 percent of the market overtook Sony, whose share had slipped to 27.9 percent. By 1988, VHS had close to 95 percent of world sales. In a show of pragmatism, Sony launched its own line of VHS machines and repositioned Betamax as a high-end system for professionals.

Group Special Mobile (GSM) Network

The development of the Group Special Mobile (GSM) network has been an essential element in the success of European wireless companies such as Finland's Nokia and Sweden's Ericsson. Analog cellular telephone systems grew rapidly in Europe in the 1980s, especially in Scandinavia and the United Kingdom. Because each country developed its own sophisticated systems and networks, the industry was characterized by incompatible equipment and operations. Since mobile phones could operate only within national boundaries, the limited market for each company's equipment meant that economies of scale were poor. It was not unusual to see executives toting multiple phones depending on the country in which they happened to be conducting business at the time. The imminent creation of the European Union (EU) made this highly inefficient situation untenable.[4]

In 1982, Nordic Telecom and Netherlands PPT proposed to the Conference of European Posts and Telegraphs (CEPT) that a new digital cellular standard be developed that would improve efficiency and help the industry cope with the explosion of demand across all of Europe. The CEPT established a body known as Group Special Mobile to develop the system. Members of the European Union were instructed to reserve frequencies in the 900MHz band for GSM to enable easy "roaming" between countries. In 1989, the European Telecommunications Standards Institute (ETSI) offered GSM as an international digital cellular telephony standard.

GSM service commenced in mid-1991. By 1993, there were 36 GSM networks in 22 countries. GSM was successful in gaining acceptance in non-European markets as well, since it was the most mature mobile digital technology. GSM also proved very successful in Asia, with its huge untapped markets that had no analog legacy to overcome.[5] By 1997, over 200 GSM networks were running in 110 countries, with more than 55 million subscribers. As of January

2001, 392 GSM networks were operational in 162 countries, with dozens more planned. GSM had 457 million subscribers (up from 162 million a year and a half earlier) out of 647 million digital subscribers; another 68 million subscribers continued on analog systems.[6]

The biggest holdout has been the United States, where the government has played no role in selecting a standard, and where a major rival to GSM, CDMA, has won many converts. Overall, the U.S. market is split among three standards: CDMA, GSM, and TDMA (a standard similar to GSM, but incompatible with it). By September 2000, CDMA had 71 million subscribers, whereas TDMA claimed 53.5 million.[7] Each network operates independently of the others.

While many technology experts argue that CDMA is a superior technology, the advantage appears to be with Europe at this point. Simply put, GSM phones are much more usable worldwide. This wider usage base has allowed Europe to move ahead in phone functionality. Nokia is leading the charge, pioneering Internet access on cell phones. Through infrared technology, phones can transmit data to each other or to a machine; in Finland, this technology can be used to purchase a Coke from a soda machine.[8] CDMA's acknowledged technological superiority is similar to that enjoyed by Betamax and the Macintosh. As history has taught us, neither was able to prevail.

The battle between CDMA and GSM may well be settled as we move to the next generation of wireless technology: so-called 3G or third-generation wireless systems featuring very high data transmission rates that will allow for two-way video communication. It is expected that most mobile operators will converge on a single worldwide standard for 3G systems.

Industry Cost Structure and Shared Infrastructure

The prevailing cost structure in an industry—those costs primarily related to production, and to some extent to management and marketing—has a deep impact on whether and how soon that industry becomes organized. This impact can be measured in terms of the relative significance of the industry's fixed costs versus its variable costs. As an industry emphasizes automation, incorporates new technology, and tries to mitigate the high or growing cost of human capital, it tends to increase fixed costs and lower variable ones.

Participation in an industry always has certain requisite fixed costs. In all aspects of business—from procurement to operations to marketing—relative market share determines spending efficiency. Thus, when it comes to national advertising and sales, for example, a company that has a 40 percent share of the market is potentially four or more times more efficient than a company with a 10 percent share. These are examples of fixed costs; that is, a company incurs them regardless of how high or low its sales are. Once a company has made the decision to target a particular market, it has to pay the piper no matter how great or small revenues promise to be. As we have observed, those industries in which such fixed costs tend to dominate are more likely to exhibit a pronounced Rule of Three structure.

If the costs to participate are high, the "minimum efficient scale" needed to attain efficiency in operations is also high. As a result, the shakeout in the industry happens sooner rather than later. In contrast, markets in the so-called agricultural age were characterized by near perfect competition: many small producers and buyers interacted in the marketplace, where prices were set according to the relative balance between supply and demand. The agricultural sector has predominantly variable costs: the costs of seed, fertilizer, and labor can fluctuate depending on conditions, but are always linked to the volume of production. About the only fixed cost is the cost of land, which is typically inherited in many countries. During the agricultural age shakeouts were kept to a minimum. As the farms have become commercialized, we see an economy of scale developing and the exit of family-owned businesses and farms.

Cost structure also makes its impact felt through the supply function. If the supplier industries enjoy significant economies of scale because of their cost structure, downstream industries also feel the pressure to consolidate, even though their own cost structure may not require or adequately support such a move. The two major suppliers to the personal computer industry—Microsoft and Intel—are dominant in their respective spaces, for example. Despite the lower entry and exit barriers associated with PC assembly, this dominance still creates pressures for concentration downstream.

Likewise, a high concentration of customers puts additional pressure on the industry to consolidate. In the industry comprising defense contractors, where the U.S. Department of Defense is by far the overwhelming customer, the number of defense contractors has fallen steeply in recent years. Also, a substitute industry that has a higher fixed-cost component will enjoy a price advantage. This too creates pressures on an industry to consolidate and become more fixed-cost intensive.

Although many people assume that fixed costs are bad for business, this is not necessarily the case. As the primary source of scale economies, fixed costs are an essential element in the competitive strategy for volume-driven players such as full-line generalists.

A Shared Infrastructure

In addition to fixed and variable costs that individual players in a market must consider, the market as a whole can move toward greater organization by developing a shared infrastructure for the purpose of increasing efficiency. Infrastructure costs are generally too high to be loaded on the transactions generated by any one company. Banks, for example, would be unable to survive if they did not share an infrastructure for check clearing, as well as for credit card authorization (through the Visa and MasterCard systems). Similarly, airlines require shared infrastructures for reservations, air traffic control, baggage handling, and ground services. Fundamentally such an infrastructure distributes the heavy cost of implementation, thereby making the system more affordable for all the players, large and small, in the industry.

To be useful in enhancing efficiency, an industry infrastructure must be:

- *Sharable:* it must allow for simultaneous access by many users.
- *Ubiquitous:* it needs to be where you want it, when you want it.
- *Easy to use:* it must be intuitive and require little or no training to use effectively.
- *Cost effective:* it must be accessible and affordable to all.[9]

By far the most significant recent example of a shared infrastructure is the Internet. Regarded as the most significant invention of our time, the Internet has become a major new infrastructure for virtually all businesses of any size, whether new or old. From an obscure tool used by researchers and academics at government-funded laboratories and universities, the Internet has exploded into the world of commerce. The starting point was a simple but brilliant innovation: the World Wide Web (see sidebar "Berners-Lee and the World Wide Web"). By general agreement it is comparable in its impact to the invention of movable type by Johann Gutenberg almost 600 years ago.

Berners-Lee and the World Wide Web

TIM BERNERS-LEE worked as a computer scientist at CERN, the international particle physics lab in Switzerland. It was his innovative idea that became the basis for the World Wide Web. In 1973, Vint Cerf and Bob Kahn had devised the Internet feature called Transmission Control Protocol / Internet Protocol (TCP/IP), which has been described as "one of the great technological breakthroughs of the twentieth century."[10]

Berners-Lee came up with two simple innovations that enable people to navigate between previously unrelated sources or Web sites. Building on the Internet technology, he created a global hypertext system by inserting links from one text to another. He named one of his innovations the Hypertext Transport Protocol, now better known to Web surfers in its abbreviated form, http. In addition, he devised a way of identifying a document using the Uniform Resource Locator, or URL. Today these are common terms used in Internet traffic, although the public may not know their full names and functions.

Created in 1989, the Web is arguably an essential element of the infrastructure, not just for business and commerce, but also for governments, personal communications, community formation, and entertainment. As with the ideal infrastructure, it is not controlled by any one commercial entity, but evolves through the collective efforts of many. Forums of engineers, such as the World Wide Web Consortium, ensure that it functions well and evolves as needed. No company can unilaterally dictate that new features be added; nevertheless, standards are set faster than ever and are completely open.

Because of this openness and malleability, the Internet has led to innovations at an incredible pace. MP3 is today's standard for compressing music files. The Java programming language has a place in practically all Web sites. Numerous other examples—digital subscriber lines (DSL), broadband, electronic mail, teleconferencing, and the like—indicate how fast this industry is moving in supplying products and services to individuals the world over.

Igniting one of the greatest explosions of wealth in history, the Web has also transformed the business community. The transformation has been both internal and external. Intranets, for example, have streamlined internal operating processes. Through extranets companies have developed closer linkages with their suppliers, alliance partners, and customers. The Web has fueled the growth of categories of commerce such as person-to-business and person-to-person.

Government Intervention

So far, most governments have resisted the temptation to try to control the Internet or regulate its functions. At the urging of their constituents, government officials have preferred to adopt a hands-off approach. Nevertheless, the government can and often does play an important role in determining an industry's structure, including triggering major consolidation. Often the government itself is a major customer—the Department of Defense exemplifies a customer with deep pockets. The significance of the government's role as a buyer is even more pronounced in Europe than it is in the United States.

A major funder of research and development as well as a major buyer, the federal government has a significant impact on the pace and direction of technological change in many industries. In some cases, the government also facilitates cooperation within an industry, especially at the "pre-competitive" stage. Japan's Ministry of International Trade and Industry (MITI) has been the most prominent example of this kind of facilitator, although governments in Europe and the United States have participated in similar cooperative efforts.

For other industries—for example, education, health care services, and computers—the government helps to move the industry toward standardized products and processes. The government may intervene, for instance, if it sees that an important market is failing to achieve efficiency on its own. When too many companies were laying cable in the telephone and communications industry, each hoping to gain monopoly power by establishing itself as the leader with proprietary products, the U.S. government intervened by creating standards or sanctioning "natural monopolies" to generate efficiency. A similar intervention in the U.S. railroad industry established a much-needed standard for operations and had immediate effects on the players' profitability.

The Railroad Industry[11]

In the middle of the nineteenth century, the railroad industry took off in the United States. Long before anyone had an inkling of the automobile industry, people saw a "natural" fit between the railroads and the physical size of the country with its vast stretches of undeveloped land. The railroads, however, developed haphazardly, primarily because the industry was so fragmented with many small, inefficient players and because there were no uniform standards. The most telling omission was that the U.S. railroad industry lacked a uniform gauge (the distance between the tracks). Goods had to be transferred between railroad carriers at points where rail lines of different gauges intersected—a highly expensive and inefficient procedure.

The U.S. government, understandably, was concerned with the speedy construction of the railroad system. In the 1850s, federal, state, and local governments stimulated the growth of the industry, granting charters (or in some cases actually building the lines), as well as providing money and credit for many private railroads. The federal government conducted surveys at taxpayer expense and reduced the tariff on iron used by the railroads. Before 1860, the government provided almost 25 million acres of land for railroad construction, with two main stipulations: (1) the railroads would transport government property and Union troops for free, and (2) Congress would set rates for mail traffic. The federal land grant program expanded rapidly after the Civil War ended in 1865.

Battles and explosions during the war significantly damaged the railway system, destroying miles of track and rendering equipment unusable. After the war ended, government officials and industry executives wisely undertook a rehabilitation program that at last specified a standard gauge of 4 feet 8½ inches for all tracks. By 1880, 80 percent of the mileage had been converted to this standard. By 1890, virtually the entire network was brought into compliance with the new standard, thereby insuring that the railroad industry became both more efficient and extended its reach to more remote regions. Now that everybody was running on the same track, the railroad companies themselves became much more serious targets for mergers and acquisitions. Accordingly, the industry rapidly became more concentrated.

The railroads increased their hold on power, such that demands for the regulation of the industry grew loud and urgent. In 1887, the federal government passed the Interstate Commerce Act, creating the Interstate Commerce Commission (ICC), which became a major force in the development of a federal regulatory policy.

The rail industry peaked in 1920; after that date, other modes of transportation—particularly the automobile and the airplane—reduced the importance of the rail system. In the 1920s severe competition from outside the industry caused many passenger railroads in their prime to cease operations. Only Amtrak would be reborn some 40 years later, and only then because of massive tax subsidization.

Industry Consolidation

Over the last several years, we have witnessed a record number of mergers, as well as numerous demergers (the spinning out of non-core businesses). As a result, the landscape of just about every major industry has changed in a significant way. The pace of this consolidation is startling: the number of mergers per year in the United States has more than tripled over the past decade, while the value of those mergers has risen tenfold. Between 1997 and the end of 2000, nearly $5 *trillion* in mergers took place in the United States alone. The most recent large mergers and acquisitions have occurred in the telecommunications, banking, entertainment, and food industries, as indicated in the accompanying tables.

While the United States has been at the forefront of this trend, M&A activity has been feverish on the global level as well. At the time, few experts believed that 1998's record of $2.52 trillion in global M&A activity would be soon broken; however, total world-wide transactions announced in 1999 reached $3.43 trillion, exceeding the previous record by an astounding 36 percent.[12] In 2000, the total reached $3.5 trillion, growing only slightly over 1999 activity. The uncertain market environment in late 2000 and early 2001 has dampened merger activity worldwide; however, we expect that it will rebound as markets recover. Appendix 1 presents an encapsulated history of merger activity in the United States during the twentieth century.

Europe has been a particularly fertile area for some of these recent megadeals, particularly in telecommunications, utilities, banking, and the retail sector. M&A activity in Europe more than doubled in 1999, totaling $1.2 trillion. This total includes United Kingdom-based Vodafone Airtouch's $203 billion offer for Germany's Mannesmann AG, the largest deal ever. France's two largest retailers and hypermarkets, Carrefour SA and Promodès, merged to form a $52 billion giant, now the world's largest retailer after Wal-Mart. The globalization of retailing, long believed to be an industry unlikely to globalize, appears to be well underway; Carrefour and Promodès are already prominent across Europe as well as in Latin America. Likewise, Arkansas-based Wal-Mart has been expanding south into Latin America as well as east into Europe.[13]

Even Japan, a nation for years thought to be an uncongenial place for mergers, is experiencing a much accelerated pace of M&A activity. Because Japanese markets and culture did not generally support mergers, most of the country's industries experienced a lot of fragmentation. In the past Japan's extremely low cost of capital and its cozy keiretsu relationships have contributed to keeping an excessive number of full-line generalists afloat. A proliferation of major players is evident in most industries: for example, seven major camera makers (Canon, Nikon, Asahi Pentax, Minolta, Yashica, Fuji, and Konica); seven big car companies (Toyota, Nissan, Honda, Mazda, Mitsubishi, Subaru, and Isuzu); and several consumer electronics companies (Sony, Matsushita, Hitachi, Mitsubishi, and Toshiba).[14] Gradually, however, merger activity has been on the increase. In

1999, M&A volume in Japan tripled over 1998 levels, though still amounting to only $78 billion. Mergers in Japan are starting to focus on industry consolidation and the "unbundling" of conglomerates.[15]

As more industries globalize, a larger percentage of mergers involve firms from different countries. Such cross-border M&A activity has risen fivefold over the past decade. In terms of total value cross-border mergers reached $720 billion in 1999. As a share of world GDP, they increased from 0.5 percent in 1987 to 2 percent in 1999.[16] Industries that previously could not expand in such a manner for operational reasons are now able to do so. Retailers, for example, can use new technologies to manage cross-border supply chains and centralized purchasing for multiple countries.[17] The following three tables present relevant statistics on merger and acquisition activity as of January 11, 2001.

U.S. MERGERS 1990–2000

Year	Number of Transactions	Value (in billions)
1990	2,074	$108.2
1991	1,877	$71.2
1992	2,574	$96.7
1993	2,663	$176.4
1994	2,997	$226.7
1995	3,510	$356.0
1996	5,848	$495.0
1997	7,800	$657.1
1998	7,809	$1,192.9
1999	9,278	$1,425.8
2000	9,602	$1,395.5

TOP TEN DEALS FOR 2000

	Seller	Buyer	Value (in Millions)
1	Time Warner, Inc.	America Online, Inc.	$166,937.50
2	Honeywell, Inc.	General Electric Corp.	$44,156.93
3	VoiceStream Wireless Corp.	Deutsche Telekom AG	$41,577.27
4	SDL, Inc.	JDS Uniphase Corp.	$38,127.61
5	J.P. Morgan Company, Inc.	Chase Manhattan Corp.	$36,540.97
6	Texaco	Chevron	$35,760.98
7	Associates First Capital Corp.	Citigroup, Inc.	$30,750.68
8	U.S. Bancorp	Firststar Corp.	$20,991.60
9	Bestfoods	Unilever NV/ Unilever plc	$20,211.50
10	E-Tek Dynamics, Inc.	JDS Uniphase Corp.	$17,410.06

TOP TEN INDUSTRY RANKINGS[18]

	Industry Classification of Seller	Total Deals	Aggregate Value (in Millions)
1	Leisure and entertainment	256	$182,599.47
2	Computer software, supplies, and services	2,431	$154,099.85
3	Electronics	225	$121,107.93
4	Banking and finance	284	$98,719.52
5	Communications	459	$83,668.15
6	Food processing	106	$78,833.12
7	Brokerage, investment, and management consulting	499	$81,985.31
8	Oil and gas	85	$51,727.25
9	Electrical equipment	287	$51,920.83
10	Electric, gas, water, and sanitary services	149	$66,015.28

Recently NationsBank completed its merger with BankAmerica in a $60 billion stock deal. SBC Communications acquired Ameritech for $62 billion in stock. British and Swedish drug groups Zeneca Group plc and Astra AB announced plans to join forces in what was until then Europe's largest merger, following Hoechst and Rhone Poulenc's merger of their life science units to form Aventis, and an all-French merger between Sanofi and Synthelabo. Ciba Specialty Chemicals and Clariant, two of the largest players in the rapidly growing specialty chemical industry, are merging. Exxon and Mobil combined to form the world's largest oil company, fast on the heels of the merger between BP and Amoco (Royal Dutch/Shell rounds out the major players in that industry). The European banking sector, following economic and monetary union, is rapidly consolidating across national boundaries. French banks Société Générale and Paribas have announced plans to combine to form Europe's second biggest bank, behind the Deutsche Bank/ Bankers Trust merger of 1999 and ahead of Switzerland's UBS AG.

Clearly we are witnessing a reorganization of the patterns of corporate ownership, as well as the risks involved in business participation—namely, those businesses a company should enter as opposed to the ones it should exit. The current wave of mergers and de-mergers represents a historic rationalization of "who does what and for whom." In general, the result is improved market efficiency, lower prices for customers, and higher returns for investors.

Industries tend to become more efficient as they undergo consolidation. In a highly fragmented market, especially one in which growth has begun to slow, numerous small, inefficient players recognize that it is to their advantage to join together or combine with larger companies that can command greater economies of scale and scope. The drive for efficiency transforms an unorganized market with myriad players into an organized one in which the number of players rapidly drops. By acquiring small companies (as General Motors did in the automobile industry) or by creating a de facto standard (as Ford did in the assembly-line process of building the Model T), one player makes the turn and becomes a broad-based supplier. From this point in the market's evolution, the Rule of Three comes into play. In most cases, two additional players are also able to evolve into full-line generalists.

The Software Industry

The personal computer software industry started up in the early 1980s. At the outset, there were hundreds of small, mostly anonymous firms vying for position. Essentially a cottage industry, software was primarily a technology business, and scale was not much of a factor. In a fateful decision, IBM selected Microsoft to provide the DOS operating system for its personal computers, thereby giving Gates's company the enormous advantage of owning the dominant standard. Over the next several years, three other companies emerged as significant players, each as a product specialist: Lotus, which had acquired spreadsheet technology from VisiCalc; WordPerfect, which fast became synonymous with word processing, and Novell, which staked out an early position in the networking arena.

Microsoft gradually leveraged its extraordinary advantage in operating system software to establish a commanding position in applications. Although it was initially unable to challenge Novell in networking with LAN Manager, it developed competitive products in word processing (Word) and spreadsheets (Excel). Microsoft was the first to sell software applications in bundled form, inventing the concept of a "suite" of applications that shared some features and allowed information to be readily transferred and accessed across them.

Microsoft thus became the first full-line generalist in the market, setting in motion an inevitable restructuring of the entire industry. Lotus, for example, soon realized that if it wanted to continue to grow, it had to reduce its overwhelming dependence on a single product (Lotus 1-2-3) and broaden its product line. By acquiring the word processor Ami Pro and developing the presentation graphic package Freelance, Lotus became the industry's second full-line generalist. WordPerfect was even more dependent on its namesake word processor than Lotus had been on its spreadsheet; it tried, but failed, to develop a viable full line of products on its own, including PlanPerfect and WordPerfect Presentations. Finally, it was forced to merge with Novell. Even so, the duo had to acquire Borland's Quattro Pro spreadsheet to complete their package of offerings.

Over time, the Big 3 added database, electronic mail, and many other categories of software to their lines. Although the market still included hundreds of specialists, they essentially ceded the large applications—word processing, spreadsheets, presentation graphics, databases, networking, and electronic mail—to the Big 3. Gradually, however, Microsoft's dominance in operating systems, superior marketing, and overwhelming financial advantage increased its dominance in the office suite domain to well over 90 percent of the market. It thus left its two main competitors with a share of less than 10 percent of the market to divide between them, in effect forcing both of them into the ditch.

To be sure, the poor execution of its competitors helped Microsoft achieve this high level of success. WordPerfect, for example, could have leveraged a major asset—its enormous number of devoted customers—to expand its product offerings in the word processing market. Instead, the company made a classic mistake: it failed to develop a version of its program for the Windows operating system until two years after Microsoft had delivered Word for Windows. By then, it was so far behind that it could never catch up. When WordPerfect later created a suite of its own by coupling its word processor with Borland's spreadsheet, the applications lacked common controls and made little headway against Microsoft's smoothly integrated products.[19]

The U.S. Airline Industry

After World War I, several European aviation companies hired wartime pilots to fly decommissioned warplanes along the first commercial air routes. Aided by heavy subsidies from European governments, a number of well-known commercial airlines such as British Airways, Air France, and KLM began operations during the 1920s.

In the United States, airlines emerged primarily as a result of the U.S. Post Office's attempts in 1919 to establish a nationwide airmail service. In fact, the Post Office played a leading role in setting up the system of airports across the nation. In 1925, Congress passed the Air Mail (Kelly) Act, authorizing the postmaster general to use private contractors to provide airmail service. The creation of a number of private air transport companies was not far behind, some of which began carrying human beings as well as the mail.

In response to this increased activity, Congress passed the Air

Commerce Act of 1926 and instructed the secretary of commerce to "foster air commerce, designate and establish airways, operate and maintain aids to air navigation, license pilots and aircraft, and investigate accidents."[20] As a whole, however, the American public was too enamored of the automobile and the Roaring Twenties to take much interest in flying. Then in 1927 Charles Lindbergh captured headlines in his solo transatlantic flight to Paris. Suddenly air travel became the rage, and new companies seemingly sprang up overnight: Pan Am and TWA were both founded in 1928; Delta followed in 1929; American Airlines was formed in 1930 out of the combination of many small mail carriers; and United Airlines was created in a merger of several older mail carrying operations in 1931.

Boeing and Lockheed introduced the first planes specifically designed for passenger service. Douglas Aircraft dominated the skies with its DC-3s, DC-4s, and DC-6s, but in 1957, Boeing beat Douglas in building the first commercial jetliner. For a time the launch of larger aircraft lowered the cost of air travel. The number of passengers grew from merely a few thousand in 1930 to about 2 million in 1939. By the end of the 1940s, the number of air passengers topped 16.7 million.[21]

Regulating this new industry, the Civil Aeronautics Board (CAB) was authorized by the Federal Aviation Act of 1958 to establish routes, fares, and safety standards. In addition, the CAB heard complaints from the traveling public and settled disputes with the airlines. Dissolved in 1984 as part of the government-directed deregulation of the airline industry, the CAB in effect gave up its responsibilities to the Federal Aviation Administration (FAA), which was entrusted with overseeing the air traffic control system, certifying pilots, and establishing standard safety precautions for the industry.[22]

Deregulation allowed the airline companies to set their own routes and, after 1982, their own fares. When the competitive forces were at last unleashed, the industry experienced rapid changes, fare wars, new incentive plans to placate employees, and innovative promotions to attract customers. Many new airlines were spawned in the deregulated industry, increasing from 36 in 1978 to 96 in 1983, most of them serving rather localized geographical niches. Between 1980 and 1983, as companies tried to compete on low prices and waged fare wars even when new competitors were flying into the market, the industry suffered losses of $1.2 billion.

American Airlines introduced its AAdvantage frequent-flier program in 1981. Lower fares and heightened competitive activity in the 1980s led to rapid industry growth in terms of customers served: an increase from 297 million passengers in 1980 to over 455 million in 1988. A decade later, that number rose to a record 551 million passengers.[23]

The financial problems that many airlines faced led to increased labor strife, bankruptcies, and for some carriers the prospect of being acquired. Delta bought Northeast; Pan American took over National; TWA acquired Ozark Airlines in 1986; Northwest gobbled up Republican; US Airways pocketed Pacific Southwest. Texas Air/Continental acquired People Express and Eastern Airlines, which shut down entirely in January 1991 after having operated two years under Chapter 11 bankruptcy provisions. In 1987, Delta bought Western Airlines. In 1989, US Airways acquired Piedmont. Continental, America West, and Pan American entered Chapter 11 in 1990 and 1991, but only the first two emerged to resume full operations. For some time TWA managed to keep body and soul together, but was eventually acquired by American Airlines in March 2001.[24]

Consolidation of the airline industry continues both in the United States and in Europe. The current Big 6 in the United States appear close to becoming the Big 3, dividing up nearly 85 percent of the domestic market. This consolidation will happen primarily through the mergers of several ditch airlines with one of the current market leaders, United, American, and Delta (see sidebar "Major Players in the U.S. Airline Industry").[25] The first salvos have already been fired: in addition to American's acquisition of TWA, UAL Corporation, the parent of United Airlines, announced in May 2000 its intention to buy US Airways Group. Meanwhile, Delta and Continental are in discussions to merge. With the advent of truly "open skies," the global consolidation of this industry is not far off.[26]

MAJOR PLAYERS IN THE U.S. AIRLINE INDUSTRY

Rank	Airline	Revenue (2000) in billions of dollars
1	American Airlines	$19.7
2	United Airlines	$19.4
3	Delta	$15.9
4	Northwest	$11.4
5	Continental	$9.9
6	US Airways	$9.3

Source: Hoover's

The Pharmaceutical Industry[27]

In the $300 billion global pharmaceutical industry, approximately 100 firms struggle for survival. The world leaders in drug discovery, U.S. pharmaceutical companies currently develop about half of all new medicines, accounting for about 40 percent of the market. European giants round out the top ten firms. But major changes now occurring in the industry illustrate the enormous effects of the four mechanisms discussed in this chapter. Consolidation over the past 15 years has whittled the more than two dozen multinationals down to about 15. Companies are exiting non-health-care businesses, increasing spending on research and development, acquiring or partnering with genomic and drug discovery companies, growing their sales forces, and increasing advertising expenditures.[28]

Which firms will be the victors? Which will be driven from the market? Currently, all major pharmaceutical companies are in or near the ditch. The largest, Merck, commands a meager 10.9 percent of the market. Growth in the industry is a direct result of new products (innovation). New drugs, however, do not come without the high risk and price of R&D. An average of twenty cents of every dollar of revenue is reinvested in R&D, but only one out of every 250 drugs that enter preclinical testing ever makes it through the approval process. The average time-to-market is 12 years, an eternity in any industry. Only a third of the approved drugs recover the cost of their research and development. When the cost of failures is amortized over that of those few successes, the estimate for bringing a new drug to market amounts to $500 million. Despite such obstacles, the demand for new drugs keeps rising.

Three key factors in today's marketplace are creating demand. First, customers—particularly those over age 65, a group that consumes three times as many drugs as those under 65—eagerly await new product releases. It is no surprise that in the past decade over 150 new medications have targeted diseases of the elderly, and currently there are more than 600 drugs in R&D aimed at seniors. Yet according to the World Health Organization, three-quarters of the 2,500 currently recognized medical conditions lack adequate therapies. With the rapid increase in the world's senior population, the demand for pharmaceutical products for society's aging will continue to rise at staggering rates.

Second, enrollment in plans such as health maintenance organizations (HMOs) and preferred provider organizations (PPOs) has swelled in the past twenty years. Managed care, which in the 1980s had approximately a 30 percent share of the pharmaceutical market, now covers 83 percent of private-sector employees. The share of market will soon reach an estimated 90 percent. It is now widely accepted that effective self-care is much more cost-efficient than treatments requiring hospitalization or surgery. Given that the leading-edge, branded drugs are fundamental in effective self-care, it is understandable that the pharmaceuticals are interested in responding to the increase in demand.

Third, since the Food and Drug Administration (FDA) has relaxed restrictions on direct-to-consumer advertisement over the past three years, advertising for drug products has surged. For instance, in 1998 Schering-Plough spent $200 million advertising the allergy pill Claritin to consumers. In 1999, pharmaceutical companies spent $1.8 billion on advertising to consumers with $1.1 billion of that going towards TV ads—a 40 percent increase over 1998 ad budgets. The result of these campaigns is increased diagnosis and treatment (with drugs) of many unreported diseases and ailments. In fact, heavily advertised products enjoy an average increase in sales of 43 percent compared to 13 percent for those products not heavily advertised.

The Rule of Three identifies four key processes by which growing markets become efficient: creation of standards, shared infrastructure, government intervention, and consolidation. In the pharmaceutical industry all of these four processes are in play. In the United

States, the FDA sets stringent standards for product safety and efficacy of drug products. Other countries and unions of countries have similar organizations. Shared infrastructure is provided by government and privately funded research organizations from around the world. The National Institutes of Health (NIH), for instance, furnishes basic scientific research to industry in the United States. Government intervention provides a level of protection for discoveries, unique processes, and intellectual property through patent laws. By allowing a short-term monopoly on a product, the innovative firm can recoup exorbitant R&D expenses.

Finally, the industry is consolidating as the Rule of Three predicts. In the past decade, there have been 27 consolidations of significant pharmaceutical companies and numerous consolidations of smaller firms. Acquisitions and alliances between big pharmaceutical and biotechnology companies have also taken place.

A leading cause of this industry consolidation is shareholder demand for high return in exchange for high risk. In evaluating a possible merger, firms look for synergies such as those that brought Pharmacia and Upjohn together in 1995. Pharmacia had many drugs in its pipeline but was weak in U.S. marketing, whereas Upjohn was just the opposite. The merger of the two companies produced a single entity with a pipeline full of products, a strong U.S. marketing presence, and $1 billion available for R&D.

Many pharmaceutical companies look to acquire competitors who have core competencies that differ from their own. Technologies such as drug delivery, drug discovery, and genomics characterize biotechnology companies but are lacking in most big pharmaceutical companies. Allowing for less expensive and more rapid development of novel therapies, these technologies complement the pharmaceutical industry's core competencies. The top 20 pharmaceutical companies combined have alliances with over 1,000 biotechnology companies.

Competitive pricing is another driver of industry consolidation. In most European countries and Japan, governments have strict pricing controls, profit controls, and prescribing controls. Such policies greatly reduce revenue and profitability for pharmaceutical companies. The United States is the only major market where pharmaceuticals are not yet restricted by government policies, but there are other agents of price controls at work. Contract purchasing by HMOs and prescription benefits managers (PBMs) has brought competition based on pricing to a new high. Replacing physicians as the gatekeepers for prescription drug allocation, powerful buying groups now demand lower prices and greater use of generic drugs. They generate preferred drug lists, or formularies, to which patients' benefits are directly linked, and they dictate which drugs can fill clients' prescriptions. The drug companies must acquiesce if they want their products to be included on the preferred drug list, even if they are sold at reduced prices.

Reduced prices, of course, reduce earnings. In response, industry consolidation can provide broader product lines and economies of scale, thus empowering the drug manufacturers in negotiations with buying groups and government agencies.

Price wars are fought on three fronts: between brand name drugs and generics, between brand name drugs in the same therapeutic category, and between comparable generics. In the United States, changes in regulatory policies have increased competition in all three areas. Each of these price wars contributes to further industry consolidation. Market share for generic drugs rose from 18 percent in 1984 to 47 percent in 1999—a rise attributed to both the purchasing power of managed care and the 1984 Hatch-Waxman Act, which abbreviates the FDA approval process for generic drugs and allows manufacturers of generic drugs to conduct their testing prior to the expiration of the brand name drug's patent. This provision has reduced barriers to market entry by lowering the cost of clinical testing and accelerating the time-to-market from the previous industry standard of three years to three months. Although patent protection is initially issued for 20 years on new brand name drugs, most new drugs are patented early in the development and approval stages. Thus, when a new drug finally enters the market, only 11 years of patent protection, on average, remain. Once a generic drug is available, sales of the brand name drug drop typically by 60 percent.

Competition between similar brand name drugs has become much more fierce because rival pharmaceutical companies have adopted fast-follower strategies. With the recent advances in information technology and drug discovery technology, the period between the introduction of a breakthrough drug and the fast follower brand name drug can be less than a year. For example, Celebrex, an arthritis medication from Pfizer, was approved on December 31, 1998. It had less than five months of true market exclusivity before Vioxx, a similar arthritis drug from Merck, entered the market on May 21, 1999. This fast competition plays a significant role in keeping prices and earnings down.

In addition, generic drugs compete with each other on price. As numerous generic products become available for a particular drug, prices are driven down. Although there are a host of independent generic drug companies, it is important to note that many of the largest pharmaceutical companies own generic subsidiaries or divisions. For example, Novartis owns Geneva Pharmaceuticals.

Other pharmaceutical companies find success in the marketplace by carving out their own niches. Certain specialties, such as cancer therapies, will most likely provide a major niche in the industry. Because cancer drugs do not require as much sales and marketing effort as other classes of drugs, companies currently specializing in these treatments or other niche market segments are more likely to remain independent.

While coalescing into a handful of large players, the pharmaceutical industry has also been exiting non-core businesses. Novartis's crop-protection and seed businesses, for example, were spun off and merged with AstraZeneca's agrochemicals business to create Syngenta AG. In early 2000, Abbott Laboratories sold its agricultural products business unit to Sumitomo Chemical Company of Japan. In June 2000, American Home Products completed the sale of Cyanamid, its agricultural business, to BASF AG.

In spite of its being a patent-based industry, which is typically not susceptible to the Rule of Three, the U.S. pharmaceutical industry actually does not present an exception to the evolution of competitive markets that we see occurring in other industries. Patent protection does not provide an impenetrable shield against competition; growth and efficiency factors will lead to further consolidation. From the current leaders in this industry, a Big 3 will eventually emerge, but not until after a big shakeout reduces the number of legitimate players.

The Dynamics of Industry Shakeouts

As we have noted above in discussions of the agricultural age, industries in which there is "perfect" competition typically do not have to go through a major shakeout. Similarly, personal care and consumer service industries such as beauty shops, plumbing and heating companies, and repair shops have not experienced significant shakeouts. These industries are characterized by a lot of individualized attention, with a high degree of manual labor. In addition, their operations are not scalable. Where consolidation is such a major driver of industry organization, however, such events can have devastating as well as beneficial effects. It is important, therefore, to look at the causes and effects of industry shakeouts in more detail.[29]

In recent years, few industries have escaped the destruction and turmoil resulting from shakeouts. Over the past two decades, victims of shakeouts (or their beneficiaries, depending on one's point of view) include airlines, automotive component producers, banks, biotechnology companies, boat builders, cable TV operators, construction contractors, defense contractors, department stores, health maintenance organizations (HMOs), hotels, minicomputer companies, newspapers, shopping malls, saving and loan companies, steel factories, trucking companies, makers of wine coolers, and woodstove makers.

An industry is considered to have experienced a shakeout if 25 percent or more of its companies have disappeared within a short period. Like an earthquake, a shakeout brings major upheaval to an industry, changing its complexion, the mix of competitors, and the rules of competitive play. Also like earthquakes, shakeouts vary in their duration, intensity, causes, and effects.

- **Duration:** The length of shakeouts and the intensity of the resulting changes vary considerably, as the chart indicates. Some industries, including trucking, soft drinks, and electric housewares, experienced massive shakeouts that lasted a short period of time (one or two years). Other industries, such as mobile home manufacturing, oil drilling, microcomputers, smoke detectors, and telephone equipment manufacturing, have experienced longer, more protracted shakeouts that lasted several years.

VARYING LENGTHS OF THE SHAKEOUT PERIOD (IN YEARS)

Shake-out Period (in years)	Industries	Primary Causes of Most Recent Shakeout
1–2	Domestic wine (U.S.)	Too many companies
	Investment banking	Deregulation
	Computer disk drive	New technology + globalization
3–10	Auto components	Globalization
	Computer keyboards	Globalization
	Color TV (U.S.)	Process technology + globalization
	Saving and loans	Deregulation
	Small commuter airlines	Deregulation
	Smoke detectors	Too many companies
	Trucking	Deregulation
10–25	Automobile	Process technology + globalization
	Commercial airlines	Deregulation + yield management
	Farming industry	Structural economic shift
	Independent phone makers	Deregulation + too many companies

• **Intensity:** If we judge the severity of a shakeout by the number of companies that exit the market, then some shakeouts have been very severe. For instance, the U.S. color TV industry lost over 90 percent of its producers in a single decade. Some shakeouts can be short in duration but severe in their devastation, as happened in the case of the TV-based home shopping industry that lost over 50 percent of its members within two years.

EXAMPLES OF SHAKEOUT SEVERITY

Percentage of Companies Exiting	Industry	Time-Span	# Companies Exiting Industry
25–30	Commuter airlines	1981–86	76
	Fasteners (adhesives)	1983–86	258
	Tobacco steaming & redrying	1977–82	22
	Quick printing services	1990–92	76
	Video rentals	1988–92	239
31–50	Building paper & board	1977–82	28
	Cigar makers	1977–82	41
	Disk drive producers	1983–86	33
	Home TV shopping	1988–90	12
	Ophthalmic goods	1977–82	224
51–75	Aircraft component producers	1945–80	20
	Smoke detectors	1977–85	16
76–95	Consumer electronics	1980–88	123
	Machine tool industry	1970–91	1790

• **Contributing causes and effects:** If the shakeout is caused by a radical shift in consumer demand—as happened when consumer preferences shifted away from electric typewriters to personal computers—the results can be severe. Shakeouts, however, occur for many other reasons, including excess supply of goods and services, the overabundance of producers, radical shifts in societal, technological, and competitive conditions, and the emergence of innovative systems of management. Frequently, several factors combine to cause a shakeout. The more radical the shift, the more swift and devastating the ensuing shakeout, as happened after the deregulation of the airline and trucking industries.

When a shakeout occurs early in an industry's life cycle, as happened in the PC industry, it can indicate either the emergence of a dominant technological design or the existence of a "majority fallacy." In the first scenario, a major technological design is widely accepted by customers as the standard, but some companies do not or cannot adapt their manufacturing or marketing operations to match that design. Their inflexibility causes those companies to fail to meet customer expectations, leading ultimately to their exiting the industry. The shakeout rids the industry of weak competitors, giving survivors a bigger share of the growing industry.

In the second scenario, large numbers of individual entrepreneurs and established companies enter an industry, attracted primarily by its promise of quick growth and easy profits. They constitute a majority, persuaded that the industry has made its transition from startup to fast growth. Well-financed and managed, the early entrants proceed either to acquire the truly pioneering companies or to replace them. Because even a growing and prosperous industry cannot always fulfill the expectations of all entrants, many fail to achieve market success. As a result, a shakeout occurs, ridding the industry of weak new entrants and inflexible pioneers. The IBM-compatible personal computer market, which in the mid-1980s went through such a shakeout, serves as an example of this fallacy.

A shakeout that occurs later in an industry's life cycle manifests a different combination of powerful forces. It often signals the industry's movement to the maturity stage, where demand plateaus, as happened in the tire industry, for example. This shift forces some companies to exit the industry because they fail to achieve appropriate profits. Moreover, as industry maturity approaches, product substitutes multiply and cause further declines in demand for an individual company's products. Further, mature industries often invite entry by foreign companies, forcing existing companies to scale down their expectations, exit the industry, or attempt to become globalized themselves.

Shakeouts in a mature industry can also be caused by "dematuring." A technologically adept competitor can open a new competitive front by deploying technologies from outside the base industry. Typically, firms use some form of information technology to transform their business, by infusing intelligence and other attributes into their products or dramatically altering their production and operating processes.[30] For example, in the late 1980s, Yamaha revived a moribund piano industry by developing a digital piano that could play itself (using instructions stored on a floppy disk), teach a novice how to play, or serve as a traditional piano. As a result, Yamaha altered the needed core competencies in the industry, and many competitors that lacked the requisite technological capabilities were forced to exit.

Industries may experience more than one shakeout. Because of the vast number of producers, the U.S. automobile industry experienced its first shakeout in 1920 and 1921. Having barely recovered from this shakeout, the industry experienced a second massive shakeout in the early 1930s, triggered by the Great Depression. Still a third shakeout occurred in the 1940s as a result of the exorbitant costs associated with competition in a growing national market. As we will see in chapter 2, this shakeout led to the consolidation of the industry in which three firms came to dominate the industry's sales.[31]

The auto industry is not alone in experiencing multiple shakeouts. The financial service industry has undergone similar changes. The early deregulation of the industry in the 1980s led to a massive shakeout. Near the end of that decade, however, global competitive forces and technological advances led to another serious shakeout.

Clearly, with rapid global and technological changes, executives can no longer accept the folk wisdom that shakeouts result just from industry maturity. Industries may experience multiple shakeouts at different points in their evolution. These shakeouts often require different strategies in order to ensure company survival.

On the one hand, forces of technology and globalization most often cause sudden changes in industry structure. These forces can be linked, as when technology diffusion across countries causes seismic changes in an industry. For example, the emergence of global players such as Airbus in the aerospace industry led to industry realignment and the exit of marginal players such as Lockheed Martin and then McDonnell Douglas from the commercial aviation business.

On the other hand, market-driven shakeouts (through mergers and acquisitions) and those induced through gradual regulatory relaxation tend to have an evolutionary impact. In the case of a historically heavily regulated industry such as telecommunications, a complex network of forces is coming into play. All four of the drivers of change discussed in this chapter are having significant effects. Changes in regulatory policies in numerous countries are rapidly creating a highly globalized industry. Technological changes are coming at a rapid pace, driven by the convergent power of digital electronics. Customers' needs are escalating. The combination of these forces is leading to a shakeout in the industry on a global basis.

Early Warning Signs for Shakeouts

Forward-looking firms can anticipate an impending shakeout in their industry by observing the leading indicators of major change. Some of these indicators are industry specific. In the personal computer software business, for example, the sales of software development kits for a new operating system provide a strong signal of coming shifts in the industry. For the majority of industries, we can identify a number of "generic" indicators of major change and possibly an industry shakeout:

- The expiration of crucial patents long held by market leaders, thereby setting the stage for a majority fallacy, followed by a shakeout.
- Sudden and large changes in trade barriers (such as the adoption of free trade agreements), leading to an unsustainable proliferation of rivals in a market.
- The rate of growth of new companies far in excess of the market growth over a lengthy period of time, such that most players cannot continue to operate profitably in the industry.
- Prolonged capacity underutilization in the industry, suggesting building pressures for voluntary or forced market exit.
- Technology breakthroughs both within an industry and in industries producing substitute products, as well as a flurry of new patent activity in a core technology for an industry.
- The sudden influx of overseas competitors into a market, resulting when key technologies become accessible to new entrants or when an industry has been targeted as "strategic" in another country.
- Shakeouts in upstream or downstream industries.

It does not take a prophet to recognize the signs of coming change, but the signals are many and varied, and they can be misinterpreted. Companies, like individuals, often see and hear what they want to see and hear. They interpret the world in self-serving terms. They view threats to the existing order with great alarm. Rather than investing real and psychological capital in the status quo, they would be far better served by adopting a "crisis imminent" mind-set, one that prepares them for an industry shakeout at any point. We take up later (chapter 8) the primary causes of market disruptions, but first we turn attention in chapter 2 to a deeper analysis of the triumvirates that dominate or that are in the process of forming in major industries throughout the free markets of the world economy. What is so special about the notion of *three* major players in a competitive market? Why are there sometimes more than or fewer than three in a given industry? And how does their dominance affect the typically smaller niche players that somehow find the means not just of surviving in a highly competitive market, but of doing quite well?

2

Where Three Is Not a Crowd

Once globally dominant, the U.S. consumer electronics industry is today virtually nonexistent, with the exception of some specialized manufacturers. In the heyday of radio, the Big 3 companies were General Electric, Westinghouse, and Emerson. With the advent of television as a major force in the industry, RCA and Zenith emerged to occupy the inner circle, relegating Westinghouse and Emerson to the sidelines. When electronics technology shifted from vacuum tubes to solid-state components, the move caught GE, RCA, and Zenith—each with a massive investment in vacuum tube technology—unprepared. Manufacturing leadership gradually shifted to relatively unencumbered Japanese companies.

Consider the case of RCA. For years the RCA dog tilted its head toward a trumpet speaker attached to an old Victrola phonograph and listened to its "master's voice." The famous logo of the Radio Corporation of America, acquired in 1929 when RCA purchased the Victor Talking Machine Company, symbolized both the dog's and the record player's high fidelity that reproduced the voice so faithfully that it must have seemed real, albeit somewhat puzzling, to a canine brain. Once a powerful company in the U.S. consumer electronics market, RCA pretty much silenced that voice when it attempted to create a new videodisk technology. Hoping this innovation would succeed videotapes, RCA lost more than $500 million in the early 1980s when it failed to convince other manufacturers to adopt the videodisk standard.

Competition completely transformed the consumer electronics marketplace in the 1970s and 1980s. In 1984 alone, the United States incurred a $9.6 billion trade deficit in such products, up a staggering 44 percent in only one year. RCA eventually merged with General Electric in 1986. As recent ads show, the RCA dog has grown up and has a pup of its own. The two, however, are sitting in awe before a giant-screen television set that has the same brand name but a very different corporate identity, now that RCA was acquired by Thomson Multimedia, S.A. in 1998, when GE CEO Jack Welch decided to get out of the consumer electronics business altogether. He sold RCA to Thomson, thereby opening the way for the government-owned French company to gain a 23 percent share of the U.S. market. No match for the real powerhouses in this industry—Matsushita, Sony, and Philips—Thomson itself now teeters on the edge of the ditch because of its weak prospects and precarious financial condition, although it has recently undertaken a joint venture with Seagate Technology to develop a digital storage capability for consumer electronics.

The rise and fall of once powerful companies have been the subject of endless speculation. Traditionally economists have theorized that most industries can be categorized in one of two groups: either a few companies dominate the market by virtue of their size, wealth, and economies of scale and scope; or numerous smaller firms, each differentiated as a specialist, jockey for position and exhibit the characteristics of monopolies. Where a few companies compete, the market is said to be *oligopolistic* (from the Greek *oligos,* a few). At the opposite end of the spectrum are *monopolistic* markets in which one company almost completely controls the niche it occupies or is so far ahead of its competitors that they pose no threat.

The Rule of Three takes issue with this dichotomy. Our observations lead us to conclude that industries such as consumer electronics, automobiles, pharmaceuticals, and a host of others evolve into a structure in which both oligopolistic competition *and* monopolistic competition occur simultaneously and in ways that are usually complementary. That is, the most efficient structure is one in which a few firms control the major share of the market, while specialists—

in effect, small submonopolies—operate in niches not served by the full-line generalists.

In this chapter we examine the first half of this theory—namely, that industries naturally evolve in ways that ultimately favor the rise and dominance of a few, typically three, major players, the oligarchs (chapter 3 takes up the second half of this theory and examines more closely the specialists, which occupy small niches). In the ideal, most efficient structure, the oligopoly comprises three major competitors. Why three is the optimal number is a question we consider at length, even as we examine those conditions in which the Rule of Three does not apply. Of course, the types and sizes of companies likely to succeed as oligopolists depend on many factors associated with the costs of competing. Any one of the top players can easily lose its dominance and fall into the ditch, where it becomes a prime target for one of its competitors. Time and again this predicament has befallen some of the best-known U.S. automakers.

The U.S. Automobile Industry

Nearly all industries start out with a lot of companies competing against each other to provide the products and services their customers want. Usually only a few survive long enough to become serious market players. When the U.S. automobile industry cranked up around the turn of the twentieth century, for example, some 500 car manufacturers competed for a share of the new market. By 1908, only about 200 of them survived. That year William C. ("Billy") Durant created the General Motors Corporation, combining the Buick Motor Company and the Oakland Motor Company (later reorganized as Pontiac) with two competitors: the Oldsmobile Motor Car Company, where Ransom Eli Olds had been making cars since 1897, including the popular "curved dash" Oldsmobile; and the Cadillac Motor Car Company, founded by Henry Martyn Leland in 1902. Durant tried but failed to convince Henry Ford to join the new company. Despite production and financial setbacks in the early years, Ford decided to pursue his alphabet of cars, and between 1903 and 1909, the Ford Motor Company produced a sufficient number of models to go from "A" to "S."

Launched in 1909, the Model T became, in Henry Ford's words, a car "for the great multitude, constructed of the best material after the simplest designs that modern engineering can devise, so low in price that no man making a good salary will be unable to own one."[1] Ford designed it so that it served as a "farmer's car": few accessories, little comfort, and a no-frills paint job only in black. With its high clearance and light weight, it was the perfect car for all sorts of chores; its engine could even run many farm implements.

By 1917, the automobile industry in the United States was down to only 23 producers.[2] GM and Ford commanded the lion's share, but a company founded by two brothers, John and Horace Dodge, both machinists and bicycle builders, began making inroads. Henry Ford used the Dodge brothers' company as a supplier of engines and other parts for his cars. This strategy enabled Ford to concentrate on design and assembly while leaving many of the manufacturing costs to his suppliers. Ford management dictated the pace of work, within limits, by controlling the speed of the assembly line. By moving the work to the men, Ford found a way to "speed up the slow men and slow down the fast men," a development that brought an incredible regularity to the Ford factory, "almost as dependable as the rising of the sun."[3] The assembly line lowered the average labor expenditure per car from more than twelve hours to just over an hour and a half. Coupled with highly standardized, interchangeable parts that required no reworking or machining, the assembly-line process allowed Ford to sell more cars for much less money. In 1916, the price of the Model T fell to a mere $360, and Ford sold 577,000—all of them in black. By 1920, 60 percent of all cars on the road were Fords.[4] In 1923, sales of over 2 million vehicles clearly established the Model T as the most popular car in America.

At the same time GM was making significant technological advancements of its own. The invention of Duco lacquer paint, for instance, cut drying time from weeks to hours. This innovation allowed GM to offer cars in many colors, giving it a big marketing advantage over Ford, whose vehicles were still restricted to one color. General Motors continued to grow rapidly into an industry powerhouse, becoming so wealthy that not even the Great Depression could stop its momentum. In 1933, needing funds for new product development that Michigan banks could not provide, GM teamed with the federal government's Reconstruction Finance Corporation to form the National Bank of Detroit.

Ford lost market leadership to GM in the mid-1920s and has played #2 ever since. The fault was partly Henry Ford's own: so attached to the Model T in design and price, he refused to modify the vehicle even as public tastes changed. If the Model T was not selling, as Ford said, it was because his salesmen were not selling it. As the decade of the 1920s came to an end, the Ford Motor Company finally developed a new model, but by then it was too late. The stock market crashed, and the Great Depression put a halt to car sales in large volume. The automobile industry would not recover for another 20 years.

By 1929, GM, Ford, and Chrysler accounted for 75 percent of all cars, but many of their competitors, some of which were industry pioneers, had already disappeared. Haynes, Apperson, Winton, Locomobile, and Stanley, for example, went under or were consolidated. Newer and highly regarded companies such as Rickenbacker and Wills Saint Claire went bankrupt. During the Depression, Pierce-Arrow, Peerless, Jordan, Stutz, Franklin, Marmon, DuPont, Durant, Auburn, Cord, Hupmobile, and many others disappeared entirely.

The economic boom following World War II, coupled with the vast national construction project known as the Interstate Highway System, helped the U.S. automobile industry to surge ahead. New car sales reached 4.8 million in 1949 and 7.2 million in 1955. Still, small companies struggled. Studebaker and Packard, for example, merged in 1954, but even combining their resources did not keep the new company out of the ditch. The last Packard was produced in 1958, and Studebaker ceased production in 1963. Similarly, Nash and Hudson merged in 1954 to form American Motors, which had a longer life span, but the company was sold to Chrysler in 1987. The industry that began with some 500 companies at the beginning of the twentieth century was reduced—through consolidation, takeovers, bankruptcy, and mismanagement—to only three players.

Until 1965, the Big 3 automakers had the U.S. market almost completely to themselves. Imports claimed only 5.8 percent of the nearly 11 million cars and trucks sold that year. The Japanese automakers managed to sell only 30,000 cars in the United States, a market share of less than 0.33 percent. When the Volkswagen Beetle started setting trends, General Motors, Ford, and Chrysler responded by developing their own "import fighters": the Corvair, the Falcon, and the Valiant, respectively.

Although they controlled the U.S. market, the Big 3 automakers developed a well-deserved reputation for being in the wrong place with the wrong product at the wrong time. In the late 1950s and 1960s, they built heavy, chrome-laden "gas guzzlers," which became the industry dinosaurs after the oil crisis of 1977. At a time when the average car sold for considerably less than $10,000, the Japanese automakers grew market share through more efficient production, by as much as an astounding $2,500 per vehicle.[5] By the end of the 1970s, the Japanese automakers were so successful that Detroit had to resort to seeking government intervention in imposing import quotas, a move that only hastened another major change in the industry. Beginning with a new Honda facility in 1982, the Japanese set up numerous production sites in the United States. Other car manufacturers soon followed, and by 1999, the "transplants" were building 3.2 million cars a year, capturing a U.S. market share of 18 percent. If the number of vehicles built abroad is factored in, the market share increases to 27.5 percent. Mercedes and Lexus took over the top spots in the U.S. luxury car market, followed in order by Cadillac and Lincoln.

As the automobile industry has become more globalized, the Big 3 companies know that to remain competitive, they must venture beyond their home markets and develop common platforms across international boundaries, as well as enter into joint ventures and partnerships to continue to grow. Worldwide today, there are 40 automakers. Collectively, they face a sizable glut in capacity and heavy pressures to increase efficiency. The result of these forces has been continued consolidation, with the expectation that another threesome will eventually rise to claim dominance, this time on a global level.

This brief review of automobile production in the United States illustrates how a fledgling industry begins with hundreds of competitors, undergoes multiple shakeouts, and eventually recognizes three dominant market players. As we will see more fully in chapter 3, an industry can experience several shakeouts over time. If and when an industry globalizes, subsequent upheavals occur. Inexorably it moves toward another Rule of Three at the global market level.

The Rule of Three—in Theory

Research has shown that, left to their own devices, industries evolve in a fairly consistent pattern. Starting from zero, the number of companies increases slowly as the commercial viability of the new industry takes hold. Small and inefficient, those start-up companies may be spin-offs of existing firms in "adjacent" industries, but they generally lack economies of scale and a well-developed supply function. As a result, they must produce many of their inputs themselves. Demand is also erratic since in the early stages of an industry, little is known about what product attributes customers will value. Companies experiment with technology, product design, and marketing. Market positions are extremely volatile, and the more efficient and innovative firms are able to overtake their more wasteful competitors, as suggested above in the discussion of the automobile industry. Examples include personal computers, electronic calculators, and customer relationship management (CRM) software.

As the number of firms continues to increase rapidly, the industry reaches a high level of inefficiency. Because of excess capacity and fragmentation, a shakeout commences, and the number of firms drops dramatically, often by as much as 90 percent. For example, most specialty e-tailers have exited the market, leaving just a handful of survivors in each sector.

After the shakeout the industry begins to become better organized. Struggling for position, the larger companies weigh financial gains against expenditures in the interest of becoming more efficient. They make strategic choices about what products to manufacture, which services to offer, and which markets to compete in. Eventually three emerge victorious from the struggle. The emergence of the Big 3, however, leaves many holes on the industry playing field, creating opportunities for new entrants or incumbents with highly focused strategies. Thus, it is not unusual to see an increase in the total number of companies in an industry following its rationalization into the Rule of Three on the generalist side.

INDUSTRY CHANGES FROM BIRTH TO MATURITY

Emerging Stage	*Shakeouts*	*Mature Stage*
Many small operators	Smaller number of larger competitors	"Shopping mall" structure
No technical standards	Multiple standards	De facto standards
Fast growth	Faster growth	Slower growth
Ease of entry and exit	Entry and exit barriers	Mobility barriers
High degree of specialization	High degree of specialization	Standardization and specialization
Excess capacity	Rationalized capacity	Renewed capacity
Local focus	National focus	Global focus
Many local or regional brands	National brands	Megabrands and niche brands

Gradually, the sudden and radical innovations give way to the incremental ones, and the industry settles into more standardized ways of doing things. As companies become close substitutes for one another, competitive intensities rise. At the same time, the compatibility in product lines and operating modes makes consolidation an attractive option, even as many nonconforming competitors rapidly exit the industry.[6]

As indicated in the accompanying comparison showing typical industry changes from "birth" to "maturity," numerous small companies in an emerging industry compete against each other. Since industry norms have yet to be established, rarely are there any overriding technical standards; each company operates on its own proprietary platform. Growth is high, and the players' lack of economies of scale means that entry and exit barriers are low. Each firm tends to be a product specialist, and there is little overlap in offerings. Often at this stage, companies have a decidedly local or at most regional flavor; accordingly, their distribution reach and their brand recognition are circumscribed by that limited geography.

When many firms simultaneously enter a fledgling industry where there are few customers, capacity far exceeds demand. After the industry grows and experiences one or more shakeouts, it presents a distinctly different profile. Through widespread exit by marginal players and the merger or "roll-up" of many others, the industry tends to be dominated by a smaller number of larger players (see sidebar "U.S. Defense Contractors"). In its evolution the industry adopts technology standards, either by consensus or by the exit of competitors opposed to the dominant standard. Growth accelerates as the industry's efficiency and standardization improve the value equation and attract more customers whose preferences become better defined and known. Companies erect substantial barriers to entry in an effort to safeguard market share, but this effort requires a major commitment of resources.

U.S. Defense Contractors[7]

TODAY the Big 3 defense contractors in the United States are Lockheed (24 percent share in 1998), Boeing (15 percent), and Raytheon (11 percent). Although together they controlled only 50 percent of the market in 1998, and received a corresponding share of the defense procurement budget, which has remained at $130 billion a year since 1994 (unadjusted for inflation), the rise of the Big 3 in this industry is a complex story of mergers, acquisitions, politics, and business decisions.

In 1991, the top ten U.S. defense contractors claimed 41 percent of the Department of Defense procurement budget, which totaled $151 billion. No single company had more than a 6 percent share of that budget. General Electric, which was then in third place with a 5 percent share, sold its aerospace business to Martin Marietta, thereby dropping to the tenth position.

In 1994, Martin Marietta merged with Lockheed, and the new company jumped to the #1 position with a 9 percent share of the market. That year all defense contractors with the exception of Lockheed Martin, McDonnell Douglas, and Northrup Grumman lost market share. Even Raytheon, which acquired the defense unit of the Chrysler Corporation, lost about a third of its defense-related revenue. By 1994, only four companies—Lockheed, McDonnell Douglas, Northrup, and GM-Hughes—had a share of 3 percent or greater of the budget. That lineup represented a significant contrast to the ten companies just three years earlier, each of which had between 3 percent and 6 percent share. Also in 1994, Raytheon had only a 2 percent share, whereas the giant Boeing Corporation claimed no more than a 1 percent share of the defense procurement budget.

For the next few years, the major contractors grew apace. In 1997, however, the number of acquisitions shot up like a heat-seeking missile. The post-Cold War defense budget was cut to $127 billion, and the major contractors scrambled to claim a piece of it. Boeing bought McDonnell Douglas in one of the ten largest mergers in U.S. history up until that time. Northrup purchased the defense arm of Westinghouse, but still fell into the ditch with only an 8 percent share of market. In buying the defense business that Texas Instruments had operated, Raytheon staked out a shaky #3 position.

That position was solidified to some extent when Raytheon beat Northrup to the punch in acquiring the Hughes Aircraft business from General Motors. The $9.5 billion purchase involved a complicated stock switch that saved GM over $3 billion in taxes, but even more significant was the fact that only one company—Raytheon—would be left to make missiles that could be launched from air, sea, and land.

It is interesting to note that GE, although a generalist in all of its other markets, has decided to act like a specialist in this market, focusing primarily on jet engines.

Exit barriers are also more significant. Because companies have invested a great deal in establishing themselves in the industry, they are reluctant to abandon sunk costs and other expenditures. Much of the industry's excess capacity is removed as inefficient companies exit, and the balance is rationalized and deployed toward the industry's most attractive opportunities. The industry evolves to a broader geographic focus, often at the national level. Commensurate with the reduction in the number of competitors, the number of brands shrinks dramatically.

Moving beyond this stage in the industry's evolution, we find that the Rule of Three comes into play, and the industry structures itself according to the "shopping mall" analogy described in the Introduction. The primary change from the previous stage is that the number of players in the industry can actually *increase* even as the large companies coalesce into the Big 3. That is, as the Big 3 stabilize their business models, they withdraw from a number of pockets within the overall market. They recognize that their competencies are an ill match for the requirements of those niches. Such market gaps never last long in a competitive market, and new entrants rush to fill them.

A mature industry is also characterized by numerous opportunities for innovation and nichemanship, and many small companies can thrive in the shadow of the Big 3. Because some of these specialized niches differ greatly from the mainstream market served by the inner circle players, they may in fact have very different technology standards. Overall, though, the bulk of the market adheres to a *de facto* standard. Reflecting its maturity, the industry grows at a rate slower than it was before and during the shakeout period, but nonetheless quite healthy, given that the industry is operating at a peak of efficiency and effectiveness. While entry barriers are low for companies aiming to be niche players, the barriers to moving from one strategic group to another are very high. Generalists and specialists cannot cross the chasm without great risk to themselves. The industry has simultaneous standardization (among the generalists) and specialization (among the specialists, of course). Specialists typically create new capacity in the industry. The industry can now begin to expand its geographic interest beyond the national scope and look to global competition. In terms of branding, the Big 3 use broadly defined "megabrands" that can span multiple products, whereas specialists have a different brand focused on each niche served. In the larger picture, a few generalists and a host of specialists can live comfortably side by side, without stepping on each other's toes. In competitive markets at least, oligopolistic and monopolistic firms are not mutually exclusive.

Why Three?

A market structure based on three major players is both more stable and more competitive than one with two players. Why this is so is one of the distinguishing features of competitive markets.

Mutual Assured Destruction or Collusion

On the one hand, when there are just two players, the outcome is either mutual destruction or collusion that is ultimately damaging to customers. Either scenario produces a de facto monopoly. On the other hand, in most markets a coalition of two out of the three is strong enough to block any predatory intentions that the third might have. Just that threat prevents an attack, since the would-be "victim" can always seek the assistance of the third to counterbalance.

The U.S. agricultural equipment market offers an interesting case in which three full-line generalists—John Deere, CNH Global, and AGCO—occupy the top positions. The #2 player, CNH Global, was formed through the merger of New Holland N.V. and Case Corporation on November 15, 1999.[8] Prior to this merger, Case and New Holland were second and third in terms of their shares of the agricultural equipment market. Case was looking for ways to cut operating costs without compromising the quality of its products, and like Deere, it wanted to penetrate emerging markets. New Holland, which was formed in May 1991 when Fiat Geotech S.p.A. and Ford New Holland, Inc. merged, produced a full line of agricultural equipment products. It wanted to expand globally while keeping its emphasis on product innovation. The combination of Case and New Holland created a strong second-place generalist to challenge John Deere, at least as part of a long-term strategy. In corporate size, product lines, and brand loyalty, CNH Global is integrating the manufacturing, engineering, purchasing, and other business functions from Case and New Holland, while maintaining both companies' widely recognized brands.[9] This merger of the #2 and #3 players, in effect, bumped up AGCO to the new #3 position, despite its large debts incurred from a string of acquisitions.

In contrast to the evolution of the U.S. agricultural equipment market, recent revelations about years of collusive behavior between the two dominant auction houses, London-based Christie's International plc and Sotheby's, based in New York, indicate the dangers of having only two major players. In 2000, the two companies, which together control 90 percent of the world market, pled guilty to having colluded in 1994 and 1995 on setting seller fees, sharing customer lists, and keeping employee salaries low.[10] Christie's and Sotheby's each have agreed to pay $256 million as a settlement to plaintiffs in a class-action suit against the companies.

With three main players, there is less predatory competition as well as a lower likelihood of collusion or mutual destruction. The third player can refuse to collude, or it chooses to cooperate with the victim to keep the other two at bay, or it skillfully pits one powerful player against the other. Analogously, during the Cold War between the two superpowers, there was in fact a third bloc that was in many ways the most powerful. The so-called nonaligned nations became quite adept at playing off one superpower against the other, usually to their advantage.

The Search for Greatest Efficiency

Our analysis indicates that an industry structure based on the Rule of Three provides the best blend of competitive intensity, overall efficiency, industry profitability, and customer satisfaction.

The well-known PIMS (Profit Impact of Market Strategies) studies concluded that market share and return on investment are strongly related. Economies of scale, the phenomenon of the "experience curve," market power, and quality of management are typically all greater in companies with high market shares. But the importance of market share varies among industries: it is greater for fragmented industries and infrequently purchased products.[11] These findings were confirmed by an analysis of 48 separate studies presenting a combined total of 276 market share–profitability relationships. In this analysis the researchers found that, on average, market share has a positive effect on business profitability.[12] Moreover, evidence suggests that lower costs rather than higher prices account for most of the greater profitability of high market-share businesses. This conclusion should allay arguments that high market share automatically leads to greater market power and price gouging.[13] Finally, economies of scale and scope benefit those companies with high market shares. They are able to make more efficient use of marketing (for example, communication efforts) and nonmarketing resources (procurement, logistics, and the like).[14]

That said, large companies in a competitive market do best when their market share does not exceed approximately 40 percent. When they grow beyond that mark, they can start losing their profitability, run into trouble with regulatory agencies, and experience the agony of no new growth. Incremental markets and customers can be more expensive to acquire and often generate less revenue. Companies with high market shares also find that the costs of subsidy across customers tend to increase as well. That is, there is always going to be a blend of profitable and unprofitable customers, and in many cases a company simply elects to put up with the unprofitable (or only marginally profitable) ones.

Some large companies go to great extremes to manipulate the

public's perception of their growth potential and to divert the eye of regulatory agencies. Consider the case of AT&T a few years ago. Before its forced breakup in 1984, AT&T was the dominant player in its market as a long-distance and local carrier. Given that it had over 1 million employees and assets in excess of $100 billion, it was by far the largest company in the United States. Indeed, it was a monopoly, as regulators determined when they forced the company to divest itself of the regional telephone companies.

In one annual report, the company claimed $70 billion in annual revenue and a 65 percent share of the U.S. long-distance market. When we read that report, we took interest in a statement the company made to its shareholders: namely, that in terms of the entire global information industry, which at the time was estimated to have some $2 trillion in annual revenues, AT&T's "share" was quite small—a mere 3.5 percent. The company concluded that despite its apparent size and market dominance, it was merely a small fish in a very large pond. As such, it had plenty of room to grow. Accordingly, investors should treat the company as a growth stock rather than just another utility. Implicit in this message was the argument that it was silly and inappropriate to continue to regulate AT&T as the dominant player in its market.

Of course, AT&T's competitors predictably took a somewhat different view of this situation. The company's own managers probably defined the scope of its business more narrowly than "the global information industry," as the annual report put it. On the one hand, that definition included TV game shows to magazines to semiconductors—all businesses that presumably would not be in AT&T's future. On the other hand, those managers who continued to view AT&T's domain as consisting principally of the U.S. long-distance market would be clearly guilty of possessing a myopic view of AT&T's business and its relevant market. After the passage of the 1996 Telecommunications Act, a broader definition—in other words, a more expansive demarcation of the "pond"—to include local telephony, wireless, and video transmission became logical and necessary.

The Equilibrium Point

Markets characterized by the Rule of Three simultaneously feature reasonable customer choice, moderate competitive intensity, and high market efficiency. No wonder it seems to be the point of equilibrium in many an industry. From a societal perspective, it is often assumed that customers suffer the most when competition dwindles, but a high degree of market concentration is not necessarily incompatible with consumer welfare. In fact, fragmented markets usually cost consumers more, since no firm is able to achieve economies of scale and all firms are expending high levels of resources on fighting one another rather than serving their customers. The Rule of Three still leaves as much as 30 percent of the market for the specialists to serve, and entry barriers are only entrepreneurial, not legal or regulatory ones. The benefits of this structure can be seen in industries that have recently achieved profitability as well as increased customer and employee satisfaction. For example, the U.S. airline industry, which greatly increased its profitability in the late 1990s after years of enormous losses, is rapidly moving to the Rule of Three. We expect that commodity industries such as aluminum and copper will also finally start rewarding their shareholders with better financial performance as they move to a Rule of Three structure worldwide.

Why Not More than Three?

Because only three players are needed to create a balance of power, the fourth player becomes expendable in the market's push toward efficiency. More important, however, we believe that the Rule of Three is strongly linked with the theory that on average customers consider at most three choices before making a purchase.[15] These options constitute what is called the consumer's "evoked set" or "consideration set," which is actually nothing more than the short list of options a typical shopper considers. Likewise, in industrial and commercial markets, customers typically consider at most three suppliers. Volume-oriented competitors such as the #1, #2, and #3 players have to be very concerned about getting into this "inner circle" that a consumer or customer first thinks about. In short, the full-line generalist has to offer one of the top three brands. Because transaction costs rise with choice, the most efficient number for gaining maximum value through competition is three.

In some industries, almost always outside the United States, a "Rule of Four" appears to be in operation. In Europe, this level of competition arose not only because of the disjointed nature of the European market in the past but also because of a long-standing sense of nationalism in infrastructure industries such as railroads, airlines, and telecommunications. Most industries support large players from Germany, France, and the United Kingdom. In addition, a fourth successful player might emerge from Italy, Spain, Switzerland, or Scandinavia. Europe's big four airlines, for example, are British Airways, Air France, Lufthansa, and KLM Royal Dutch Airlines. The most significant phone companies are British Telecom, Deutsche Telecom, France Telecom, and Telecom Italia. In a short time, however, these Big 4 players are likely to lose one of their own. As the European economy evolves toward unification, and as barriers to cross-border consolidation dissolve, we expect to see the Rule of Three come more fully into play. On a country-by-country basis, the Rule of Three is clearly evident, as examples cited earlier suggest (see also Appendix 2 for a sampling of Big 3 companies by nation).

The pattern is seen elsewhere, but for different reasons. Japan, for example, currently has four big stockbrokers (Nikko Securities, Daiwa, Nomura, and Yamaichi), four major convenience stores chains (7-Eleven's 6,400 stores, Lawson's 5,700 stores, Family Mart's 3,400 stores, and Sunshop Yamazaki's 2,700 stores). Among car companies, several of the "minor majors" have decided to focus their operations more narrowly (for example, Isuzu around sport utility vehicles, Subaru around four-wheel-drive vehicles). Of the remaining Big 5 automakers—Toyota, Nissan, Honda, Mitsubishi, and Mazda—it appears evident that Mazda cannot make it on its own. Ford already owns 33 percent of the company, and we predict that that level of ownership will soon increase to 100 percent. An anomaly in this market, Mitsubishi Motors produces a full line of vehicles even though its market share is very low. As a member of the mammoth Mitsubishi corporate empire, however, the company's automotive operations have been propped up by other diversified operations. Also, it produces cars for other car makers. If it does not merge with another automaker, the company will have to retreat into a narrower profile, either producing cars to be sold under other brand names or focusing on a limited number of successful products such as its popular sports cars. In 2000, DaimlerChrysler agreed to acquire a sizable stake in the company, signaling a now familiar turn in the automobile industry toward fewer players.

The Big 4 inevitably become the Big 3, as one falls by the wayside or two of the companies merge to become the new #1 or #2. For example, until 1996, there were four major manufacturers of computer disk drives. Seagate merged with Conner Peripherals early in 1996, and became the top-selling disk drive vendor, ahead of Quantum, which had held the top position since 1993. The new #3 player is Western Digital Corporation. The rapid rate of technological change, intense margin pressures, and relative lack of specialization opportunities in this market caused some weaker players such as Hewlett-Packard to exit. Other marginal players sold out to more diversified electronics companies. For example, Hyundai Electronics took over former #5 Maxtor, and Singapore Technologies purchased Micropolis.

In the gas turbine business, the four major players until recently were General Electric, Westinghouse Electric, Siemens, and ABB. The business is highly competitive, margins are razor thin, prices are falling, and there is substantial industry overcapacity (estimated to range from 25 to 40 percent) despite repeated downsizing by the four major players. The core markets of Europe and North America are stagnant, while prices in emerging markets are cutthroat. Given these conditions, it became likely that one of the Big 4 would have to exit the market. In fact, Siemens has recently bought Westinghouse's gas turbine business. Having spun off its industrial holdings, Westinghouse has reinvented itself as a media company.

In the liquor business, the big four spirits makers are Guinness's United Distillers, Grand Metropolitan's IDV, Allied Domecq, and Seagram. This business is rapidly globalizing. For example, it has resulted in the steady consolidation of the Scotch whisky industry, where Guinness, through United Distillers, controls 26.5 percent of Scotland's malt whisky production capacity. Seagram's is the second largest player with 14.7 percent, and Allied Domecq is third with 11 percent. With continued globalization, there will no longer be room for four big players, and one of them will retreat to a specialist position or merge with another company.

Barriers to the Rule of Three

These instances suggest a trend in industry consolidation toward the conditions favorable for the dominance of three major players, but by no means do they indicate that this trend is happening everywhere. The Rule of Three does not apply when naturally occurring competitive forces are thwarted by regulatory and protectionist impediments. We would not expect three full-line generalists to emerge in markets where any of the following conditions—all of which are artificial creations—occur:

- **Regulation:** The industries most susceptible to government regulation include those that directly serve the public: utilities, highways, airports, telephone, and the like. Government agencies act to limit competition in order to allow incumbents to serve everyone and to recover their capital investment. If regulatory policies hinder market consolidation, as they have in Japan, India, Russia, and other countries, or allow for the existence of "natural" monopolies, as was the case with the local telecommunications market, the Rule of Three is not operational. With deregulation, it comes into play, as illustrated by the consolidations in the U.S. long-distance telecommunications industry, leading to the emergence of AT&T, MCI, and Sprint as the Big 3. The 1984 breakup of AT&T created seven regional "Baby Bells," which over the years through mergers and acquisitions have regrouped themselves into three: the #1 provider, Verizon (a combination of Bell Atlantic and NYNEX, as well as GTE); SBC Communications (formed from Pacific Bell, Southwestern Bell, and Ameritech) in second place; and the #3 player BellSouth, which is expanding operations in Latin America. In the wireless industry, the Big 3 are Verizon Wireless, Cingular, and AT&T Wireless.
- **Exclusive rights.** If licenses, patents, and trademarks are major factors, the market in question must be viewed as a collection of monopolies, which are not subject to traditional competitive forces. In the chemicals industry in the United States, where patents are not so paramount as they are for the large pharma-

ceutical companies, the Rule of Three has selected E. I. Du Pont de Nemours, Dow Chemical, and Monsanto. In the specialty chemical markets such as pharmaceuticals, which have traditionally been heavily restricted by patents and licenses, we would not expect to see the Rule of Three govern market evolution. However, as we discuss later, recent changes in the pharmaceutical industry have shortened the exclusivity window on patents and hastened a move toward the Rule of Three structure.

- **Major barriers to trade and foreign ownership of assets:** In this case, we see the Rule of Three operating at the national level but not at the global level. The Rule of Three may still be seen in the formation of global groups or alliances, as we believe is likely to occur in the global telecommunications market. Other examples include the airline and railroad industries, as well as national postal systems.

- **Markets with a high degree of vertical integration:** To the extent that certain customer groups are captive to in-house suppliers or vice versa, the emergence of three full-line players in the supplier market is unlikely. For example, GM had its AC Delco unit, whereas Ford had Visteon. Vertical integration impedes traditional competitive market forces by tying up suppliers and customers internally and preventing them from buying and selling freely in the open market. Over time, many such arrangements are likely to break down, triggering the Rule of Three in the process. In fact, both GM and Ford have spun off their auto supply units. The oil industry is another example of the breakdown of vertical integration, in this case between refining and distribution.

- **Markets with combined ownership and management:** If ownership and management are combined, as in the case of professional services, the market process is not allowed to work. Owner-based businesses, in general, including most professional services such as law firms, accounting firms, consultants, and advertising agencies remain an exception to the Rule of Three. Ownership creates emotional attachment and inhibits purely efficiency-driven, economic decision making. This is one explanation why the Big 5 accounting firms—PricewaterhouseCoopers, Arthur Andersen, Ernst & Young, Deloitte Touche Tohmatsu, and KPMG International—may not become the Big 3. That said, it should be noted that those five firms are themselves the products of acquisitions that have reduced the number of major accounting firms from the Big 8 of only a few years ago. Moreover, as these industries go public and as ownership is separated from management, we expect to see the Rule of Three become operational.

- **Licensed economies:** In years past, many countries placed limits on production, chiefly in the former Soviet bloc of countries, as well as in China, India, and emerging economies. Companies in India, for example, were required to obtain government licenses to raise production levels. This type of regulation effectively prevented any one company from growing large enough to initiate a Rule of Three within its industry. This exception to the Rule of Three is temporary, although the path to free-market-driven economies is sure to be longer for some than for others. Examples of licensed economies include Mexico, Brazil, India, Russia, and many former Soviet-bloc nations.

When these barriers fall, markets move quickly toward the ideal equilibrium and stability that the Rule of Three posits. Nearly all of the barriers noted above are starting to crumble. As a result, an increasing number of industries in more countries are likely to come under the sway of the Rule of Three. But numerous stumbling points remain in the path of even the best-managed companies, especially those pondering whether to stop competing against the #1, #2, and #3 companies in order to pursue a life as a specialist. This is one of the key questions we take up in chapter 3, which examines in detail the complementary relationship between generalists and specialists in competitive markets.

3

Specialists and Generalists

As in life, so in business, there is no one formula for success. Each company must develop a strategy that best fits its capabilities, resources, circumstances, and opportunities. The failure of company leaders to understand this basic principle is one of the key reasons why their companies slide into the "ditch," described in chapter 1 as that unenviable trough between the full-line generalists and the specialists. Commanding only a small percentage of the market, the ditch-dwellers are squeezed between the generalists on the right, which control the largest share of the market and succeed on the basis of high volume, and the specialists on the left, whose individual market shares may be no more than 5 percent, but who stay successful because of their high margins.

The present chapter examines more closely the contrasts between generalists and specialists. It argues that rather than being seen as outright competitors, these two groups are better conceived as occupying complementary positions within a market. In most cases, they are neither going after the same customer, nor interested in selling the same products. The poet Rudyard Kipling once said of East and West that "never the twain will meet" (outside of Heaven). Given our earlier depiction of these two competitive groups, it could be said of the generalists and the specialists that Right is Right and Left is Left—and if they meet, it's probably going to be in the Ditch.

Economists and experts in market structures have traditionally assumed that firms in the same industry are, by virtue of that fact, competitors. We now understand, however, that firms within an industry do not constitute a monolithic whole, but group themselves according to any number of similarities and purposes—size, products, customer segmentation, targeted markets, processes, and the like. For identification purposes, we can call them "strategic groups." That is, they follow strategies that are consistent within their group but quite different from those adopted by other groups.

Most industries have at least two strategic groups: a small group of oligopolists or full-line generalists (the Big 3, for instance), and a large number of product and market specialists (or in some cases super-nichers, which specialize in both a product and a particular market). Within the two general groups, we can identify five major types of market players:

1. **Full-line generalists** cover the major product categories and market segments within the overall market, as Kellogg's does in the breakfast cereal market, or the Ford Motor Company does in automobiles. Ford, for example, offers vehicles of all sorts to fit practically every budget and purpose, from the modest Taurus to the most luxurious Jaguar or Lincoln Navigator. Most full-line generalists have extensive fixed assets in place, a powerful corporate identity that also doubles as a product brand name, and high levels of efficiency. Both Ford and Toyota have much invested in fixed assets, and both enjoy a corporate identity known around the world.

2. **Portfolio generalists** constitute a special category of full-line players. They cover a market in its broadest range but also participate in adjacent or unrelated markets. Kraft Foods, for instance, competes in the broad cereal market through its Post unit, but also has a wide range of products including Maxwell House coffee, Stove Top Stuffing, Jell-O, and Velveeta. Other famous examples of portfolio generalists include Procter & Gamble, the king of household products as well as the maker of Iams pet food, toothpaste, and beauty care products. The General Electric Company, another portfolio generalist, competes in various industries such as aircraft engines, generators, turbines, medical imaging equipment, and television broadcasting.

Leveraging key assets across their various business units, often by using a common brand name as GE does, portfolio generalists have the additional burden of maintaining the status of a full-line generalist in each of the markets in which they compete. Blending full-line and specialty businesses rarely works well because culture or brand clashes between the two types are bound to arise. Kmart, for example, has experimented—not always successfully—with specialty retailing as in its attempt to sell designer jeans for women or books under the Walden name. In contrast, the Martha Stewart line of linens has proved a popular addition. Unilever's recent acquisition of Ben & Jerry's premium ice cream business may suffer from this problem. In the mainstream ice cream market in the United States, vanilla is the most common flavor, accounting for 30 percent of sales. Known for its slogan "something unexpected and original," Ben & Jerry's developed a reputation for creating the most unusual flavors and combinations—practically anything other than plain vanilla. Unilever's decision to go after vanilla aficionados by creating and marketing a Ben & Jerry's vanilla runs counter to the brand identity of the company it acquired.[1]

3. **Product specialists** are typically technology-based monopolistic competitors. They focus on one product category that has wide appeal for various customers; accordingly they know a lot about the products they sell, but less about the people who buy them. Most product specialists confine their activities to one product category (for example, Just Jeans, The Athlete's Foot, and Toys "R" Us), whereas a few others span multiple categories. Other examples of product specialists include Southwest Airlines, which got its start by providing short-haul air travel; Bose speakers, which are widely said to be the best in the industry; Bang & Olufsen, which concentrates on premium, stylish consumer electronics; and in the biotech industry California-based Amgen, which received almost 95 percent of its $3.6 billion in sales from two drugs—Epogen, used to treat anemia, and Neupogen, which stimulates the immune system.

4. **Market specialists** seek to meet the needs of a specific geographic, demographic, or vertical market. Many exploit their strong relationship with a market by adding offerings that may be related to their initial core product offering. For example, The Limited has a number of retail options to meet the tastes and price preferences of

many women shoppers, including Lerner Shops, Express, Victoria's Secret, and Structure (for men's apparel). The insurance specialist USAA has become a full-line financial services company that remains focused on its core market, namely military officers and their families. German automaker Volkswagen nearly perished in the United States in the early 1980s, but the company has rebounded lately by successfully appealing to a small but loyal market of Generation X customers.

5. **Super nichers** simultaneously specialize in both products and particular markets. Most are intensely focused, single-product, single-market companies. Appealing to a special type of customer and offering a set of unique products and services, super nichers tend to operate under conditions approaching those that characterize a monopoly. The product specialist Foot Locker, for example, has become a super-nicher by adding stores such as Kids Foot Locker and Lady Foot Locker, which focus on athletic shoes for their defined market. Similarly, the Snoopy Store appeals to the under-10 set that has an insatiable appetite for an endless number of products, all on the same theme.

As two strategic groups, specialists and generalists are fundamentally different economic creatures. They are relatively insulated from one another; accordingly, their actions and strategies have the greatest direct impact, not on each other, but on the members of their own strategic group. When one of them decides to change a product or pursue a different segment of the market, members of the other group may hardly feel a ripple—unless, of course, they are targeting the same share of the market or offering similar products and services. Should Foot Locker, for example, decide to expand its product offering by adding women's dress shoes or pocketbooks, it would be seen as infringing upon the territory of full-line generalists.

Respecting each other's unique features and reasons for being, neither a specialist nor a generalist would be advised to try to become the other—not at least without due preparation for what amounts to a major transformation of genetic makeup. Indeed, among strategic groups "mobility barriers" prevent firms from readily moving from one group to another. Akin to entry barriers at the industry level, mobility barriers are a key factor in the formation and operation of the Rule of Three. They reinforce the fact that specialists and generalists are so fundamentally different there is little crossover between the two. As outlined later in this chapter and discussed in chapter 6 in greater detail, specialists need to follow certain paths to success, which differ markedly from those chosen by the Big 3. There are clear guidelines as to the kinds of strategies that different types of players—for example, regional airlines or local banks—should pursue, and research has demonstrated that firms actually perform better to the extent that their competitive behavior conforms to the industry norms for their type of player.[2]

Even though the members of a strategic group may follow similar strategies, it does not follow that they are direct competitors of each other. Thus, two companies could both be market specialists, but target different markets—for example, Dr. Martens boots have a fiercely loyal following of men under 25, whereas Johnston and Murphy (a division of Genesco, Inc.) markets dress shoes to men over the age of 25 and still makes shoes for every U.S. president, as it has done since Millard Fillmore was the chief executive. To the extent that the market definitions are distinct, as they are in this example, the two firms do not compete with one another, although each faces distinct competitors in its chosen market.

As a rule of thumb, the more specialized the player, the more likely that company is to find little or no direct competition. This, of course, is the essence of what economists call monopolistic competition. Relying on high margins, these specialists are found at the extremes of the market's high and low ends, catering to smaller, more concentrated, and often more loyal sets of customers or end-users than their generalist counterparts. They usually command anywhere from 1 percent to 5 percent of the market, but frequently do well within their special niches.

The biggest pitfall for either the specialist or the generalist remains the ditch. Specialists that attempt to expand product offerings in order to compete with the Big 3 can slide down the steep slope of their declining margins as measured against the modest gains that they make in acquiring new customers. In contrast, full-line generalists, especially the #3 player and the ditch players, may feel the need to try to compete with specialists. Unless well planned, such a strategy can have ill effects, pulling the generalist into the ditch from which there may be no escape other than bankruptcy or a merger or both. It usually takes an extraordinary effort and time to develop specialty products and the market for them. As in the case of Kmart's ill-fated attempt to run specialty retailing businesses, when it comes to generalists and specialists, it is best that never the twain should meet.

The Primary Characteristics of Generalists and Specialists

As indicated in the list of contrasting characteristics given below, full-line generalists within an industry are first and foremost volume-driven players, as opposed to the specialists, which are driven by high margins. For the generalists, which exist on the right side of the ditch, financial performance is positively correlated with market share. On the left side, in contrast, the relationship is negatively correlated: the specialists live with a much lower market share, but must depend on a high margin to succeed.

Specialists	*Generalists*
Focus on high margins	Focus on high volume
Emphasis on service and selection	Emphasis on scale and speed
Advantage in exclusivity of product offering	Advantage in high asset utilization
Focused products or services	Full line of products or services
Target market positioning	Broad market positioning
Image- and experience-based competition	Value- and promotion-based competition
Focused channels	Hybrid channels
Multibusiness enterprise	Integrated enterprise
Innovation in products and marketing	Innovation of processes
Multiple brands identity	Single or dual corporate identity
Effectiveness with small trade-offs in efficiency	Efficiency with small trade-offs in effectiveness

High Margins vs. High Volume

The most significant distinction between the two strategic groups is that generalists succeed by virtue of their high volumes, whereas specialists sell fewer products but reap healthy returns because of greater margins. Capitalizing on their great size and on their economies of scale and scope, full-line generalists can attract consumers through "Everyday Low Prices," as Wal-Mart says. The company has made its inventory process both a mark of its excellence and a familiar selling point for consumers (it can replenish its stores much faster than its competitors). Because it deals in such large bulk and controls the supply chain, Wal-Mart can keep its average and marginal costs low. In contrast, the specialist, which stocks and sells fewer products, stays alive by targeting such a narrow audience that it can predict their needs and desires with near absolute accuracy. As illustrated by the check-cashing facility in many urban ghettos, it can keep prices high because it is, in effect, the only show in town, and customers will travel long distances to do business there.

Service and Selection vs. Scale and Speed

Another significant difference is that generalists are scale and speed driven, whereas specialists are driven by service and selection. The generalist reduces costs through task specialization, volume discounts for component parts and raw materials, the deployment of expensive but highly efficient equipment that would not be possible with lower output levels, and the ability to spread overhead costs over a large volume of output.

The enormous power of scale economies is evident in numerous industries. A classic example comes from the early years of the petroleum industry. After the Standard Oil Trust was formed through an alliance of 40 companies, it controlled 90 percent of the kerosene market in the United States. In the 1880s, the trust decided that it should close small refineries and concentrate production in three huge new ones, which would together produce 25 percent of the world's kerosene. This reorganization of its production process greatly lowered the cost of kerosene. The smaller plants' average cost of production had been 2.5 cents a gallon, whereas the new plants were able to produce kerosene for less than a fifth of that cost. As a result, the trust's profit per gallon doubled from half a cent to one cent, while the price declined sufficiently to allow Standard Oil to compete in Europe with Russian producers, despite the shipping costs the trust had to add to the price it charged. For a long time, no other companies in the world could match Standard Oil's economies of scale, nor could any one of them afford to invest on the scale that Standard Oil had.[3]

The second factor that has become increasingly important in recent years for generalists is speed. Whereas in the past we used to speak of large companies moving very slowly—they were often compared to supertankers trying to turn around in a narrow harbor—today the successful generalists can be nimble and quick. Once they decide on a course of action, they are able to move rapidly in that direction. Companies as huge as Microsoft and General Electric have repeatedly demonstrated their ability to make and implement quick changes in their strategy and direction.

After the early success of Netscape Explorer, for example, Microsoft turned on a dime and quickly implemented an Internet-centric strategy, producing three generations of its Internet Explorer browser within nine months. Likewise, under Jack Welch's direction, General Electric moved rapidly in the 1980s to reinvent itself as a more streamlined company; more recently it has aggressively embraced e-commerce and is now in the midst of transforming itself into more of a services-dominated company. Answering a similar call for speed, Chrysler benchmarked the fast product development processes at Toyota and Honda in order to bring its Neon to market in less than 30 months and for less than $1 billion.

In contrast, some full-line generalists continue to move slowly and deliberately, almost to a fault. General Motors took ten years and spent $5 billion from concept to product for its Saturn division. At a development cost of $6 billion, Ford took six years to bring its Mondeo world car to market

Exclusivity Advantage vs. High Asset Utilization

Full-line players have a cost structure that is dominated by fixed costs. They maintain extensive operations facilities, sophisticated and flexible manufacturing systems, huge amounts of retail floor space, sometimes even a fleet of airplanes or automobiles, for example. For the incremental transaction, variable costs tend to be low. The opposite is true for most successful specialists: by keeping the number of fixed assets to a minimum, they can rapidly scale their costs down if the need arises.

Because they have so much invested in hard assets, full-line generalists, if they are to remain successful, must use them profitably and track them constantly. Whatever the asset—technology, equipment, or working capital—the generalist is always on the lookout for ways to gain an advantage by putting its assets to good use. A company, therefore, will take pains to quantify that use and measure it against what its competitors are doing. One such measure is the ratio of the company's sales to its assets (adjusted for inflation): the higher the ratio, the better. In addition, the most successful generalists are constantly taking their own pulse, as measured by the turns in all cost centers, from accounts receivable to human resources to information technology to inventories.

Computer manufacturers Gateway and Dell, both known for their efficient business models, deliver asset turns of 3.8 and 4.7 times per year, respectively. In contrast, a more traditional computer manufacturer such as Compaq Computer turns assets at just 1.88 times per year.[4] Wal-Mart, the leader among discount retailers, considers its high asset turns a key factor of success. Its asset turn ratio is much higher than that of Kmart. In terms of the Rule of Three, however, being the low-cost provider isn't enough. In fact, it is worthless if you are not increasing value.

When asset turns are low or declining, margins have to improve in order to maintain profitability. Generalists have a hard time achieving this goal, whereas specialists clearly have an advantage here. They tend to focus more on their margins, less on asset turns. The specialists that can deliver and maintain an exclusivity advantage experience higher margins than those whose products are more easily duplicated. For optimum success, customers should not be able to find the specialist's products anywhere else. In Manhattan customers stand on line for hours to buy Krispy Kreme doughnuts, called "sugared air" by those who love them. Often imitated but never duplicated, the best recipes at the most exclusive restaurants command the highest prices and never disappoint the customers.

Tiffany's promises exclusivity as part of its brand appeal, even though its products and styles are copied the world over.

Full-Line vs. Focused Products and Services

Successful generalists offer a wide range of products and services, and are able to meet the needs of customers for ancillary products as well, either through horizontal integration or alliances with other firms. Market specialists, in contrast, offer a range of products to a well-defined segment of customers, whereas product specialists provide deep selection within a defined product category to a wide variety of customers. In retailing, for example, Staples, Toys "R" Us, and Tower Records stand as "category killers." That is, each company took a product category—office supplies, toys, and music CDs and records, respectively—from a full-line generalist and turned it into a stand-alone business for itself, "killing" the category for the generalist, at least for a time. As the market evolves, generalists may step back in and reclaim the product category, as discount retailers have done with all three of these product groups, but they may not be able to loosen their competitors' tight grip on the market.

Target-Market vs. Broad-Market Positioning

Positioning refers to a company's attempt—through marketing, advertising, production processes, financial standing, and the like—to shape both the public's and the business community's perception of the company, especially in relation to its competitors. The generalist needs to position itself as a leader in its industry and to develop an image that is broad enough to have value for all the segments the company serves and all the products it offers. This objective requires more than just a good slogan, of course, but in terms of the public's perception a number of generalists have done well to capture in a few words the essence of their business mission. General Electric's motto "We bring good things to life," for example, conveys the company's involvement in businesses and products that have a positive impact on the quality of customers' lives. The slogan avoids too high a degree of specificity about a particular product or market. Likewise, Panasonic came up with the phrase "Just slightly ahead of our time," which captures well its broad portfolio of technology-based consumer products and conveys the message that its products are near the cutting edge while not necessarily being radical innovations. BASF proclaims that it doesn't make the products the customer buys, it makes those products better.

For specialists, the positioning must evoke the specific markets they seek to serve or the products they offer. They must identify what matters most to that market and position themselves accordingly—for example, as the "safety leader" or "prestige leader." Examples include Tiffany's in fine jewelry and Boston Coach in more luxurious and reliable local transportation services for business clients. On the low end of the retail market, Dollar Stores cater to customers who care much more about price than about product quality or the experience of shopping in luxurious surroundings.

Image and Experience vs. Value and Promotion

In the world of discount retail, Wal-Mart is legendary for providing good value to its customers. By far the world's largest retailer, Wal-Mart wins its customers' loyalty by competing not so much on price (although it does position itself as a price leader through its slogan "always low prices always"), but on value for its customers. Here "value" is defined broadly as the sum of all elements that enhance a consumer's experience such as availability, store access, convenience, added product features, maintenance contracts, and the like. Low price is obviously a big part of value, but not all. Although the customer doesn't see it, Wal-Mart's famed supply chain helps keep those prices low and customers happy.

While their prices are competitive, generalists may not always match the lowest prices in the marketplace. They can save on costs, however, by integrating both internal and external operations, as Wal-Mart does with its logistics and inventory system. Through advertising and other mass marketing approaches, the generalist builds a single corporate identity, gains efficiency advantages from scale economies, and offers superior value to many customer groups.

In contrast, specialists at the market's high end compete on image and the quality of the experience enjoyed by customers. Staging memorable experiences is more important for specialists because customers come to expect unique values. No other automaker can match Rolls Royce for certain features that provide a unique driving experience for customers. Luxurious, hand-sewn leather upholstery is only a part of that experience, which derives much of its value from the connotations of Rolls Royce as the automobile chosen by royalty and heads of state, not to mention the world's richest entertainers and business executives.

Focused vs. Hybrid Channels

Because their market success depends on high volume, generalists need to attain the highest possible coverage of the market in order to make their products available to all potential customers. Accordingly, they use hybrid distribution systems. Inevitably, however, channel conflicts arise. A consumer who wants to purchase a personal computer, for example, has many channels from which to select: she can call Dell or Gateway or any number of manufacturers directly or order the computer at an Internet site; she may elect to visit an electronics retailer, a computer superstore, or a department store; or she may purchase her PC from a value-added reseller. Many computer manufacturers now recognize the advantages, as well as the disadvantages, of making their products available through such channels. For one thing, the company extends its reach and makes the purchasing as convenient as possible for each consumer.

Sony is a full-line generalist that has adopted this approach. As one of the most successful Japanese manufacturers of consumer electronics, Sony is not restricted to any one channel. Rather it reaches consumers through a wide variety of distribution outlets. The issue is not one of avoiding channel conflict but knowing how to manage it effectively.

Specialty businesses, however, tend to use much more focused channels, typically distributing their products through specialty retailers or dealers rather than through volume-driven mass merchandisers. Product specialists such as high-end luggage and leather goods manufacturer Tumi have unique distribution channels. Tumi has no qualms about restricting its reach to selected well-to-do neighborhoods, upscale shopping malls, and its own outlet stores in New York and a few other cities. The rather narrow set of distribution channels is, indeed, one characteristic of the niche that Tumi fills. Given that exclusivity is an integral part of the brand's appeal, wide distribution would dilute that competitive advantage. Market specialists, in contrast, have unique suppliers. Columbus, Ohio–based Limited is a specialist in women's apparel, but owns a major interest in Intimate Brands, which operates Victoria's Secret stores, a super-nicher in women's lingerie. These stores provide a restricted focus on products and markets, presenting a unique and exclusive offering to a select audience.

Multibusiness vs. Integrated Enterprise

Ask most people under the age of 50 to name the vehicles that General Motors produces, and chances are that few will have a clue. To those in the market for a new or used car, GM appears to be a collection of 11 separate car companies rather than a single integrated company with one recognizable brand.[5]

Whatever the public's reaction, the integrated approach to the business enterprise proves much more economical and efficient. While the road to efficiency still appears long at GM, management has not been blind to the need to strive for seamlessness and shared operations. Indeed, all successful volume players make these attributes a top priority in their enterprise design. To that end, many generalists resort to a hybrid or matrix organizational structure, by which they hope to avoid duplication of effort and generate higher asset turns.

Generalists also seek to improve their economies of scope by making extensive use of "flexible" fixed assets. These are hard assets—for example, production lines, facilities, information technology systems, and the like—that can readily be reconfigured to meet the most pressing demands of the moment. Toyota's globally integrated production and marketing system is a hallmark of success for the Japanese automaker: the same Toyota assembly line, for instance, can produce the Tercel, the Camry, and the Lexus LS400. Had DaimlerChrysler had a similar capability, the company perhaps would not have found itself in the unenviable position of having created a very popular vehicle—the "retro" PT Cruiser—but underestimating the demand for the car and thus losing sales to competitors.

Specialists pay much less attention to this kind of enterprise integration and synergy across business lines. In their management structures, multispecialists resemble large umbrellas or tents under which various business lines exist as largely independent operations. While such a structure pays off for the specialist, it usually proves dangerous for the ditch-dweller that is losing both effectiveness and efficiency by not integrating as well as its full-line competitors have done.

Product or Market vs. Process Innovation

Cisco Systems is extraordinarily good at process innovation and virtual integration, but in comparison with its rivals the company has very few patents—only 68 between 1994 and 1999, compared to 1896 for Lucent, 510 for Alcatel, and 844 for Ericsson in the same period. Like most full-line generalists, Cisco is more interested in efficiency as the means of lowering transaction costs than in product innovation, as a niche specialist would be. Generalists concentrate on strengthening their operations management and fully exploiting communications technologies in order to make business processes faster and cheaper. Virtual integration with suppliers and customers allows them to develop the kind of close relationships enhanced by technology that lead to reduced operating costs.

When they do engage in product innovation, generalists aim for incremental rather than discontinuous development. Their motto is "better, faster, cheaper" rather than "brave new world." To keep costs earth-bound, they formalize the process for developing new products and add layers of management oversight and budget controls.

Product specialists, in contrast, direct their innovation efforts to their core offering rather than trying to increase process efficiency. Moreover, since their customers may defect to the generalists if they become dissatisfied with a product's values, specialists are always looking for that next big change or new idea that signals much more than another incremental innovation. This contrast between product specialists and generalists is often evident in the release of new models. Specialists are more likely to completely revamp one of their models than generalists, who tend to favor new models that offer some interesting but only minor changes in design or added features.

Market specialists can also create products with major innovations, but unlike their product specialist brethren, they do so because they see a trend developing in the market or because they wish to initiate such a trend. Most of their innovations, however, are directed to the market itself and their marketing efforts: they are highly creative in developing new marketing campaigns, creating new ambiance that appeals to their market, and adding new products and services that consumers consider valuable. Retailers such as the Gap, Banana Republic, and Old Navy are all well tuned to the interests and preferences of their loyal customers.

As we will see in greater detail in chapter 7, gaining competitive advantage as either a generalist or a specialist involves a paradox. The generalist needs to take a page from the specialist's book, whereas the specialist must look to the generalist for direction. Because all the generalists in a given market are trying to make their processes more efficient through incremental innovations, they are all adding the same or similar values to their products and services. A primary means of distinguishing oneself from the rest of the pack, therefore, is to engage in something the others are not doing—in this case, product innovation. The #3 companies in the inner circle, being the ones closest to the product specialists, are more likely than their #1 and #2 counterparts to bring out important product innovations. Chrysler's minivan innovation is a well-known example.

Specialists, in contrast, already differentiate their markets and products; therefore, process innovation becomes the key to their competitive advantage. One of the major challenges for Krispy Kreme, as it expanded beyond its Winston-Salem, North Carolina base, has been the technological innovation both in its production process and in its supply chain, which now must stretch across large geographical regions.

Multiple vs. Single Brand Identity

Generalists need to pursue a broad market positioning and promote a single corporate identity. A full-line generalist such as IBM offers various products to diverse segments under its own name, thus establishing a common market identity. Citicorp, with thousands of locations in close to 100 countries, offers financial and brokerage services, loans and credit card accounts, insurance and other products, all under a single corporate identity. For both IBM and Citicorp, the corporate positioning is broad enough to allow for wide applicability across products and segments.

Specialists need to position themselves in ways that are different from what the generalists are doing. Product specialists need an identity that is virtually synonymous with a product category, as Stamford, Connecticut–based Pitney Bowes, Inc. has achieved in the area of mailing services primarily for businesses. Market specialists, in contrast, have to define themselves almost entirely in terms of categories of customers or segments of the customer base. Since each brand stands for something distinct, specialists with more than one focus must keep the identity of each separate.

Effectiveness vs. Efficiency

It is a given that successful companies in any industry, whether generalists or specialists, must deliver efficiency through low costs and as well as achieve effectiveness: gaining the loyalty of best customers by providing a strong fit with their needs and wants. A subtle distinction exists between generalists and specialists on this score, however. Generalists enjoy an overwhelming advantage over specialists in being able to exploit great economies of scale; thus, they can keep their costs low and operate more efficiently. For generalists the key to success is efficiency, even if it sometimes requires small trade-offs with effectiveness. Because they serve customers whose needs are not stringently defined and who are rather easily satisfied with mainstream products or services, the generalists need not be so concerned as specialists with the detailed fit between products and customers' desires. In other words, the generalist's customers are typically looking for the product that gives them a good value and simply "does the job."

In contrast, specialists offer highly differentiated products and services that cater to the distinct needs or wants of a narrowly defined segment of customers. Specialists live or die based on the degree of their effectiveness. To be successful, they must ensure a high level of fit between their offerings and the needs of their more exacting customers. In order to do, they may have to sacrifice some efficiency in the process.

A generalist may actually gain competitive advantage by studying the specialist's dimension, just as the opposite is true for the specialist. Assuming that two or more generalists in the same market are equally efficient, the one that is most effective will have the competitive advantage. Although under normal conditions two specialists would not engage in head-to-head competition, when and if they do meet and are equally effective in "satisficing" the customer, the specialist that is more efficient will win. Southwest Airlines is a highly effective market specialist that has one of the airline industry's lowest complaint rates. Incorporating its "no frills" approach into its branding, Southwest continues to be a leader among its competitors because it is so highly efficient. As a result it is one of the few consistently profitable airlines year in and year out.

These points of contrast between generalists and specialists give only a hint of the shape of competitive markets and the rules that govern them. As we draw the lines connecting the dots in later chapters, it will become evident that in specific cases many important differences exist between members of each competitive group, as well as between the two groups themselves. Many of those distinctive features depend on a company's position within its industry. For the moment, however, we turn attention next to several major guidelines first for the generalists, then for the specialists.

Implications for the Growth of Generalists and Specialists

As the Rule of Three stipulates, generalists and specialists experience quite different effects from the relationship between market share and return on assets. On the left side of the ditch, the slope of the line depicting this relationship is very steep for the specialists; that is, their market share may vary from, say, 1 percent to 5 percent, but as that share increases, their financial performance declines sharply. The opposite is true for the generalists—up to a point. So long as their market share stays below about 40 percent, the financial picture for them slows a gradual rise. Gaining more than 40 percent of the market comes with mixed blessings: The price a generalist has to pay for small increases in market share may be quite high in terms of overall financial performance.

In other words, a small change in market share for a specialist can have a dramatic impact on performance, whereas an equally small change for a generalist would not have much impact at all. Thus, incremental market share gains are not very worthwhile for generalists to pursue, as the gains tend to be expensive and short-lived. It is more worthwhile for generalists to gain share by taking quantum jumps. Acquisition through one of two strategies can achieve such a goal:

- **Buy market share:** If there are more than three full-line generalists and if the largest has a market share below 40 percent, there is still room to grow. At present such openings exist in the airlines, banking, and supermarket industries, among others. This type of merger is relatively straightforward to integrate, since the companies in question tend to have similar cultures and growth strategies. When the leader's market share exceeds 40 percent, however, the advantages of further gains through acquisition are offset by the drawbacks, which include greater regulatory scrutiny as a "dominant competitor" and diminishing returns resulting from customer acquisition costs exceeding the value of acquired customers.
- **Buy product lines:** A second growth strategy for the generalist is to take a fast-growing specialty and make it a category within the full line of offerings. This approach is common, for example, among industry leaders in pharmaceuticals and processed foods. The generalist targets specialists that are closer to the ditch, rather than those at the extreme left, as these are less expensive to acquire as well as less specialized. The best option is to pick up any floundering competitors that are already in the ditch. This strategy brings the dual advantage of making an acquisition at a fire-sale price and removing a desperate competitor from the market. In its recently announced acquisition of US Airways, United Airlines snapped up parts of a competitor that had grown through merging local carriers with strong geographical markets, but that at the time United sought to acquire it it was clearly in the ditch. In the process United will gain valuable new markets in the Northeast corridor, the Mid-Atlantic region, and the South.

Market Dominance

Some industries—automobiles and wireless communications, for example—are controlled by the full-line generalists. The specialists hardly seem to have a chance. In other industries, however, the opposite is true. Close examination of competitive market factors such as barriers to entry and the distinction between customers' needs and their wants suggests why these differences exist and point to the implications that lie in them.

First, in an industry with high entry barriers, generalists are more likely to be dominant. If large capital investments are required for a specialist to enter an industry, the incumbent generalists have a tremendous advantage in terms of both scale and complexity. They are likely to have already in place a firmly loyal supply chain, wide-ranging distribution channels, conveniently located brick-and-mortar outlets, and customer-friendly Web sites. Specialists are well advised to measure carefully just how high those barriers are.

Second, if an industry revolves around customers' needs, as distinguished from their desires or wants, generalists are more likely to have the upper hand. In industries such as steel, aluminum, copper, cotton, and tobacco—in effect, all the commodities—generalists rule. Their customers are interested in the functional, not the psychological attributes of the products and services. Generalist strategies are more profitable when customers are looking for a fairly standardized offering and refuse to pay a premium for specialized products. The full-line generalists can procure, manufacture, and deliver that functional value at a much lower cost than the specialists.

Third, if the industry is characterized by customers with strong wants, as opposed to needs, specialists tend to dominate. The perfume industry is a clear example. Specialist strategies are more profitable when the market rewards specialization—that is, when customers' needs are truly different in a tangible way that relates to the competencies of providers to serve them adequately. Furthermore, the specialists can be either product-oriented or market-focused. Where those specialized niches proliferate, generalists have more difficulty achieving the economies of scale and scope that give them advantage elsewhere. In these cases the specialists have the advantage, but maybe not for long. As technology becomes more sophisticated, customization can become less costly and more of an advantage for the generalists, especially where customers prefer one-stop shopping and immediate access to products and services. True customization, however, requires more than merely providing the core product on terms the customer demands. It also means that the brand, the distribution, and the pricing need to be customized.

Dell Computer Corporation is well known for its highly efficient "Dell Direct" business model, whereby it deals with its customers directly by telephone or Web site rather than through intermediaries. Operating on this model, Dell has risen to the top of the PC manufacturing industry. Recently, however, growth has slowed considerably, presumably because of market saturation and the new competition from hand-held devices. A more significant problem for Dell's continued growth and market dominance lies in the business model itself. Dell loses many sales because some customers want to go to a store and bring home their computer, just as they would a television set or a VCR. The "direct" sales model—which requires a customer to postpone satisfaction until the personal computer can be built, shipped, delivered, and set up—may be reaching its end, or if not its end, at least its current viability as the *only* channel. To succeed as a full-line generalist, Dell will have to tap some indirect channels, such as value-added resellers (VARs) and the superstores.

Fourth, if customer needs are relatively equal in importance to their wants or preferences, generalists tend to be less dominant, and there is plenty of room for both groups to exist in complementary distribution and do well. Some recent developments in the hardware retailing industry help to illustrate this rule. Home Depot dominates this industry in the United States because of its huge selection and low prices. Many thought that the business model would put the specialists—the local, family-owned stores that provide friendly service and convenient locations—out of business. Indeed, some did change their specialties, filling other niches such as locksmith services. But many of the local hardware stores joined cooperatives such as Ace Hardware and TruServ, enabling them to save on procurement costs by as much as 20 percent. As a result, there are still over 21,000 hardware stores in the United States, down only 12 percent since the meteoric rise of Home Depot in the mid-1970s. It turns out that Home Depot's growth has come primarily at the expense of national chains such as Sears and Montgomery Ward, as well as the regional chains of midsize "home center" stores, which were too big to match the personal service of small stores but too small to challenge Home Depot on costs and price. Consumers needed the access, the convenience, and the friendly advice of the local hardware dealer, even if the price was higher.

Home Depot is now extending its presence in the market. In launching its EXPO chain of upscale home-decoration stores and its Villager's Hardware stores in New Jersey, the company is reaching up as well as down, much as a product and market specialist would do. As we examine these initiatives in light of the Rule of Three, we believe that the EXPO venture will succeed, as do most upscale initiatives of full-line generalists. The Villager's Hardware strategy, which offers a new chain of midsize stores that aims to duplicate the service and convenience virtues of local hardware stores while still offering low prices, is a nonstarter. It promises to play out as a classic case of being "caught in the middle," and we predict that it will fail, as did Home Depot's earlier foray into rural hardware stores, CrossRoads, in the mid-1990s.[6]

Growth through Acquisition

Because they are so fundamentally different, full-line generalists and specialists have approaches to business that rarely mix well. That is, both a margin-driven company and a volume-driven one would be better served if they looked at each other as good neighbors rather than good partners in a marriage. Their contrasting styles, however, need not be an obstacle to their looking for a company to rescue out of the ditch. Not only are they likely to discover bargains there, but they may find fewer contradictions in culture and strategy to overcome.

The same logic applies to partnerships and alliances as it does to acquisitions and mergers: specialist manufacturers that try to sell their products through generalist retailers are headed for trouble, just as generalists that try to run specialty businesses in addition to their core business find that they have no talent for it. Kmart's attempt to foster a range of specialty businesses such as Walden Books and Sports Authority failed. Likewise, JCPenney is struggling as it tries to balance its department stores with specialty businesses such as its subsidiary Eckerd Drug Stores.

The only way generalists can succeed with such a strategy is by maintaining strict separation between the two sides. Attempts to extract synergy between the operations—for example, by creating overlapping assortments or by sharing brand names—will prove counterproductive, since they dilute the uniqueness and specialty nature of the specialist. The Venator Group (formerly the Woolworth Corporation) has been only moderately successful running a wide variety of specialty retailers, which at one time included Kinney Shoes, Richman Brothers, Champs Sporting Goods, and Foot Locker. Today, only the latter two remain as subsidiaries of the company.

In a fast-changing industry where boundaries are like lines drawn in the shifting sand, new full-line generalists can arise through the acquisition of startups. The optical networking industry offers examples in the numerous small companies that Cisco and Lucent Technologies have bought up for their technology assets. A full-line generalist can best manage research and development in two ways: integrating some portion or all of a promising startup that has received significant venture capital investment from the outset, or applying a reverse "D&R" effort that emphasizes the lessons learned by innovative competitors and applying them to the business, as Microsoft and Intel have done in the software industry.

Specialists take a different point of view. Recognizing those products or markets that are no longer truly specialized, a specialist would be advised to sell these off to a full-line generalist, thereby freeing up the specialist to focus on a more profitable business elsewhere.

Marketing Advantages and Branding

Successful full-line generalists, as well as some specialists, are good marketers, but the generalists devote a significantly greater amount of resources to marketing and do so in a manner that is highly productive. They have learned to manage their marketing function by not confusing a "full product line" with product proliferation, and they seek to globalize their brand portfolio even as they offer products in the full range of the industry's price points.

As manufacturing systems have become more flexible, manufacturers can increase the assortment of their products without greatly increasing unit costs. Efficient production does not mean that products can be sold efficiently, however. Many firms have expanded the range of their product offerings beyond what the market needs. To get rid of unsold inventory, they need to add advertising and sales people, thereby increasing the marketing costs for the product line substantially. At the time it sold its housewares business to Black & Decker, for example, General Electric made 150 different products in 14 categories. The company even produced 14 different irons. To obtain distribution support for its entire line, the company had to administer a whole range of incentive programs for retailers, including early-buy allowances and "full-line forcing" programs. After acquiring the business, Black & Decker gradually moved away from the proliferation approach by pruning the product line and developing a replenishment logistics approach that achieves the ideal of "Sell one, ship one, build one."[7]

Brand proliferation is wasteful and destroys profitability, a lesson many full-line generalists, especially in the consumer goods arena, have learned the hard way. Each brand requires its own hefty advertising budget, and synergy across brands is often nonexistent. As a result, in recent years many companies, including Nestlé, Procter & Gamble, and Diageo, have drastically reduced the number of their brands. Some of the most drastic cuts are occurring at Unilever, which is reducing the number of brands in its global portfolio from 1,600 to 400.[8] We believe that even that number is way too high: Unilever would be better off by reducing the portfolio to no more than 40 brands.

Product proliferation can lead to brand proliferation, which lowers the economies of scale associated with advertising. Since each new brand requires a high threshold of advertising spending just to be noticed, the break-even market share becomes very high. The typical "national" brand name can cost as much as $100 million a year to support.

Companies are finding, however, that they can achieve the benefits of a powerful brand name without investing in the resources to create a new one. Procter & Gamble, for example, discovered some years ago that "Ivory" was really an umbrella brand, not just one that stood for soap. The company has since leveraged Ivory's considerable brand equity into leadership positions in dishwashing liquid, shampoo, conditioner, and laundry detergent. The strategy of utilizing an existing brand name is feasible provided the same image is appropriate for all the products under that brand umbrella. Matsushita (Panasonic), Mitsubishi, and Yamaha stand as strong models for successfully using their brand names across an extremely wide variety of products. Likewise, General Electric has successfully used its brand name across a wide variety of businesses.[9]

Generalists, however, need to be careful with this kind of marketing. On the one hand, a problem with brand extendability has been that many brands have been defined too narrowly (mostly through past advertising); as a result, they have become too product- and function-specific, and thus too difficult to extend. On the other hand, some firms have been slow to recognize the value of the brand equity in some of their products and have underutilized those assets.

Another powerful factor in making the marketing efforts of full-line generalists more productive is the use of the corporate name as the umbrella brand. In a study of 130 companies, McKinsey consultants found that those with strong, diversified brands earned total returns to shareholders that were 5 percent higher than average.[10] Examples included Disney, GE, and American Express, all of which achieve more leverage across product categories. Others such as Matsushita, Sony, Toyota, and Ford are also in a strong position in this regard. Recently, Kellogg, Nestlé, and Cadbury have made concerted efforts to feature their corporate names more prominently on all of their products, thereby extending the brand recognition while lowering some of the costs associated with product promotion.

Yet another important way to reduce brand proliferation is to globalize the company's brand portfolio. Generalists in major industries, if their resources support the effort, can take on this major challenge by gradually transferring the brand equity of local brands onto the chosen global brand. In some cases, entirely new global brands may need to be created. Several giant companies in the United States and in Europe have recently created new names and rapidly turned them into recognizable entities. Lucent (formerly a part of AT&T), Verizon (formerly Bell Atlantic), and Agilent (formerly part of Hewlett-Packard) fall into this category. Ahold of the Netherlands, which owns major supermarket chains around the world including Giant and Stop & Shop in the United States, suffers from the fact that it has different brands in each country. By contrast, its two major global competitors, Wal-Mart and Carrefour of France, use the same brand name everywhere.

A name by itself is not enough, however. Full-line generalists must offer distinct products at all of an industry's major price points, and with minimal overlap with one another. If not, they leave an opportunity for a competitor to position itself. For example,

Ford's acquisitions of Volvo and Jaguar give it a full range of price points in Europe: Jaguar price points are at the high end, Volvo comes in below that, and Ford's European cars are all priced below Volvo.[11] Another example of this strategy is Sears's former policy of offering customers three quality and price points in most product categories: good, better, best.

This chapter's comparison of generalists and specialists reveals major differences in their means to profitability, as well as their attitudes toward such issues as branding, speed, scale, channel distribution, and integration. It suggests that responsible strategizing rests on a clear assessment of where a company is positioned vis-à-vis the two groups, what its share of market is, and how the competition is arrayed. While these choices are nowhere near the status of default selections, the marketing principles implicit in the Rule of Three indicate that managers are not completely without a compass when it comes to setting direction for their companies. As we will see in chapters 6 and 7, the Rule of Three can be a kind of global positioning satellite by which managers can locate their companies and assess the competitive landscape. But first we need to look at that landscape in greater detail, particularly at the feature called the Ditch. Chapter 4 describes how a company can be either pushed or pulled into this undesirable and unforgiving place, from which it is extremely difficult to escape.

4

The Ditch

The Rule of Three posits a model of market competition in which two diametrically opposed strategies can be viable and successful. A veritable Bermuda Triangle of competitive strategy, however, lies in the middle. Both generalists and specialists can generate attractive returns, provided they follow strategies appropriate to their position in their industry and stay out of the ditch. The way out of that trough can be long and possibly fatal. It is far easier to stay out of the ditch in the first place.

The ditch represents a market position between the generalist and specialist positions. Companies that fall into the ditch are weakened financially or too small to be full-line players such as their competitors on the right. At the same time, they are too big to be focused, margin-based specialized players such as those on the left. The ditch thus consists of *overgrown* niche players and *undersized* full-line companies, neither of which has much of a claim on long-term viability.

Ditch companies soon discover that few customers want what they have to offer. Mainstream customers have needs that the big generalists, thanks to their economies of scale, can meet better than their smaller competitors: they offer superior value in the form of highly standardized products at good price points. While a company can now customize and personalize aspects of its interactions with customers, many customers do not value this capability highly, or they have come to expect such personalized attention and factor it into their expectations. First-class passengers on the major airlines, for example, are no longer surprised when a flight attendant greets them by name; they have come to expect such treatment, which all carriers nowadays provide.

In banking, most customers are satisfied with large-scale, mass-produced products and services. They respond well to the lower prices that a "financial factory" offers and the promise of consistency and uniformity in services. Service is good, but not tailored to each individual customer.[1] If customers have highly idiosyncratic needs, it is unlikely that the full-line generalist will find it worthwhile to serve them. Those that try to do so soon discover that their cost structure simply does not allow it, and they walk away from such customers.

In a competitive market with relatively few entry barriers, however, such customers do not go wanting for long. Product or market specialists soon move in to serve customers whose needs are not met by the generalists. These players are highly attuned to customers' demands. In some cases, the customer's specific needs revolve around simply getting the right product, in which case a good product specialist will rise to the occasion; in other cases, it is a market specialist that comes forth to satisfy the customer's multifaceted needs.

Ditch companies can do neither very well. They are caught between the proverbial rock and a hard place. Those aspiring to be generalists have all the costs and complexities associated with that strategy, but lack the customer base over which to spread their costs. They must either charge higher prices, which customers simply will not pay, or offer less value, which customers will soon resent, or just make less money, which shareholders will find untenable. In such a predicament, the ditch player cannot long survive. On the other hand, if the ditch company is an overgrown specialist, it will find that it cannot match its more focused, left-side competitors on the qualities that customers care about. Product selection will not be focused enough, or the company's ability to assemble a comprehensive solution to satisfy customers' particular needs will be weak.

How Companies Fall into the Ditch

Stronger competitors on the right side push small generalists into the ditch, whereas specialists tend to be pulled in by the lure of rapid growth. Undermining both the generalist and specialist are the seismic changes that can affect any industry, resulting in major shakeouts and the demise of players on both sides—a subject we will take up in chapter 8, "The Disruption of Markets." In the present chapter we look more closely at the reasons why many generalists and specialists slide into the ditch, and we suggest some means by which ditch companies can pull themselves out.

The Lure of Fast Growth

Specialists often fall victim to the demands of stakeholders to grow beyond their means. They engage in a policy of seeking "too much, too soon."

Consider the fate of a specialist pen manufacturer Excalibur, a fictional company whose plight is all too real. Here's what might happen if Excalibur leaders were tempted to do business with the giant retailer MegaMart (another fictional character in this parable), in direct violation of a basic principle of the Rule of Three—namely that in regards to generalists and specialists "never the twain should meet." The following account shows how such a marriage of unequals might evolve:

Year 1 (The Selling of the Soul): Under intense pressure from its board, Excalibur tries to grow. The company seeks to broaden its market reach and approaches MegaMart about carrying its offerings. After much haggling, MegaMart agrees to offer the product, provided Excalibur lowers the price somewhat and invests in creating an electronic link with the giant retailer's ordering system. Buoyed by the sudden growth in volume at a relatively modest reduction in its margins, Excalibur reports record sales and a big jump in market share, profits, and stock price. In order to meet increased demand, the company takes on debt to build an additional factory and provide greater automation for its existing plants. Executives receive big bonuses, and the manager in charge of the MegaMart relationship is promoted.

Year 2 (The Pound of Flesh): At the end of the first year, when it is time to negotiate the contract, MegaMart asks Excalibur to lower its price still further. It hints that it has an alternative supplier in Taiwan ready and waiting to offer comparable products on better terms. Now dependent on the higher volumes and committed to an expansion of its manufacturing facilities, Excalibur has little choice but to agree. In anticipation of still higher production volumes, the company adds third shifts at all its plants. Production managers report that quality problems are on the increase, but management is too preoccupied to focus on the issue. Sales increase, market share climbs, but profits head down as margins are squeezed. Sensing distress, investors begin selling. Excalibur's board cancels bonuses for all executives.

Year 3 (The Indecent Proposal): Once again MegaMart asks Excalibur to lower the price on its pens. The company pleads with the retailer that it has already taken as many costs as it can out of the system. Its pen's metallic cylinder requires precision machining and expensive materials; cutting costs further can be done only at the expense of quality. MegaMart managers suggest that Excalibur look at creative ways to cut costs. After tortured searching by all parties, one MegaMart executive poses the fateful question: *"Could you make it in plastic?"*

Excalibur has grown its way into the ditch, as this scenario presents. One fact is clear: Excalibur cannot stay in the middle. The ditch is an inhospitable home for any company. What then are Excalibur's options? It must first decide which side of the ditch it wants to play on. If, on the one hand, it wants to go back to its specialist position, it must systematically exit certain markets and drop some products. It must reestablish its quality image. In going down the path that it has taken, however, Excalibur may have already closed this option; its image has been severely tarnished in the eyes of its previously loyal customers. Its specialty retail partners have already abandoned it since its products are now available at Mega-Marts everywhere.

If, on the other hand, the firm wants to become a volume-driven player—that is, a generalist on the order of PaperMate, Bic, and Scripto—it must recognize that its effort to climb out of the ditch will be immediately opposed by the #3 incumbent, if not all the full-line generalists. A costly fight for market share will likely ensue, and profits will dry up completely for perhaps several years. Specialists can "make the turn" out of the ditch and into generalists' territory only if there is vacancy in the inner circle. Since three large players already exist, this route too is blocked for Excalibur.

Allowing itself to be lured into the ditch, Excalibur took on additional fixed costs and destroyed its image and core competence. Ignorant of the Rule of Three principle, the company sought to grow "too much, too soon," boxing itself in so that it could not say no to MegaMart's demands.

Examples abound of misguided attempts to grow out of specialty status. After years of being a great niche player, American Motors slid into the ditch when it tried to expand into a full line of automobiles. Lacking the resources to do so, it came up with a single car, the Hornet, masquerading as everything from an "econobox" to a luxury sedan.

In the U.S. market for stereophonic speakers, Harman International Industries, Inc. has been a major challenger to the Bose Corporation, a highly profitable, privately held company based in the Boston area. Smaller rivals in this competitive market include Boston Acoustics and Cambridge Soundworks, but major competition comes from Japanese manufacturers. In 1994, after a time of big losses and layoffs, Harman made the classic mistake for a specialist: it became obsessed with market share. Harman merged the design, marketing, and sales forces and greatly expanded its JBL and Infinity product lines. The two brands accounted for over 80 products. As margins dwindled, the company's positioning became more muddied. "It was tempting, so I chased market share," admits CEO Sidney Harman. "It turned out not to be the best move."[2]

Harman pulled out of discount retailers and smaller specialty stores. He reduced the JBL and Infinity lines to 25 products each and focused on the professional market that supplies products to theatres, stadiums, and studios. In addition, Harman International now supplies speakers to numerous automobile and personal computer manufacturers.

In retailing, the market specialist Nordstrom provides a clear warning to others. Having successfully navigated its growth from a shoe store chain to full department store, this West Coast department store chain acquired a sterling reputation for customer service, setting the industry standard for personal service. Then in the late 1980s the company decided to expand rapidly. Around the country, mall developers were eager to land Nordstrom as a tenant. In some cases they were willing to offer Nordstrom a lease for a token $1 a year, an offer the company could not refuse. By 1999, Nordstrom had grown to 99 stores in 22 states.

In effect, Nordstrom lost its regional specialty status and became another mid-sized retailer in the industry. The company's growth undermined its reputation for service as well as its fashion leadership. Its information systems were woefully antiquated; for example, salespeople still wrote notes by hand to remind themselves about customer preferences. Moreover, the company was highly decentralized and fragmented: its 900 buyers caused serious efficiency problems. There was no national marketing effort; advertisements were created regionally. With its poor information systems, decentralized operations, and lack of national marketing, Nordstrom runs counter to our prescriptions for successful generalists. In contrast, the much larger R. H. Macy & Co. has only 100 buyers, sophisticated IT, centralized operations, and national marketing.

Another company guilty of "too much, too soon" is Einstein/ Noah Bagel Corporation, which found itself in Chapter 11 in April 2000. Riding the low-fat craze of the mid-1990s, the company expanded indiscriminately; in some years, it opened as many as 200 locations. Its capital spending program left the company with a huge mountain of debt that it had no prospects of being able to pay off. At the same time the bagel market cooled. Coffee bars such as Starbucks and doughnut shops such as Dunkin' Donuts, not to mention even supermarket bakeries that offer freshly baked goods, have left the market crowded and very competitive.[3]

Loehmann's, the legendary New York retailing institution, thrived for decades as a store offering designer clothes at attractive prices to fashion- and budget-conscious women. Seeking growth, the company added gifts and men's clothing. It began expanding geographically, reaching 69 stores in 19 states. The new lines carried good margins, and the company might have been able to pull off the transition—except that it also lost its focus on designer clothing and began stocking clothes that could be bought practically anywhere. Having borrowed $100 million to finance its ill-conceived growth, the company was forced to declare bankruptcy in May 1999. After closing 14 stores, Loehmann's now seeks to recapture some of its lost magic, offering more designer clothes and returning to its core customer base.[4]

Sometimes, specialists get into trouble by attempting to grow through forward integration. A manufacturer, for instance, seeks to get into retailing. The name London Fog has been synonymous with quality raincoats for decades, and the company still enjoys tremendous brand equity. In 1995, this quintessential product specialist embarked on a four-year retail store strategy, building 140 London Fog stores, including 30 factory outlets. This strategy, however, put the company into direct competition with the department stores that carried its products. Not surprisingly, London Fog's trade partners were upset. In September 1998, the combination of high capital costs and weaker sales combined to send London Fog into Chapter 11. Having recognized the folly of its ways, the company has decided to close 110 of its stores, leaving only the factory outlets. Once the company emerges from the fog of bankruptcy and returns to its core competencies, its prospects should be quite bright.[5]

Outside investors are often to blame for a specialist company growing too fast and falling by the wayside. In their eagerness for rapid growth and a strong return on their investment, they can cause the company to destroy the very qualities that made it special. For example, the catalog retailer J. Peterman started in 1987 out of the founder's home in Lexington, Kentucky. At first, the company sold a small number of eclectic clothing items, but soon grew rapidly to $20 million in sales and 75 employees by 1990. With the financial backing of outsiders, Peterman began to invest heavily in retail outlets, new catalogs, and hundreds of new products. Soon, growth spun out of control, and the company's unique culture and aesthetic sensibility rapidly deteriorated. Though revenues grew, profits suffered. By 1995, the company was losing money. Peterman's investors, however, continued to exert pressure for faster growth, even if it meant taking on more debt and adding more products. The company soon was caught in a liquidity squeeze as vendors would not extend credit and lenders would not finance more inventory. The company was liquidated, and the founder lost the rights to his own name. As he later reflected, "I should have trusted myself—over anyone else—and I should have known when to say no."[6]

Specialists sometimes flounder when they add unrelated products to their portfolio that have little production or marketing synergy with their core product. For example, Whistler is the leader in the radar detector category, with an estimated market share of 35 percent. Seeking growth, the company acquired the garage door opener business from Stanley in 1997—a business in which it had no expertise and which required different production, distribution, and marketing approaches. As the pattern has shown, the company ran into trouble and was forced into Chapter 11 in June 1999. The company is now selling its noncore businesses and is expected to regain financial health by focusing once again on its core market.[7]

Such examples show that forced growth of any kind can be fatal to specialist companies. Their growth needs to come organically, as they remain within their specialty and grow only in carefully considered directions. We examine these options more closely in chapter 7, "Strategies for Specialists."

The Fatal Push into the Ditch

In contrast to specialists that grow "too much, too soon" and are pulled into the ditch, generalists are pushed into it by their head-to-head competitors on the right. In this sense specialists can be their own worst enemies, doing to themselves what no competitor is forcing them to do. Generalists, however, often wind up in the ditch because of the actions of others. By the time they become aware of what is happening to them, their efforts to extricate themselves are usually a case of "too little, too late." Generalists, therefore, need to anticipate such an eventuality and ensure that they stay out of the ditch in the first place.

Highly competitive markets in the process of consolidating typically have six to eight companies vying for the three available slots that form the inner circle. In the process, some rise to the top. Some get merged and some get purged.

When market growth slows or becomes negative, it is usually the

#3 player (and any other aspiring full-line generalist) that is *pushed* into the ditch when the two leading competitors fight for market share. This phenomenon is most common during tough economic times such as the high-inflation 1970s or the low-growth early 1990s. As a result, the #1 and #2 players raise the competitive stakes and try to take market share away from the easiest target: player #3.

It is important to note that specialists are not directly affected by the tumult among the generalists. The competitive challenge from full-line generalists affects other generalists and would-be generalists. The specialists are far more secure in their own niches. For example, Chrysler's descent into the ditch in the mid-1970s had little to do with Japanese competition and everything to do with the fight between GM and Ford. After the 1974–75 energy crisis, GM redesigned the Chevrolet Caprice, a car that had great fuel efficiency and was rated by *Consumer Reports* as a "best buy" for several years running. As a result, GM's market share in full-size cars jumped significantly. Ford was able to keep pace, but Chrysler couldn't. It slid into the ditch, reemerging—only after its bailout—as a marginal full-line player with an emphasis on minivans. Chrysler could have remained in the ditch, giving Honda or Toyota an opportunity to become the #3 player in the U.S. market. Instead, the automaker pulled ahead by acquiring AMC from Renault, while Honda and Toyota failed to expand their product lines rapidly enough to include minivans and sports utility vehicles.

The movie theater business, currently beset with growing overcapacity and attendance numbers that are flat or declining, provides another example. In recent years, large theater chains have invested heavily in new state-of-the-art megaplexes with stadium-style seating and expanded amenities to attract moviegoers. At the same time, they have been slow in closing down their older complexes. The result: an oversupply of seats. The struggle has affected the Big 3—United Artists Theater Company, Loews Cineplex Entertainment Corporation, and AMC Entertainment, Inc. As is usually the case, however, such market conditions may give the Big 3 a cold, but companies hovering near the ditch get struck with pneumonia. In this case, Carmike Cinemas, Inc., a ditch player with a 7.4 percent share of screens nationally, was pushed into bankruptcy in August 2000. Given that the industry has an estimated 25 percent overcapacity, it is unlikely that the chain will be rescued by one of the Big 3 or be able to revive on its own.[8] In fact, several of the large players have also entered Chapter 11, but are likely to emerge stronger than before as the weeding out of weaker players reduces the industry's overcapacity.

Crown Books was an odd hybrid of a company: a discount bookseller which grew to 179 stores in several far-flung metropolitan areas, such as Washington D.C., Chicago, San Francisco, and Los Angeles. The company operated traditional stores with 30,000 titles as well as superstores with 80,000 titles. By 1997, Crown had grown to become the fourth largest bookseller in the country. However, it was far behind the two dominant players, Barnes & Noble and Borders, and somewhat behind the fast-growing Books-A-Million chain. The emergence of Amazon.com as a significant player in the industry and the combative efforts of the market leaders to respond to the challenge soon enough had the expected impact: Crown was pushed into the ditch and into Chapter 11 by May 1998. With its spotty market coverage and unfocused retail platform, Crown stood little chance against the big incumbents or the new upstarts. The company emerged from bankruptcy with a new lease on life and half the outlets it had before. However, Crown was less than half the size of Books-A-Million, Inc., the #3 company.[9] Down to 43 stores, Crown again declared bankruptcy in February 2001 and started liquidating its assets. Many of its store leases have been assumed by Books-A-Million.

Exiting the Ditch

Few companies actually *stay* in the ditch for very long. Either the company realizes its problems in the nick of time and takes steps to become a niche player, or a generalist looking to solidify its position on the right side acquires it. Either result beats the alternative, which is simply to declare bankruptcy and expire.

The ditch, in fact, could be considered the bankruptcy court's waiting room. The majority of companies filing for protection under Chapter 11 are in highly competitive, consolidating industries. They have been forced into the ditch by changing conditions in the market or as a result of their own strategic missteps. In recent years, these marooned businesses have become increasingly attractive targets for generalists looking to grow quickly by paying just pennies on the dollar.

Salvaging real value from the ashes of corporate failures has become a big business. As many as 200 private equity-based "phoenix funds" have been formed to buy and revive troubled companies, mostly those operating in bankruptcy.[10] Generalists often bypass these funds to pick up such "distressed assets" themselves. Athletic footwear retailer Footstar, for example, bought 79 superstores and 23 specialty retail stores of Just for Feet, Inc. In most cases, the acquiring company immediately increases the value of assets it is acquiring by linking them with its own successful business model. To vary the old proverb, "One man's disaster is another man's opportunity."

In early 2000, McDonald's purchased Boston Market, which had declared bankruptcy. A relative bargain at $173.5 million, this acquisition gave McDonald's rights to the Boston Market name, 751 restaurants, and franchises for 108 additional units, locations that the company can use to open additional McDonald's outlets, as well as its two new chains, Chipotle Mexican Grill and Donato's Pizza.[11]

Not all ditch companies, of course, are in Chapter 11. In Japan, ditch companies are often kept afloat by their business partners or the government. Several years ago, Mitsubishi Motors, for example, was #3 in the Japanese market with a relatively low 15 percent market share. Nevertheless, the company offered a product line ranging from luxury cars to sports utility vehicles to sports cars and minivans—an undistinguished line that was broader than that of Toyota, which was triple its size.

Despite its struggles at home, Mitsubishi aggressively entered the highly competitive U.S. market, where it discounted its vehicles heavily to gain a real market presence. Its share, however, remained stuck under 2 percent. As its share in Japan slipped below 10 percent, Honda stepped in to claim the #3 position (and soon overtook Nissan to claim the #2 spot). By 1998, the company was desperate, having piled up $15 billion in debt. Thanks to more loans from banks in the Mitsubishi keiretsu, which held 70 percent of the company's shares and loyally purchased its cars, the automaker continued to exist.

In April 2000, DaimlerChrysler purchased a 34 percent stake in the company for $2.1 billion. With a debt topping $16.5 billion, Mitsubishi needed the strategically sensible solution to its problems that the combination with DaimlerChrysler provided. Having long enjoyed a partnership with the former Chrysler Corporation, producing several of its cars in the United States, Mitsubishi could offer its production operations in Japan, Indonesia, Malaysia, the Philippines, Taiwan, Thailand, and Vietnam, to help fill out DaimlerChrysler's product line in Europe.[12] Although Mitsubishi insists it will remain an independent company, it is only a matter of time before it is completely taken over.

From Ditch to Niche

Perhaps the most common strategy employed by struggling ditch residents is to beat a strategic retreat and become a specialist or collection of specialists. They identify how they can present a unique profile to the marketplace and divest themselves of all assets that do not fit the chosen profile.

Furniture maker KI of Green Bay, Wisconsin, for example, now tops some $500 million in annual sales. With sales that large, it is too big to compete with true niche players but too small to take on the industry's full-line leaders, Steelcase, Haworth, and Herman Miller. To compete effectively, the company focuses on tailoring unique solutions to 17 vertical markets (for example, college, K–12, high-tech, government, health care). The company emphasizes immediate response and personal service, in keeping with its position as a collection of several market specialists. This strategy has proven highly successful, enabling the company to grow much faster than the industry.[13]

In its relatively brief history, Apple Computer had two opportunities to become the market leader. The first came in 1986, when Apple passed up the chance to license its operating system to Apollo Computer and others. At the time Microsoft was still working on its Windows Release 1.0 and had a nonexistent user base for its graphic user interface (GUI). Had Apple moved aggressively at that time to broaden its market, it would likely have established itself as the dominant GUI standard and become a software as well as hardware leader.

The second opportunity arose about 1996, at a time when no PC manufacturer had a clear leadership in the market. Compaq and IBM were struggling against the low-cost business models of Dell and Gateway. Had Apple separated its software and hardware divisions and jumped aggressively into the Wintel business (dominated by Windows and Intel), it could well have become the largest computer maker of all. Instead, the company chose to continue on its "Macevangelical" path, which led to further loss of market share. Apple found itself pushed into the ditch.

The return of Steve Jobs to head the company heralded a successful shift to a specialist strategy. Whereas Jobs once dreamed of changing the world with Mac computers, Apple is now content with targeting two markets: on the consumer side, the K-12 education market, and on the business side, design and publishing professionals. Jobs has simplified and reduced the company's product lines, down from 15 to just four today: desktop and portable Macintoshes for professionals and consumers. He has also centralized the organizational structure and pared down distribution channels. The strategy worked well; Apple's revenues initially declined, but profits soared. Over time, revenue growth resumed, and the company even started to convert a small number of PC users to the Mac platform. Apple's future is as a niche player; it can no longer aspire to be one of the industry's behemoth leaders.[14]

Other ditch residents in the PC industry may not be so fortunate. Packard Bell and NEC merged in order to compete, but the combination of two weak players does not usually result in one strong player. Whereas the top-tier companies in 1998 (HP, Compaq, IBM, and Dell) were growing at between 20 and 70 percent a year, the second tier or ditch companies were actually experiencing revenue declines, at a time when the overall PC market was growing at about 25 percent a year. Companies in the third tier (niche players) were growing at 6 percent.[15]

Sometimes, when ditch players try to become specialists, they find that smaller, nimbler companies are waiting to eat their lunch. Consider the plight of Acer. In 1996, the company occupied a position near the top of the consumer PC market, driven by its innovative design and ease-of-use features that appealed to first-time buyers. The Acer Aspire was the first PC to be offered in a color other than putty; however, some of Acer's bundled software was too complex for new users, who flooded the customer service center with calls. By the time the company fixed its problems and came out with a second-generation machine, the market had matured, and first-time customers were hard to find. Competitors such as Compaq and HP had incorporated new styling and functionality features. Acer also had a mismatch in its marketing; it advertised nationally but did not have distribution everywhere.

Struggling greatly, the company decided to do a 180-degree shift: it would target the commercial market. To broaden its product offerings for business customers, the company purchased Texas Instruments' mobile division. This strategy, however, stood little chance of succeeding. First, corporate buyers valued different things than consumers, and Acer was only known for its consumer-oriented innovations. Second, competitors were even more deeply entrenched in the business market than they had been in the consumer market. Third, Texas Instruments' mobile business was weak to begin with, and the additional brand confusion did not help. Finally, the company had to build new business-oriented sales channels from scratch. Facing huge challenges, Acer decided that the only way to succeed was to create application-specific devices for customer groups such as educators and real estate professionals. This "XC" strategy includes devices such as a kid's computer (KC), an educational computer (EC), home banking computer, or e-mail computer.[16]

Not surprisingly, Acer is still floundering. The company plans to market a mobile phone and has created Acer Neweb, a division to market wireless devices to consumers and businesses. Its Acer Nexus will offer local area networks and related networking solutions. Acer still faces powerful, entrenched competitors such as Cisco Systems, Lucent Technologies, Nortel Networks, and 3Com Corporation. Rather than attempting to enter all of these new markets, the best option for Acer is to become a PC specialist in Asia, where it has strong brand equity and a position of strength.[17]

Leveraging its brand name and distribution channels, Kodak found a way out of the ditch for its battery business. Having entered that market to build on its strength in chemicals, the company has had to abandon ambitions of becoming one of the Big 3 in the battery category. Long-time incumbents Duracell and Energizer are too well entrenched, and Rayovac at the #3 position has been aggressively challenging them for market share. Instead of challenging them head on, Kodak decided to become a niche player by focusing on batteries for cameras. It created the Photolife line of photographic battery products, with the intention of offering a line of batteries to fit every camera in the marketplace. Given that the camera battery market is growing at 10 to 15 percent a year—much faster than the battery market overall—and that 90 percent of all lithium batteries sold are for cameras, Kodak seems to have chosen wisely. The rising popularity of digital cameras will only increase the demand for batteries, which Kodak hopes to capture by placing its batteries in the electronics and photographic sections of retail stores.[18]

Likewise, in the computer business, Unisys successfully navigated its way from the ditch to a defensible niche. Formed in 1986 by the merger of the Burroughs and Sperry corporations, Unisys nearly perished in the early 1990s, in part because the merger was plagued by incompatible computer designs and corporate cultures. In 1997, the company began a transformation process by exiting from the personal computer business and focusing on services, a narrow customer base (banks, airlines, and governments), and off-the-shelf or "repeatable solutions." Deriving two-thirds of its revenues from services, Unisys has a bright future in services, but it is still identified with the hardware business, making mainframes based on Intel chips and Microsoft Windows NT. On this side it faces strong competition from several other vendors with comparable products.[19]

Honda and a Future Focus on Women

In the midst of the consolidating global auto industry, Honda seems to be an anomaly. The company is now #2 in Japan (having moved up from #4 just a few years ago), #5 in the United States, and #8 worldwide. By any measure, it is one of the most successful and admired car companies in the world. But how can that be if it is a ditch player?

The company's annual output of approximately 2.5 million cars is comparable to that of PSA Peugeot Citroen, and barely a third that of market leaders General Motors and Ford. Peugeot, clearly a market specialist, focuses on its regional strategy. Honda's outstanding engineering prowess is reflected in its worldwide strength in engines: it sells five million engines for boats, lawnmowers, and hedge trimmers a year. It is the world's leading maker of motorcycles, selling 4 million a year. All told, it produces 11.5 million engines a year, only 2.5 million of which are for automobiles.[20]

Honda has a relatively full line of products and is highly globalized, although its presence in Europe is weak. Can it sustain such a broad market position in the face of competitors several times its size? The company has thrived so far on its efficiency, flexibility, and time-to-market, but the large companies have benchmarked most of Honda's innovative practices in manufacturing, supply chain management, and quality assurance. Many have already closed the gap significantly.[21]

We see two interesting long-term possibilities for Honda. First, the company could narrow its geographic scope. With 85 percent of its operating profits from North America, it could become a very successful market specialist in this region. No other companies currently occupy this niche, whereas there are several in Europe. This idea is not as far-fetched as it sounds; a few years ago, the company actively considered moving its headquarters to Hawaii.

The second possibility is even more intriguing: Honda can become a global market specialist focusing on women. Worldwide, women have become much more active in purchasing cars, especially in the United States and Europe. In fact, 61 percent of car buyers under 25 are female, and 49 percent of 25 to 44 year olds.[22] No car company as yet has tried to capitalize expressly on this fact, and Honda is in the best position to do so. Of the five most popular cars with women, three are Hondas. A J. D. Power study of women car buyers found that the Honda Accord was their favorite car. Already, 70 percent of Honda Civic buyers are women. Furthermore, this success has come despite few concrete efforts to appeal directly to women buyers. If Honda were to focus on creating products with great appeal for women, and then advertising and selling them in a way that also appealed to women, the company could create enormous growth.

Honda, however, finds itself in an industry that is moving from the multinational to the global level. Whenever an industry undergoes such changes, it can suddenly lose its secure domestic position and become vulnerable to new competitive forces. Nowhere is this principle more evident than in the global markets that are now opening up, markets that have deep implications for players great and small. As market boundaries expand both regionally and globally—for instance, through free trade zones such as NAFTA, the European Union, and ASEAN—the number of shakeouts in individual industries will increase, and the threesomes that form the inner circle of those industries are likely to see many replacements in the ranks. The move toward globalization is inevitable, and sooner or later everyone engaged in competitive markets will need to deal with its far-reaching effects. As we discuss in the next chapter, this move represents an extension of the Rule of Three on a much broader scale. Competition is as fierce as ever, if not more so, and companies that seek to compete in these broader markets must adopt strategies far different from those followed by companies that seek to remain more localized.

5

Globalization and the Rule of Three

Marking a milestone in the history of the aviation industry, the last jet planes bearing the name McDonnell Douglas rolled off the assembly line in February 2001. Founded in 1920, the company had once been the #1 manufacturer of military aircraft and the second biggest recipient of U.S. defense contracts. Originally known as Douglas Aircraft, it made the first plane that flew completely around the world and created a series of aircraft whose names all began with the famous letters: the DC-3, the DC-9, the DC-10, for example. Acquired by the Boeing Corporation in 1997, McDonnell Douglas continued producing jets and other aircraft for commercial airlines, but primarily for the U.S. Department of Defense and its squadrons of military transport planes, helicopters, and fighter planes.

The aerospace industry, of course, attracts the deep interests of the U.S. Defense Department, in ways that few other industries can match. It is fair to say that the department essentially bankrolled the industry's technological superiority, which helped make the Big 3 in the United States—Boeing, McDonnell Douglas, and Lockheed Martin—the three largest aircraft manufacturers in the world.

In the recession of the late 1970s, the intense fight for market share between Boeing and McDonnell Douglas in commercial aviation pushed Lockheed into the ditch. In the 1980s, Airbus came on strong and became #2 in the industry, pushing McDonnell Douglas into the third slot. Then in the late 1990s, the fierce global rivalry between Airbus and Boeing pushed McDonnell Douglas into the ditch, with a market share below 10 percent. McDonnell Douglas's only real option to remain a full-line player was to make the Asia market its second "home." To this end, it tried to ally with Taiwan Aerospace, especially to get access to the huge Chinese market (with its $20 billion in backlog orders), but the deal fell through for political reasons. The company's other option was to give up on being a full-line generalist and become a product specialist based on its popular DC-80 platform. In the end, McDonnell Douglas decided that its best bet was to merge with Boeing. Since the merger, Canada's Bombardier has emerged as potentially the new #3 player in the industry, based on its popular long-range, smaller capacity jets that have found a lot of customers among big airlines looking to replace their turbo-prop fleets and add new longer routes with smaller passenger counts.

The remarkable change in the inner circle, which now includes Airbus, has evolved largely because several European countries, recognizing an opportunity to gain a foothold in an important global industry, banded together to support the Airbus consortium and lift it to the #2 position. As this evolution demonstrates, a government or one of its agencies—if the stakes are high enough and the political unit powerful enough—can boost a local player, or two or three, to the position of a global leader.

Clearly, there are many companies that need not and should not venture into global operations: great Parisian restaurants, some retailers (even large ones), and smaller financial institutions do best when they stay local.[1] It is also a dangerous strategy for most market specialists, whose focus is likely to be more regional or based on customer characteristics.

If a company does decide to go global, the transition from local or national player to global leader does not always come smoothly. When a market globalizes, many full-line generalists that were previously viable as such in their secure home markets are unable to repeat their success on the global stage. But even in the wider global setting, the Rule of Three eventually holds sway, after one or more shakeouts occurs. It is often the case (but not always) that each of the three survivors comes from one of the three primary economic regions, which Kenichi Ohmae identifies in his book *Triad Power* as North America, Western Europe, and Japan.[2] While each market in this triad is expanding regionally today, the basic concept that the world's economic markets are divided into three main areas gains validity from empirical observation and presents a logical connection to the Rule of Three. We have observed that to survive as a global full-line generalist, a company has to be strong in at least two of the three triad areas. For example, Ford is strong in North America and Western Europe, whereas Toyota is strong in Asia and North America.

An implicit principle in this book's argument is the law of expanding markets from a local to a regional base, then to a national one or often a multinational base, particularly when encouraged to do so by regional trade pacts or political alliances such as the North American Free Trade Association (NAFTA), the European Union (EU), or the Association of Southeast Asian Nations (ASEAN). To become *global* is to move one step beyond these regional arrangements, establishing supply chains, distribution channels, and markets in various—but obviously not all—geographical and cultural areas of the world.

The Shift from Local to Global Thinking

Globalization is by no means a new or recent phenomenon. In fact, over a century ago a number of countries traded with a high degree of economic openness. In the early twentieth century, however, nationalism increased dramatically and figured as a major cause in two world wars. At the same time, economic thinking became polarized, and there was a sharp decline in worldwide trade. Influenced by powerful ideological arguments, government officials in many countries, especially in South America and South Asia, embarked on misguided strategies predicated on achieving "self-sufficiency" in every major sphere of economic and cultural activity. Rather than emphasize and leverage their comparative advantages, these countries erected onerous tariff and nontariff barriers to trade. Consumers worldwide had to pay the price.

These obstacles to globalization slowly eroded in the second half of the twentieth century as the benefits of freer trade and capital flows became more apparent. The trend accelerated in the 1980s and became especially pronounced in the 1990s. Four factors contributed to the rapid rise in globalization over the past decade: (1) the collapse of communism; (2) increased economic pragmatism; (3) extensive privatization of publicly owned assets; and (4) a greater focus on shareholder value creation.

The first two of these factors are clearly related. As communist governments started to fall with astonishing speed in the late 1980s and early 1990s, the newly minted democratic regimes in these countries quickly adopted a free market orientation. Most did not have a choice in the matter; they desperately needed to attract investment capital from developed countries and had to restructure their economies in adherence with guidelines set by the International Monetary Fund and the World Bank. One result of these changes was that successful companies in other countries found enormous opportunities for growth opening up in these new markets.

In India and China, which did not see such a drastic change in political ideology, a new attitude of economic pragmatism nevertheless came to the fore. Both countries dramatically lowered entry barriers and eased restrictions on foreign ownership of domestic assets. They attracted huge amounts of investment capital as well as technology inflows from developed countries, using access to their large domestic markets as a bargaining chip. Even as economic pragmatism has spread like wildfire around the world, some countries remain driven by strong ideologies, in effect erecting barriers around themselves and lagging far behind other countries in economic development. The Middle East and much of Africa, for example, have seen little economic growth, as these areas continue to be mired in ideological debates and doctrinaire positions.

On the more pragmatic side, many countries soon realized that the biggest drag on their economic growth was the public sector. Where there was extensive government ownership of economic assets, often exceeding 50 percent of a country's gross domestic product, the state-owned "corporations" were highly inefficient, rife with corruption, and generally incapable of competing in a more open market. Many were losing enormous amounts of money as well.

Following the lead of Chile in the 1970s and the United Kingdom in the 1980s, countries started to privatize many government-owned businesses, resulting in a huge economic bonanza as multi-nationals from around the world bid for the right to acquire those entities. The impact was greatest in infrastructure industries such as telecommunications, electric utilities, basic metals, and transportation. Although slowing, the privatization process still continues. Foreign direct investment related to privatization in Brazil, for instance, represented 28 percent of total inflows in 1999.[3] In Mexico, the government plans to privatize Aeromexico and Mexicana, which control two-thirds of the domestic market and operate international flights to three continents. Major American airlines are certain to be among the bidders.[4] Europe alone has seen $200 billion worth of privatization in recent years. In Great Britain, for example, privatization led to the creation of 14 regional electricity companies, seven of which were acquired by American companies.[5] More than half of all new foreign direct investment worldwide is related to cross-border merger and acquisition (M&A) activity.

As privatization has increased, companies worldwide are putting greater emphasis on creating shareholder value. As Daniel Yergin, co-author of *The Commanding Heights,* observes, "one of the primary forces tying the world together during this sometimes unsettling period of globalization is the rise of the global shareholder. This global equity culture is redefining capitalism and the New Economy in every corner of the planet."[6] Accordingly, large companies are intensifying their pursuit of efficiency by leveraging global economies of scale in sourcing, producing, and marketing. Of all the world's economies, the United States has long been the one most heavily driven by considerations of shareholder value. Now, however, with the liberalization of financial markets and the need for capital, the rest of the world is experiencing the pressures for financial accountability that money managers can bring to bear. In Europe, for example, companies in the past could simply ensure that they were able to meet their payroll and pay their bills. If they did so, they faced few pressures to reform. Now, companies are under increasing scrutiny by analysts and more activist shareholders.

Capital markets are rapidly globalizing. During the 1990s, non-U.S. listings on the New York Stock Exchange increased by more than 300 percent. The "Wall Street ethos" has truly arrived, not just in Europe but also around the world.[7] The impact is by no means limited to institutional shareholders. In Australia, nearly 54 percent of adults own stock in companies directly or through mutual funds, followed by Canada with 52 percent and the United States, with just under 50 percent. In Germany, the share is rising but still very low, increasing slightly from 11 percent in 1998 to 13 percent in 1999. In Japan, the figure is just 7 percent. These numbers will surely rise in the future.[8]

Since greater efficiency typically leads to greater profits, and profits are the key driver of increased shareholder value, it stands to reason that industry structures that promote those attributes are the most favorable. Above all else, the Rule of Three encourages the creation of the most efficient industry structure and thus can contribute greatly to shareholder value.

While globalization has its critics, the evidence suggests that it has been a huge boon to living standards all over the world. Incomes and life expectancies are rising in most countries (particularly those that have embraced globalization); food production is growing faster than the population; literacy rates and education levels are rising, and communications technology is empowering people around the world.[9]

Moreover, approximately two-thirds of all industries are either already globalized (such as tires, computers, and aerospace) or in the process of becoming globalized (such as autos, auto parts, and appliances).[10] Many companies get half or more of their revenue and profits abroad; in the case of big companies from small countries, such as Nestlé and Nokia, it can be as high as 90 percent. In 1993, the General Electric Corporation received 16.5 percent of its sales from outside its home market, a figure that increased to just over 30 percent in 1999. Wal-Mart, which had no sales from outside its U.S. market in 1993, received just under 14 percent of sales from its worldwide markets by 1999. And McDonald's, which has invested heavily in franchising abroad, took in 61.5 percent of its 1999 sales from its worldwide markets, as opposed to just under 47 percent in 1993.[11] Overall, U.S. companies now derive about one third of their total net income from operations outside the home country, compared to less than 10 percent in 1950. Despite this impressive growth, it is widely believed that globalization is still at an early stage in many markets and industries.[12]

The Rule of Three and Geographic Market Scope

This important shift toward global markets leads to a significant observation about the Rule of Three: no matter how large the market, the Rule of Three prevails. That is, when the scope of a market expands (whether from local to regional, regional to national, or national to global), the Rule of Three forces further industry consolidation and restructuring.

Many companies, once regionally dominant, find themselves trailing badly when the market broadens to a national or global level. For example, although U.S. banks are still prohibited from true, no-holds-barred interstate banking, they are working around those restrictions with holding company structures, making de facto regional banking the norm. Consolidation through mergers and acquisitions proceeds apace toward a national Rule of Three market structure, led by Bank of America, J. P. Morgan Chase, and Citigroup. Such a structure already exists in Germany and Switzerland. Among wireless communications companies, Verizon Wireless (through mergers of regional companies), Sprint (through building out on a national basis), and AT&T (through acquisition of McCaw Cellular and others) occupy the top three positions. Cable television franchises, once the most local type of business, have consolidated into large regional players, with national and international consolidation following close behind.

Because local or regional markets are relatively rare, usually maintained only through regulatory mandate, the most significant transition occurs when a market organized on a country-by-country basis moves toward becoming truly global in scope. A distinct pattern emerges when markets move to this level, offering some of the most powerful evidence for the Rule of Three.

When a market moves to global competition, the first casualty is typically a European company (though not usually a British company). European markets have historically been geographically fragmented, highly protected, and often dominated by public sector concerns. In addition, they have had to contend with country-by-country standards and very small home markets. The German drug industry, once known as "the world's pharmacy," provides a case in point.

Drug Manufacturers in Germany

In the late nineteenth century, companies such as Hoechst AG and Bayer developed many of the first synthetic drugs such as aspirin and Novocain.[13] Today, however, German drug companies are no longer among the leaders of the global pharmaceutical industry: Hoechst, which until 1980 was the world's largest drug company, comes in at #13; Bayer follows at #16, Boehringer Ingelheim at #20, Schering at #22, and BASF at #27. Consolidation with other European players is now occurring: Hoechst has become a part of the French company Aventis SA. Bayer may soon be acquired as well, having "missed its chance to become a global pharmaceuticals leader," according to a J. P. Morgan research report.[14]

The complex reasons for the German drug industry's decline include stifling regulations and the "old-school chemist" mind-set at the leading companies. The biggest factor, however, has been the industry's aversion to biotech research, in part a response to environmental pressures from the German Greens. In addition, German companies were slow to embrace combinatorial chemistry, which can increase the likelihood of creating successful drugs. In terms of developing the technology, those companies fell behind the competition by as much as 15 years. Despite the efforts of the German government, which in 1994 sought to reverse this trend by providing $2 billion of subsidies for biotech research, the additional capital has not brought the major companies back into contention with industry leaders worldwide. In 2000, those leaders were Merck (U.S.), Pfizer (U.S.), and Johnson & Johnson (U.S.).[15]

In other industries many European companies are handicapped in the transition to global markets. Despite efforts at consolidation resulting from the newly formed European Union, they face high barriers to becoming successful global players, such as higher labor costs, lower operating efficiencies, and less effective use of enabling information technologies for operations as well as management. The home appliance industry offers an example.

The Home Appliance Industry

In 1986, the globalization of the appliance industry began in earnest when Europe's leading appliance maker—and the world leader—AB Electrolux of Sweden acquired White Consolidated of the

United States in an unsolicited bid. White sold refrigerators, freezers, and other appliances under the Frigidaire, White-Westinghouse, Kelvinator, and Gibson brands. These would complement Electrolux's U.S. subsidiary Tappan Company, which sold gas and electric ranges. Moreover, White was the third-largest appliance maker in the United States with 15 percent of the market, behind GE and Whirlpool, which controlled between 25 and 30 percent each.[16] With a full line of appliances, Electrolux was thus positioning itself to compete head-on with GE and Whirlpool.

Meanwhile, Whirlpool, looking to bulk up in the U.S. appliance market, purchased KitchenAid early in 1986. Within six months of the White acquisition, mergers had left four companies—General Electric, Whirlpool, Electrolux, and Maytag—in control of about 80 percent of the U.S. market. Maytag, which up to then had been a laundry specialist, purchased MagicChef in order to make a push into the fast-growing refrigerator market and Jenn-Air to gain entry to the high-end of the cooking range market. In 1988, General Electric outbid Whirlpool to acquire stove maker Roper.[17] Ditch companies included #5 Raytheon (see sidebar "Raytheon's Path to the Ditch"), which once sold appliances under the brand names Amana, Caloric, and Speed Queen.

Raytheon's Path to the Ditch

USING radar technology it developed for the military during World War II, Raytheon invented the microwave oven in 1947, but did not introduce the first commercial microwave until 20 years later. For some time Raytheon was the only company selling microwave ovens, commanding a 30 percent margin. After acquiring Amana Refrigeration, Inc. in 1965, Raytheon bought Caloric (ovens and ranges) and Speed Queen (washers and dryers), but soon ran into trouble. The growth of imports from the Far East (particularly South Korea) reduced Amana's market share in microwave ovens from 17 percent in 1980 to 7 percent in 1984. Amana and Caloric both lost sales because neither could offer retailers and builders a full line of products. Raytheon tried to rectify this problem by having Amana make refrigerators for Caloric and Caloric make ranges for Amana—with little success.[18]

Meanwhile, Raytheon's defense businesses grew and became more profitable: the company is now the #1 U.S. manufacturer of missiles and ranks third behind Boeing and Lockheed Martin in the aerospace and defense industry. Outside analysts, however, saw the appliance unit as a distraction and urged the company to sell it and invest the proceeds in more profitable businesses. Disregarding such suggestions, Raytheon in 1994 bought UniMac, a maker of commercial washing machines, increasing the number of brands in its appliance group to include Huebsch, Menumaster, Modern Maid, and Sunray.

Deciding in 1996 to compete with Sub-Zero Freezer Company in the high-end market, Amana introduced a new $1,749 refrigerator and planned to debut a $3,600 model later that year. Although the high-end market represented only 3 percent of a $4.45 billion market for residential refrigerators, Amana decided it was better to become a high-end specialist than to compete with the industry leaders for the middle of the market. However, this strategy failed to dislodge the strong incumbents on the high end.

In February 1997, Raytheon succumbed to the inevitable and announced that it would sell its appliance businesses and use the proceeds to reduce debt associated with its purchase of defense-industry assets from Texas Instruments and GM's Hughes Electronics. With those purchases, Raytheon became a leading defense contractor, with sales of more than $20 billion and 118,000 employees. It sold three segments of its appliance group—Amana home appliances, heating and air conditioning, and commercial cooking—for $550 million to Goodman Associates, a private holding company. In 1998, it sold its commercial laundry business (Speed Queen, UniMac, and Huebsch brands) for $358 million to a Boston-based investment firm and a group of Raytheon executives. From a company that once dealt in radar systems, textbooks (D. C. Heath), home appliances, petrochemicals, optical systems, and computer terminals, Raytheon is now resolutely focusing on its core defense business.

The European appliance market was far more fragmented than the U.S. market: 300 local manufacturers competed for business, most of them focusing on the idiosyncratic preferences of consumers in one European country.[19] In France alone, 55 appliance makers once sold products under more than 150 brand names.

Whirlpool and Electrolux continued their head-to-head competition in a series of acquisitions. In August 1988, Whirlpool acquired a majority stake in the large appliance division of N.V. Philips of Holland, which sold clothes dryers, refrigerators, and microwave ovens under the brand names Philips, Bauknecht, and Ignis. That acquisition gave Whirlpool Philips a 13 percent share of the European appliance market, a distant second to Electrolux's share of 25 percent. Germany's Bosch-Siemens followed with 12 percent, and Italy's Merloni Group had a 9 percent share.

After acquiring the rest of Philips's appliance business in 1991, Whirlpool eliminated several national brands, such as Phonola (Italy), Siera (Belgium), Radiola (France), and Erres (Holland). It became the first appliance maker to embrace a pan-European strategy, with centralized operations in areas such as procurement, product development, and brand marketing and advertising, rather than on a country-by-country basis. Its branding strategy was rationalized to include three clearly defined tiers: Bauknecht, for medium-range to high-end; Whirlpool for the broad medium range; and Ignis for the value-priced segment.[20]

When Whirlpool came to Europe, Electrolux was highly diversified: in addition to appliances, the company manufactured artificial flowers as well as road-paving equipment. After Whirlpool's entry, Electrolux immediately started to exit all its noncore businesses, cutting its payroll by 15,000. The company set its strategy to adopt a single global brand, Electrolux, and three pan-European brands, Electrolux, Zanussi, and AEG, while retaining strong local brands such as Faure in France, Tricity Bendix in the United Kingdom, and Zanker in Germany.[21]

Europe's enormous brand fragmentation decreased dramatically from 1982 to 1992, as the number of brands fell from 350 to 100. Most of the smaller companies became well-defined niche players. Fifteen firms controlled 80 percent of the market, still a far higher degree of fragmentation than the U.S. market, where the top four had 80 percent market share.

Meanwhile, Bosch-Siemens countered Whirlpool and Electrolux's aggressive moves by introducing a completely new line of products. Over a three-year period, it replaced every washer, dryer, dishwasher, and oven. It also stepped up its overseas activities, investing in Peru, China, Turkey, Spain, and elsewhere and raising its non-German business to two-thirds of revenue from one-third between 1994 and 1999.[22] In 1997, Bosch-Siemens also entered the U.S. market, first opening a dishwasher factory and then buying Thermador in 1998.

On another front, Maytag purchased the parent company of vacuum specialist Hoover, Chicago Pacific, but because of the aggressive moves by Europe's Big 3, Maytag decided to quit the European market in 1995. It sold its Hoover unit at a loss of $130 million. In August 2000, Maytag approached three companies to explore a possible acquisition, including Bosch-Siemens and Sanyo. Having purchased the Regina Company to boost its presence in the vacuum cleaner segment, Electrolux emerged as the leading candidate to acquire Maytag. Maytag's reputation as an innovator and industry quality leader are strong attractions. For example, the company recently launched a bagless vacuum cleaner and a flash-roast oven costing $3,500 that can cook a 10-pound turkey in an hour. Maytag also has a sizable commercial business, selling its washers and dryers, industrial cooking equipment, and vacuum cleaners to laundromats, restaurants, and hotels.[23] As the appliance market settles down from these consolidations and acquisitions, the emerging leaders are General Electric, Whirlpool, and Electrolux.

This brief survey of the global home appliance industry highlights four fundamental corollaries to the Rule of Three:

- In the globalization process, the #1 company in each triad market is best positioned to survive as a global full-line generalist.
- When foreign competition enters, the first casualty is usually the #3 company, since it is by far the weakest.
- When government subsidies are kept to a minimum, the default position is that each member of the global Big 3 comes from a different region in the triad of North America, Western Europe, and Asia.
- To be successful as a global full-line generalist, a company needs to have a major presence in all three areas preferably, or, barring that, in at least two of the three regions.

In consumer electronics, the U.S. market is now experiencing a fierce fight for market share between the Japanese (Matsushita/

Panasonic and Sony) and the European firms Philips/Magnavox and Thomson/RCA/GE. This battle will determine which players survive as global full-line generalists. The United States presents an ideal battleground because there is no U.S. company with a "home court advantage." Since there is no major domestic consumer electronics player, there is little danger of substantial government intervention. It is conceivable that neither of the European companies will be able to make it, and a third Japanese company (perhaps Toshiba) or a Korean company (such as Samsung or Daewoo) may emerge as a global full-line player.

Also as we have seen, when foreign competition does gain entry into one of the triad markets, the first casualty is usually the #3 company. White-Westinghouse was the #3 player in the U.S. appliance industry and would have fallen into the ditch were it not for its being acquired by Electrolux, which saw a way of entering that market.

The Rule of Three and National Competitiveness

In many countries competitive market forces are not allowed to operate freely. The heavy hand of government lays down excessive controls, or industries themselves institute practices that are intended to shield local companies from foreign competition but turn out to be counterproductive. As we have noted in chapter 2, few industries in these countries are allowed to evolve toward the Rule of Three. Evidence indicates, however, that if the Rule of Three is thwarted by such restrictions, the country in question will be at a competitive disadvantage in an industry that is rapidly moving to globalization.

Japan provides a good example. Eleven major automakers continue to exist in Japan, kept alive by government incentives, major barriers to exit, and a regulatory climate that discourages mergers. In addition, the keiretsu system, which has shielded unprofitable companies from market forces, has prevented the Rule of Three from developing domestically. Many of the automobile companies continue to struggle, including Nissan and Mitsubishi, which are reporting huge losses and have enormous debt burdens. In recent years, several of the weak Japanese companies—such as Mazda, Nissan, and Mitsubishi—have had to sell significant stakes to foreign car companies in order to survive. Renault, for instance, now owns a 37 percent stake in Nissan, Japan's #3 automaker (behind Toyota and Honda). Also, DaimlerChrysler owns 34 percent of Mitsubishi.

Until recently Europe has had the largest numbers of would-be full line generalists, often several in each country. Following 1992 and the move toward a common market, cross-border consolidation has greatly increased, and we are seeing the emergence of a Europe-wide Rule of Three in many industries. As a result, European companies are now competing with renewed vigor in the world's most open market, the United States. In the automobile industry, several years after Fiat, Peugeot, Sterling, and several other European automakers were forced to exit from the U.S. market or reduce their presence, companies such as Volkswagen, Mercedes-Benz, and BMW have come back strong. To ensure their success, however, players in the global markets need to heed some primary rules for competing.

Rules of Engagement in Global Markets

When venturing abroad into an industry poised to move from a domestic Rule of Three to the global level, companies can benefit by observing the following rules of engagement.

1. **Shore up the domestic market first.** A successful international assault cannot be launched from a weak domestic base. Companies must ensure that they are not vulnerable in their home market before looking at other opportunities. General Electric's Aircraft Engine (GEAE) division, for example, consolidated its strong lead over Pratt & Whitney before it went abroad to work with the emerging aerospace giant Airbus Industrie. It then took on the industry leader, Rolls-Royce plc (not to be confused with the maker of luxury cars). Now the world's largest maker of jet engines with 1999 revenues of $10.6 billion, GEAE builds engines to power both military and commercial jets used by the world's major airlines. The Stealth bomber, for instance, uses GE engines, as does Air Force One, not to mention thousands of other aircraft worldwide.

2. **Have the right attack strategy.** It is very important to attack with a superior weapon. The best way to enter a market is to offer a

better product at a lower price, rather than a better product at a premium price. The second best approach is to offer a low-end product at a low price and gradually move up. When Michelin entered the U.S. market, it had a superior product—the radial tire—that was also cheaper on a per mile basis. Michelin ensured that its products were priced such that there was enough margin for all value-chain members to make money, including retailers and service providers. Japanese automakers entered the U.S. auto market by following this second strategy. The Toyota Corolla, Datsun 210, and Honda Civic first appeared as relatively inexpensive models, whereas today's Toyotas, Nissans, and Hondas are much higher in the lineup of high-quality, mid-priced automobiles.

Successful Japanese companies have always used their domestic market to create a superior weapon. Like Toyota, they recover much of their development cost in the domestic market and ensure that the supply chain is lined up.

3. **Counterattack in the attacker's home market.** If attacked in its home market, a company is best advised to return the favor. After Electrolux made the first move into the U.S. market by acquiring White-Westinghouse, Whirlpool countered by scaling the barriers to the European market. Similarly, after Michelin attacked its home market, Goodyear immediately countered by entering the European market. As discussed below, this strategy hurt Michelin's profits in its sanctuary at home and caused it to ease back in the U.S. market.

4. **Time the entry right.** Foreign companies can make the most advantageous entry when domestic players are preoccupied with other issues or just after they have completed a major capital spending program. For example, when Michelin entered the U.S. market, the tire industry had just gone through a round of capital spending to upgrade its technology for manufacturing tires. The changes it made, however, were incremental, allowing the companies to continue to use the same factories and the same machines. Given that the move to radials represented discontinuous technological change, it required companies to set up new factories and adopt very different production processes. With the long depreciation schedules typical of the U.S. industry, American tire makers were at a disadvantage.

In the telecommunications industry, Nortel employed a similar strategy to leapfrog Lucent (at that time AT&T Network Systems). Lucent was selling, for example, Dimension analog PBXs, when Nortel came in with digital technology. Nortel took over the enterprise PBX market and eventually the carrier switch market from Lucent. The company is trying to repeat this performance as the industry evolves toward optical networking technology.

5. **Don't go into foreign markets alone.** Companies going global and moving from one nation to another should not go alone. Like a squadron of fighter planes, several of them should touch wings and fly in together. Japanese and Korean companies prefer to move into new territory together, whereas European companies are less likely to enter at the same time. Typically, three or four companies attack at the same time, segmenting the market and going after slices of it. They don't directly help each other, but together form a complementary front. Many major companies, for instance, are moving quickly into India and other areas with potentially strong economic futures.

The Global Tire Industry

These fundamental propositions related to the Rule of Three can be seen in the tire industry, which in the last few decades has taken extraordinary steps in its journey toward globalization. Until the early 1970s, this industry showed little interest in going global. For the most part, homegrown tire manufacturers remained comfortably in control of their national markets. Goodyear, Firestone, and Goodrich ruled the U.S. market; Michelin, Pirelli, Continental, and Dunlop kept their focus on Europe; Bridgestone, Sumitomo, Toyo, and Yokohama controlled the Japanese market. So long as they didn't bump into each other, the Big 3 in each triad market—Western Europe, North America, and Japan—maintained an easy truce.

The first salvo in the globalization of the industry was fired by Michelin of France. Company executives believed that expanding in Europe would be difficult since they were blocked from growing in the United Kingdom, Germany, and other nations.[24] Other than its home market, the company had few places where it could sell its innovative products. Michelin, which began as a maker of pneumatic tires for bicycles, pioneered an automobile radial tire in 1946. For over 25 years, radial tires were very popular in Europe, but American tire companies ignored the new technology in favor of bias-ply tires. Sears, however, began selling Michelin radials under the Sears name in the mid-1960s, and the tire maker experienced an explosion of exports to the United States in the early 1970s. Soon thereafter the company announced plans to invest $300 million to build radial tire plants in North America.[25] It opened its first factory in South Carolina in 1975.

When U.S. companies could no longer ignore consumers' demand for radials, most responded to Michelin's attack by getting into the radial business themselves; however, their hasty efforts produced poor-quality products (for example, the Firestone 500 resulted in a major disaster). It was several years before the industry learned to operate efficiently, cut excess capacity, and build modern radial plants.

Meanwhile, several players began looking at markets beyond those for traditional or innovative tires. By 1981, Uniroyal was focusing on its non-tire operations; Goodrich decided that its future was in specialty chemicals, and General chose to diversify. Like a classic specialist in a time of great change, however, the Cooper Tire and Rubber Company held its course and concentrated on the low-end, bias-ply niche of the replacement market.

These changes left only two major U.S. tire makers—Goodyear and Firestone.[26] Michelin recognized the opening and overtook Firestone in 1980 to become the world's second largest tire company. It then mounted a challenge to Goodyear, the world leader, for the #1 position. To expand its North American market share, Michelin cut prices, hoping that strategy would prove successful in attracting new customers without incurring Goodyear's retaliation. Counterattacking in its competitor's home territory, Goodyear targeted Europe, dropping the prices of its tires in an attempt to erode Michelin's profit base. That strategy worked, and Michelin was forced for a time to reverse its plans to expand its share of the North American market.[27]

During the 1980s, Goodyear continued to hold off Michelin's challenge, but it had to sell most of its non-tire businesses to fight a takeover threat from financier Sir James Goldsmith. Saddled with an enormous debt burden of $3.7 billion—1.7 times its equity—and looking at a mature and globalized industry, Goodyear had apparently few opportunities for differentiation and low-profit margins. The global tire industry was ripe for consolidation, and all the major players believed that growth into other countries held the key to the economies of scale that would be crucial to success.

Thus, the market for acquisitions heated up. Outbidding the Italian operating company Pirelli S.p.A., Japan's Bridgestone acquired Firestone for $2.6 billion, until that time the largest Japanese acquisition of a U.S. manufacturer. This purchase had the added advantage of bringing Bridgestone closer to the Japanese automakers then in the process of setting up U.S. factories. Bridgestone, which had almost no European business, was also interested in Firestone's loose foothold in Europe, where it had only a 4 percent share, but a share nonetheless. With a presence (however limited) in each triad region, Bridgestone publicly announced that its strategy was to become the #1 tire manufacturer in the world.

Michelin also had visions of global operations. In 1989, Michelin spent $1.5 billion to purchase Uniroyal Goodrich, raising its debt to almost $6 billion, nearly three times its total equity.[28] Still, the acquisition helped improve Michelin's presence in the United States. After a major restructuring of operations and a cut of nearly 30,000 jobs, Michelin regained some of its financial footing and began looking elsewhere for potential purchases. In 1995, the company bought a controlling interest in a Polish tire manufacturer; in 1996, it took a 90 percent share of the Hungarian rubber company Taurus; and in 1998, it acquired the Colombian tire group Icollantas. Such actions spoke clearly of the company's intentions to go global.

By 1990, foreign companies had bought six U.S. tire makers. In Europe, Pirelli S.p.A. and Continental AG of Germany engaged in acrimonious merger talks. Goodyear was the only major company that had not had any mergers. However, the company made a disastrous diversification move into the oil pipeline business, on the dubious logic that the industry was less cyclical than the car business. At a cost of $1.6 billion, the company's pipeline between California and Texas lost $53 million in 1990, and Goodyear could not find a buyer to take it off its hands.[29]

Even as the industry's giants struggled with their acquisition-related debts and post-merger integration challenges, the relatively small Cooper Tire and Rubber Company prospered. In 1990,

Cooper's profit rose 14 percent to $66 million on sales of $896 million. With only 1.5 percent of the world market, Cooper was a classic specialist: it stuck to the market for bias-ply replacement tires. The company spent very little on R&D, preferring to stay with mature products. Shunning company-owned stores, it did business with independent retailers, which preferred to buy from suppliers without a competing retail network.[30]

By 1998, Goodyear slipped to third place in the industry behind Michelin and Bridgestone, but regained the lead in 1999. That year the company acquired the Dunlop operations from Japan's Sumitomo Rubber Industries and came out with some new products such as its run-flat tires for the mass market. At least for the moment it is the world's #1 tire maker. The jockeying for market leadership remains close, however, with Michelin currently in the #2 position and Bridgestone not far behind. The Bridgestone/Firestone disaster involving Ford Explorer SUVs that roll over when tires blow out stands as a warning to any company in any industry, however, not to be lulled into thinking that market position, once attained, is forever.

This survey of the tire industry in the three major geographical markets illustrates many of the situations that players in any industry can expect to encounter as they seek to expand their global presence. While conditions will vary—depending, for instance, on whether an industry is in a mature stage as the tire industry was, or whether that industry is still evolving and thus more favorably disposed to innovations—an understanding of the fundamental rules of engagement can help any company develop a winning strategy for globalization.

So long as a market remains relatively free of artificial constraints, the Rule of Three will eventually impose an order on the players, distinguishing the three major participants and encouraging the rise of any number of niche players. The primary concern for any player remains staying out of the ditch. Insofar as it is possible to design one's destiny—as opposed to being designed by it—a company is best advised to keep one eye on the competition and another on its core business, whether that is providing a needed specialty or successfully playing the role of a full-line generalist. Trying to do both is certain disaster. Knowing when and how to challenge the competition is a major key to success, which the Rule of Three can offer to those leaders who are the most perceptive and courageous.

6

Strategies for Generalists

The quickest way to lose market leadership is for a company to pursue strategies that are inappropriate to its industry position. One of the most aggressive challengers in recent memory, Wal-Mart toppled Kmart from its #1 spot by taking advantage of the leader's miscues and constructing a well-designed strategy of its own centered on steady growth in smaller towns at first, superior logistics, firm control of the supply chain, everyday low prices, and well-trained employees in a family-focused culture. Doing much of the work in-house, Wal-Mart developed an impressive and sophisticated logistics system to track inventory and build a sales force of local heroes.

Market leaders are assumed to have a lot of advantages: size, wealth, breadth of offerings, economies of scale and scope, the presumed loyalty of customers, for instance. If they appropriately exploit these advantages, they should exhibit the best financial performance of any of the major players in their industry. Most assuredly they should show results superior to those of most specialists.

Disruptive forces external to a company can rapidly undermine its market position, however. The best-managed companies see the gathering clouds before the storm hits and are able to make the appropriate preparations to protect themselves. But that's often not enough. Internal disruptions can upset any company.

The failure to achieve the great promise of performance can be viewed as a failure of management. Responsibility for recent stumbles at market leaders Kellogg, United Airlines, and AT&T must be borne, in large part, by the leaders of those companies. At Kmart the loss of the #1 position is a story that points to a veritable conspiracy of external and internal forces. Unwittingly Kmart's own management was partly responsible for the ultimate rise of Wal-Mart to lead the discount retail industry. Despite valiant attempts to recover from that loss, Kmart may soon slip to third place behind rival Target Corporation.

The discount segment is growing faster than any other sector of retailing. In 1999, Wal-Mart, Kmart, and Target together accounted for approximately 80 percent of the segment's total $225 billion in U.S. sales.[1] When Wal-Mart went public in 1972 to raise money to build its first warehouse, it had only 30 discount stores in rural Arkansas, Missouri, and Oklahoma. Embarking on a trajectory of steady growth, the company set a strategy for building large discount stores in small rural towns, where its operating expenses, especially for payroll and rent, were low. Meanwhile, industry leader Kmart focused only on towns with populations of more than 50,000.

Wal-Mart grew steadily, capturing a high share of its served markets, which remained below its competitors' radar screens. When market leader Kmart finally did notice Wal-Mart, it determined that it did not make sense for it to launch its own stores in such out-of-the-way locations. This "natural market monopoly" became a significant entry barrier that shielded Wal-Mart from head-on competition. Within ten years, Wal-Mart had grown to 650 stores and $4.7 billion in sales. Still, Kmart continued business as usual, not viewing Wal-Mart as a major threat.

By 1987, Wal-Mart had over 1,200 stores—half the number that Kmart had. Its revenues topped $16 billion, about 60 percent of Kmart's revenues. Even more important, Wal-Mart had taken the lead in using computers to track sales and inventory as well as automatically replenishing its stores. Despite its smaller size, Wal-Mart was already more efficient than Kmart.[2] Having outgrown its rural base, Wal-Mart started to encroach on Kmart's territory in larger towns and cities. Instead of facing its new competitor head-on, Kmart tried to diversify by buying a number of specialty retail chains and upscaling its image.

Both strategies failed, and in 1991, Wal-Mart surpassed Kmart in sales. By 1993, it had $67 billion in sales, a full 50 percent more than

Kmart. More significant was the asymmetry between the two companies: whereas more than 80 percent of Kmart's stores faced direct competition from Wal-Mart, only half of Wal-Mart's stores faced competition from Kmart. After all, location is said to be the most important thing in real estate and in retail.

In 1994, Kmart announced that it would spin off its specialty stores and concentrate on its core discount store division. The companies Kmart eventually divested included OfficeMax, PayLess Drug Stores, Pace Membership Clubs, Coles Myer, Borders, Walden Books, The Sports Authority, and Builders Square.[3] With the erosion of its market share and its failed investment in specialty retailing, Kmart was so strapped for cash that it could not properly renovate its stores or invest in new technology. When it was finally able to do so, investing in computerized scanners and new product procurement and inventory control systems, the discount retailer found that it was still far behind its rival from Arkansas. There was no short cut for Kmart, and the company had little hope of regaining its leadership.

While Wal-Mart's greater efficiency and more popular approach to pricing (through its "everyday low prices" strategy) were undercutting Kmart's leadership position, another major competitor, Target Corporation, was successfully crafting a slightly more upscale image for itself. Although smaller than Kmart, Target made ten times as much profit in the first quarter of 2000. In August of 2000, Kmart announced that it would close 72 stores and take a pretax charge of $740 million to reorganize. It also announced that it would spend $460 million to upgrade its information systems and $210 million to upgrade its logistics.[4]

Wal-Mart's net sales in fiscal 2000 were more than $165 billion, up nearly 20 percent over the previous year's sales. Its international sales are almost $23 billion, including sales of the large U.K. retailer Asda, which Wal-Mart purchased in June 1999. Now dominating the discount retail category, Wal-Mart is looking to food sales to grow revenue. It already has a 12 percent share of all U.S. food sales. With 1,104 supercenters now in operation and a yearly growth rate of 15 percent, it is expected soon to become the #1 grocery retailer in the country. Both Kmart and Target have sought to emulate Wal-Mart by creating their own "super" formats that include groceries and fresh foods.

The rivalry between Wal-Mart and Kmart illustrates a number of basic principles about competitive market leaders. First, the leader is always the main focus of its competitors, whether or not they appear on the leader's radar screen. For years, Kmart ignored the threat from Wal-Mart, having assumed that the rival was little more than a country bumpkin. Kmart management simply did not think its market leadership was vulnerable. Second, a market leader has to guard against the danger of investing too much in the status quo. Should it succumb to the dangers of inertia, wily competitors can surround it like an overweight animal in the mudflats of a drinking hole. By the time that Kmart recognized the threat from Wal-Mart, it had already become stuck in excessive sales promotions and inefficient operations. Other recent victims of this inertia include Kellogg and AT&T. Third, a market leader becomes the "rule maker" of its industry or category, much as Wal-Mart has done in several areas, including logistics and inventory replenishment. By the time Kmart turned its attention to the technology it needed to compete, it had already lost its leadership position. Now it is just trying to play catch-up.

In this chapter we examine various strategies for the #1, #2, and #3 market leaders. Given that #3 players are concerned either with maintaining that position, fighting off challengers, or trying to overtake rivals, it follows that the strategies they should adopt are not the same as those chosen by the market leaders. In addition, conditions specific to each market and leadership position have an impact on the strategies managers select.

Strategies for #1 Companies

Founded over a hundred and twenty years ago, Anheuser-Busch took more than 50 years to become the first nationwide brewer in the United States, a position it attained in 1957. When the company started, the beer industry had only regional and local brewers. Quality control was practically nonexistent. The first company to make beer of consistently high quality, Anheuser-Busch relied on volume production and aggressive pricing to stake out its leadership position, which it has never relinquished. It is now approaching a 50 percent market share in the United States.

The company has been a masterful marketer; indeed, *Advertising Age* named it the fourth best marketer of the twentieth century. It has had consistently memorable advertising—the advertising for Bud Light has been described as the "gold standard" for beer advertising—and the company has been a pioneer in sports sponsorship and event marketing. Although it does not seek to be an innovator in developing new types of beer, the company moves aggressively when it decides that the market has responded favorably to the innovations of others. When rival Miller Lite was introduced in 1975, Anheuser-Busch responded with Bud Light five years later. While this go-slow approach avoids disasters such as Coors' ill-fated Zima, it can prove costly, and clearly the company will need to pick up the pace a bit! Although #1 companies do not need to be innovators in order to be successful, they must be *fast* followers.[5]

This brief overview of the #1 brewer in the United States suggests several of the basic strategies a market leader needs to consider in order to remain at the top of its game. Among these are the following seven:

Strategies for #1 Companies
- Be a "fast follower" in innovations
- Push for the adoption of industry-wide standards
- Develop world-class marketing and advertising through single or dual global brand positioning
- Use multiple distribution channels
- Emphasize both low costs and product differentiation, and focus on volume over margin
- Grow the market
- Avoid dogmatic thinking

Be a "Fast-Follower" in Innovations

The first strategy is probably the most radical and counterintuitive. For #1 firms—but not for the others—the risks of innovating in the market outweigh most of the benefits the innovation brings. Instead, a #1 company is more likely to profit from being a "fast-follower" rather than a market pioneer. As we have seen in the case cited above, Anheuser-Busch allowed the Miller Brewing Company to go through all the costs of developing and marketing its Lite beer, testing the waters to see how eagerly consumers would accept the new taste. While Anheuser-Busch waited too long to respond, and accordingly lost a great deal in market sales, the company nonetheless did not risk damaging the Budweiser brand. Eventually its "second but better" strategy paid off. In January 2001, the company announced that Bud Light—the second largest beer brand in the world behind Budweiser—registered its ninth consecutive year of double-digit growth.[6]

In 1966, marketing pioneer Ted Levitt wrote about the virtues of "innovative imitation"—taking an existing idea and creatively expanding on it.[7] Evidence is growing that this is indeed a smart—if seemingly heretical—way for large companies to grow. Peter Drucker also endorsed the idea, suggesting that creative imitation works if the innovation is considered from the customer's viewpoint. Indeed, the imitator must understand the innovation's application better than its creator does. Drucker suggested that creative imitation requires a fast-growing market and is most appropriate for major products, services, or processes—precisely the domains in which the innovator is at the biggest disadvantage relative to the market leader.[8]

The #1 company should heavily emphasize competitive intelligence, especially on the #3 company, which is typically the most innovative of all the market leaders. Since innovation is a requirement for survival for most #3 companies (as discussed below), the best strategy for a #1 company is to learn from the #3 and improve upon it. AT&T adopted many consumer marketing innovations from MCI and Sprint, and IBM and Microsoft have learned many lessons from Apple. Many Japanese companies follow the same principle. In consumer electronics, #1 Panasonic (Matsushita) has been a fast-follower of #3 Sony. With the Acura, #3 Honda preceded #1 Toyota's Lexus in the luxury car market.

The market leader should also be highly flexible and capable of speeding products to the market—a most difficult assignment, given that most large companies tend to be slow and excessively bureaucratic. It should adopt a "D&R" approach—rather than an R&D one—thereby spending more on development and less on research. As we will see, the opposite is the best strategy for the #3 company.

In addition to practicing creative imitation, market leaders must make their market entry rapidly, as soon as the pioneer has validated the market. Companies that enter a market in its growth stage—that is, when its viability has already been demonstrated—outperform pioneers. They achieve faster sales growth and find customers more responsive to their higher-quality products. The trick is to enter in the early growth stage of the market rather than waiting until the market is already mature. For example, Microsoft in browsers and IBM in mainframe computers have both taken the "second but better" strategy. Brands that enter in the mature stage tend to perform poorly.[9]

Most successful #1 companies have shown themselves to be very adept at this rapid response. Although it almost missed the boat, Microsoft did respond to the success of Netscape's Internet browser: within 22 months (an eternity in Internet-related matters), it launched four successive versions of Internet Explorer, eventually overtaking Netscape with its Version 4.0 and never looking back. In contrast, some #1 companies are slow to respond to pioneer innovations; for example, it took GM many years to come out with a minivan after Chrysler launched the category.

The fast-follower strategy is successful because #1 companies tend to have a strong market presence and are very good at marketing a proven product concept. They use sophisticated market research techniques to fine-tune product features and functionalities. In comparative evaluations of similar products, those by Microsoft, for example, usually receive all the reviewer's "check marks." The market leaders have well-developed distribution systems and the resources to invest in the advertising necessary to create market pull.

One landmark research study found that pioneers were market share leaders in only four of the 50 product categories studied.[10] Examples of markets in which late movers eclipsed pioneers include personal computers, wine coolers, and video games. Late movers—if not excessively late—can win in several ways. They can leverage their understanding of buyer preferences to craft a superior product, improving quality and features. They can offer better prices, even as they spend more on advertising and distribution. Market leaders excel at incremental rather than discontinuous innovation, a capability they can use to their advantage as part of a fast-follower strategy.

To help justify the heretical advice to embrace a fast-follower strategy, we recall the fate of RCA in its $500 million debacle with laser disc players, discussed at the beginning of chapter 2. The price of failure can be very large for a market share leader, and trying to absorb too many such failures will weaken the company's reputation among investors, depress its returns, and even put it out of business. Coca-Cola eschews radical product innovation, preferring to exploit opportunities identified by others; for example, Coke emulated RC Cola's launch of a diet cola as well as its packaging in aluminum cans. While many of its attempts at innovation have failed, Microsoft has been enormously successful at crafting follower products with meticulous attention to customers' needs. Though the company did not pioneer any of the major software application categories (word processing, spreadsheet, presentation graphics, database), it has now become the leader or near-leader in each. Microsoft's success in operating systems was also based on this pattern; the original DOS was licensed from another company, and Windows was inspired by the Macintosh interface.

The market leader should try to be an innovation leader only when it has the ability to secure monopoly power through patents or other means. General Motors, for example, worked with the Department of Transportation on catalytic converters and established a stranglehold on the market for many years. Given the huge advantage of "Intel Inside," an icon that consumers have come to demand, the Intel Corporation is almost assured that any new microprocessors it develops will succeed if they are competently executed. For the most part, Intel's Pentium processors are incremental innovations, each one a bit faster and more powerful than the previous. Our caveats with regard to radical innovation still remain.

Push for the Adoption of Industry-wide Standards

Market leaders are the "rule makers" of their industries. They set the norms by which the rest of the industry must operate and by which competing companies are judged on quality of products and services. Microsoft not only governs the technological standards for the PC industry but also sets price points and affects business models. Dell Computer Corporation once set the standard for customer service, as computer magazines frequently pointed out. Cisco Systems, IBM, UPS, Wal-Mart, and Home Depot have in various ways established standards for their industries such that customers use them in comparisons with market rivals. As has been pointed out in *The PIMS Principles,* a mark of the successful market leaders is that the quality of their products and services is higher than that of other companies in the same category.[11]

Nokia has become the world leader in cellular telephones in large measure because of the widespread adoption of the GSM standard. In 1976, the Sony Corporation lost out on its Betamax VCR when its rival Matsushita set the industry standard with its VHS, but Sony has come back with other products that have established a dominant standard such as 8mm camcorders.

Develop World-class Marketing and Advertising Through Single or Dual Global Brand Positioning

The strongest core competency of successful #1 companies is marketing. They are the most customer-driven, market-oriented companies in their industry. They make it their business to understand why their customers buy what they do, and they have highly developed and sophisticated marketing systems to cater to them. They also excel at advertising. The five "Marketers of the Century" named by *Advertising Age* are all market leaders: Nike, Anheuser-Busch, Coca-Cola, McDonald's, and Procter & Gamble (a marketing innovator that invented brand management as well as soap operas).

Many leading companies, especially in the United States, have spent too many resources on launching and sustaining multiple brand names, and they are tempted to do more market segmentation than they should. Such companies lack an overarching brand identity that can be leveraged across all their products. To be successful, #1 companies should pursue a broad market positioning and promote a unified corporate identity, usually by means of a global umbrella brand. Because they are volume-driven, these full-line generalists need to offer a variety of products to as diverse an audience as feasible. Their corporate positioning should be broad enough to allow for wide applicability across products and segments.

Japanese companies such as Yamaha, Panasonic, and Mitsubishi have demonstrated for decades that brand names are far more powerful when defined broadly and applied widely. Most #1 companies would be better off if they reduced their proliferated brands to one, or at most, two umbrella brands, with subbrands as needed. Companies focused on the business market typically only need one brand, while those that target the consumer market may need a second brand for the premium segment—for example, Toyota/Lexus, Honda/Acura, Nissan/Infiniti, VW/Audi, Ford/Jaguar, Marriott/ Ritz-Carlton.

The case of consumer packaged goods (CPG) companies is somewhat different. These companies tend to offer a line of products within a product category, and may require a large number of brands. However, many CPG companies are guilty of having too many brands. Long characterized by its brand proliferation, Procter & Gamble has almost no corporate identity in the minds of consumers. People know the products by name—Tide, Pampers, and Iams pet food, for instance—but have no knowledge that these products are part of the P&G family. In this regard, P&G is at a disadvantage compared to Unilever and Colgate-Palmolive. The company is now systematically reducing its stable of brands and more aggressively marketing those that have a global appeal.

Use Multiple Distribution Channels

Since #1 companies seek volume, they must strive for full market coverage; that is, they must be readily accessible to all mainstream customers. They should use multiple third-party channels, such as institutional, retail, private label, and original equipment manufacturers (OEMs). Excessive loyalty to any one channel is dangerous for #1 companies. Furthermore, they should particularly avoid vertical distribution channels, in which they own a part or have a controlling stake. Both IBM and AT&T flirted in the past with excessive concentration of distribution and sales responsibilities internally—a strategy from which they were eventually forced to distance themselves.

Emphasize Both Low Costs and Product Differentiation, and Focus on Volume over Margin

Companies in the #1 position are successful because they are highly efficient, usually the most efficient in their industry. Their overhead expenses should be lower than their competitors' when expressed as a percentage of revenues. They must also ensure that they do not have too much excess capacity. The #1 company must not only emphasize the low-cost position, which is based on superior sourcing or more efficient manufacturing, but also practice product differentiation in order to generate more revenues. Failing to add value through their product lines, many #1 companies slowly lose market share to the #2 and #3 players, as Kmart did when it lost its leadership position to Wal-Mart and now finds itself threatened by Target.

Too many #1 companies make the mistake of believing that they are leaders because of some extraordinary and sustainable core competence, when in fact their #1 position might result from a short-lived proprietary technology or a situational advantage. Apple briefly enjoyed a period of industry leadership in the mid-1980s with its proprietary operating system and hardware architecture. However, Microsoft rapidly recognized an advantage in licensing its operating system to the PC clone makers, and the rest is history.

To guard against competitive vulnerability, #1 companies have to figure out how to make money based on high volumes rather than high margins. If they remain margin-driven (because they have a lock on the market, or a monopoly, or strong patent rights), they are liable to collapse quickly. High margins attract aggressive lower-cost producers to a market, as we see now in the long-distance telephony business, where a number of companies are able to undercut the pricing of long-distance companies such as AT&T, Sprint, and MCI WorldCom. It happened previously to many U.S. companies against Japanese competitors, especially in automobile manufacturing, consumer electronics, copiers, and the like. Born of decades of high returns, complacency caused many #1 companies in the United States to falter. For example, the extraordinary margins commanded by IBM PCs in the early years of the PC industry provided a window through which clone-makers could emerge. Had IBM been more aggressive on pricing and focused on volume, there would have been almost no opportunity for those competitors. In the early 1970s Xerox left the door open to Canon and Ricoh. Because they refused to reduce their margins and emphasize volume, companies such as General Motors and RCA saw their market shares dwindle.

Grow the Market

The strategy of increasing volume rather than margins would seem to be a formula for lowered profits, were it not for the corollary that reduced margins must be accompanied by market growth. The #1 company is much better off growing the total market than continuously fighting for a larger share of a stagnant market. Such companies have a difficult time gaining incremental shares of the market. This is especially true for companies with dominant shares—that is, anything over, say, 40 percent. In the long-distance calling market, AT&T's market share is nearly five times greater than that of Sprint. For AT&T to gain merely a 1 percent increase in market share at the expense of Sprint, Sprint would have to lose 10 percent of its customer base. Such surrender would not come without a fight.

Leading companies have many ways to grow their markets, starting with international expansion. Once they have established a secure position in their home market, #1 companies should consider defining their geographic market more broadly. Having built up its base in the United States, Wal-Mart became the #1 retailer in both Canada and Mexico, then set its sights on the European market, where it has already presented a challenge to industry leaders. McDonald's captured the U.S. market, then took aim at Japan, the easiest target it could find. Subsequent forays into various markets around the world have proven more difficult but by no means impossible: McDonald's now operates restaurants in 120 countries, and some 60 percent of its sales revenues are non-U.S. based.

The #1 company can also broaden the category definition of the market it competes in. For example, local telephone companies are now looking for a high "share of wallet" within the broader communications market, which includes their core business of local calling, but also includes long distance, wireless, and Internet access. Currently, their share of this expanded wallet is just under 20 percent. Leaders should leverage their base of satisfied customers to offer related products and services.

Carnival, for example, now defines itself as a vacation company, not just a cruise line. The #1 cruise company, Carnival has been on an acquisition spree, acquiring a 40 percent share of NCL Holding, which operates Norwegian Cruise Line. Its financial performance is worthy of its status as the industry's volume leader: the company's earnings growth averaged 23 percent between 1996 and 2000, and its profit margin stood at almost 32 percent. Having solidified its position as the global leader in its industry, Carnival is taking the next logical step: it is now broadening its market definition to being a "vacation company." Recently it spent $775 million to buy out time-share marketer Fairfield Communities. At a time when Disney has aggressively entered the cruise market, Carnival's actions make a lot of sense.[12]

Another attractive growth vector for leaders is to move aggressively into downstream value-adding activities, as General Electric is doing by playing a more active role in providing "productivity solutions" for customers and helping them derive more value from its products and services. GE's division for jet engines places greater emphasis on obtaining long-term service and maintenance contracts than it does on landing the initial sale. An important corollary to this strategy is that companies should seek growth from services if they are primarily a physical product company, and from physical products if they are primarily a services company.

Companies can also grow the market by broadening their product lines to include new products aimed at attracting new users into the marketplace. As the #1 company in the soft-drink industry, the Coca-Cola Company now faces this challenge. The public's growing preference for juice, bottled water, tea, and other noncarbonated beverages has forced Coke to target these markets more aggressively. Coke already sells over 230 such beverage products worldwide, and CEO Douglas Daft believes that the company may one day sell as many as 2,000 different drinks, including new hybrid drinks such as carbonated tea. Coke-owned brands such as Fruitopia, Nestea, Dasani bottled water, and Powerade sports drinks are all also-rans in their product categories, none of them even approaching the strong positions of Coke's carbonated brands. Daft wants to remake Coke into "a leader of the beverage sector, as opposed to a soft-drink company."[13]

In addition, the premium segment of any market is particularly attractive nowadays, as evident in the automobile, appliances, professional services, and tourism industries. Market leaders, however, should stay away from the ultra-premium segment, which remains the domain of specialists. They should address only that portion of the premium market that is amenable to their volume-driven approach.

A good growth vector for #1 is to become the supplier of private label products, for example in packaged goods or telecommunications. As a part of the recommended hybrid channel strategy for top generalists, this strategy is not recommended for #3 companies, which tend to have less leverage with large downstream players and are thus more vulnerable. These competitors also have less of a scale advantage than #1 companies and are thus not able to offer the same value proposition to downstream players.

Avoid Dogmatic Thinking

Market leaders should have no sacred cows. They must be prepared to change technologies, kill old products, and adopt new marketing approaches. Peter Drucker once defined "intellectual integrity" as "the ability to see the world as it is, not as you want it to be."[14] This ability is the hallmark of pragmatic leaders. Pragmatism requires an uncoupling of means from ends, a willingness to alter or even reverse course if strong evidence clearly points in that direction.

Bill Gates is a maestro at the art of pragmatic corporate leadership. Time and again, he has steered the ship of Microsoft into new waters, even reversing course with a degree of alacrity that would be remarkable in a company a tenth the size of Microsoft. The company is often derided, with some justification, for not being an innovator, and the majority of its successes have come slowly, the result of superior implementation of the ideas of others. Yet, it is the very essence of the pragmatic company, with a focus on results, on learning from others, on identifying large opportunities when they are barely noticeable. Every time a competitor or a new technology appears to present a threat to the company, it mobilizes quickly to turn that threat into yet another growth opportunity. Microsoft is largely reactive, to be sure, but most of its reactions have had a greater impact on the industry than all the actions that inspired them.

The degree to which pragmatism dominates in management and strategy can determine whether a market leader creates shareholder value or destroys it. Pragmatism in business builds shareholder value; dogmatism sacrifices it to ideological purity. Pragmatic companies are capable of being passionate and dispassionate at the same time—passionate about uncovering new opportunities and superior execution, dispassionate about particular products, technologies, or even customer groups.

A lack of pragmatism can cause leaders to miss opportunities for growth, as Apple did by choosing to ignore over 90 percent of the world's PC market that is wedded to the Wintel standard (that is, the Windows operating system and Intel's processors). Microsoft, by contrast, embraced the Internet opportunity as well as the emerging wireless sector. It even invested in Apple, despite the rivalry between their operating systems, and today Microsoft is by far the largest developer of applications for the Macintosh OS.

When emotion or inertia dominates logic, companies have a tendency to squander resources on lost causes. IBM spent billions on the development of its OS/2, even though it was starkly evident that it had no chance whatsoever of displacing Windows on the desktop. Likewise, Motorola pursued the Iridium satellite project, the $5 billion consortium that promised to build a global communications network in space, but has recently declared bankruptcy and been sold.

Pragmatism should *not* be equated with a lack of principles or the absence of vision. In recognizing the fluidity of the external environment—major opportunities occur less by grand design than by serendipity—the pragmatic leader calls for the company to constantly adjust its strategies to new realities rather than proceed resolutely under obsolete assumptions. Visions and principles are defined in a manner that accommodates such adjustments, although even they are willingly junked when they prove no longer valid. Companies are much better served by becoming strategic opportunists rather than resolute implementers of rigidly defined strategies.

Strategies for #2 Companies

"If you've ever been #1, it's no fun being the #2 sled dog and looking at the lead dog's you-know-what." So observes Robert "Bob" Tillman, the chairman and CEO of Lowe's Companies, and he should know. Until the mid-1970s, his company was the leader in the building materials retailing industry.[15] While some company managers are perfectly content to remain #2 in their respective industries, most would share Tillman's assessment of being on the south end of a north-bound sled dog.

The appropriate strategy for #2 companies depends on two key factors: the position relative to the #1 company, and the rate at which the market is growing. The first three strategies presented below are generic for all #2 companies. The second group of four strategies is conditional on the market context. To restate the obvious, we do not intend to suggest that *every* #2 company adopt these strategies wholesale; rather, leaders need to weigh each strategy against company goals and pragmatic realities.

Generic Strategies	*Conditional Strategies*
• Engage in productive marketing	• Clone the leader—but be smart about it
• Focus on value	• Topple the leader
• Close the efficiency gap with the #1 company	• Challenge the leader
	• Co-exist with the leader through segmentation

Engage in Productive Marketing

In contrast to the industry leader, a #2 company often has to invest disproportionately in marketing. In 1998, for example, Pepsi's promotional budget exceeded Coke's. The danger for #2 companies is that they spend marketing money indiscriminately, relying on the usual marketing gimmicks. Instead, they must be creative and spend in a more selective manner, focusing, for example, on key customers in key markets, much as MasterCard is now doing. The #2 company should reduce subsidies across customers so that they can cherry-pick the best ones from the #1 company, which tends to rely heavily on customer cross-subsidies.

Focus on Value

While it is never easy existing in the shadow of a successful market leader, #2 companies can succeed by emphasizing greater value. They must be competitive with #1 companies on price. If they try to price higher for a comparable product, it will not work.

In some cases, however, targeted price reductions can work to the #2's advantage. The reason is that price elasticities tend to be better for the #2 company than for #1, especially if the share gap is large. If a #2 company drops its price 10 percent, it is likely to get a larger share from #1 than #1 could gain by dropping its price an equivalent amount. If the market share ratio is large (say, two or three times), the 10 percent drop in price will generate a much greater impact for the #2 company than it does for the #1. To illustrate this point, consider the case of MCI, which gained large chunks of market share from AT&T through its "Friends and Family" program. By selectively discounting rates for MCI customers who called other MCI customers and by giving them an incentive to persuade others to switch to MCI, the company was able to raise its market share from 13 percent to 20 percent in less than three years. Had AT&T retaliated in kind, it would have suffered a large decline in profitability because of lower margins.

This case also points out that #2 companies should emphasize value-added services while maintaining price parity. The Ford Motor Company's recent purchase of Kwik-Fit, a leading after-market service chain in the United Kingdom, indicates the direction the company is taking. Given that the automotive manufacturing industry is characterized by low growth, low margins, and low price-to-earnings ratios, Ford embarked in 1999 on a program designed to increase what it calls its "customer touch-points" and decrease "asset intensiveness." CEO Jac Nasser wants to change Ford from a manufacturing company to a "consumer company," by which he means that Ford wants to leave a larger share of its manufacturing activities to its suppliers, while it focuses on market research, product development (even noncore engineering activities will be outsourced to suppliers), and most important, the downstream activities such as service, financing, and communications where extra value can be added for the consumer. As Ford sees it, the typical customer spends $60,000 over the ten-year life of a car, only $18,000 of which comes to the manufacturer. Ford wants to follow the consumer throughout those ten years and capture as much of the remaining $42,000 as possible—and do it with less asset intensiveness than its manufacturing operations. With the Kwik-Fit acquisition, Ford plans to translate its close customer relationships into better products and higher profits. At the same time, it must guard against losing its vital core competencies in product design and quality production.[16]

Close the Efficiency Gap with the #1 Company

Provided their execution is comparable, #1 companies enjoy an efficiency advantage over #2 companies due to their superior economies of scale. The #2 company must close this gap or risk losing ground to the market leader. To this end, the #2 player has to improve asset utilization, as Ford, for example, is doing by decreasing "asset intensiveness" as part of the new initiative described above. By entering into long-term strategic relationships with best-in-class suppliers, the #2 company can begin to reduce vertical integration and outsource more functions than the #1 company is doing. In essence, this is one of the strategies that Wal-Mart used when it lagged behind Kmart. The strategy allows the #2 company to use other companies' resources and capital (for example, those of suppliers). Also #2 companies must seek to improve process efficiencies to minimize #1's scale advantage.

Closing the efficiency gap should not be confused with compromising the quality of products, however. The example of Fruit of the Loom stands as a *memento mori* that all market leaders should take to heart. The venerable 150-year-old Fruit of the Loom Company was forced to seek bankruptcy court protection in December 1999. This popular American institution, with a brand name trademarked in 1871, had a 32 percent share of the market for men and boys' underwear—a close second behind the 37 percent share controlled by Hanes, a part of the Sara Lee Corporation. Between mid-1997 and early 2000, the stock price of Fruit of the Loom had declined precipitously from $44 to a mere 56 cents.

In terms of market share, however, Fruit of the Loom could have been counted as a success. How, then, could such a well-known company end up in Chapter 11? To lower its costs, Fruit of the Loom had shifted a major portion of its production to offshore locations in the Caribbean and elsewhere. And that's when it ran into problems with product quality and availability. By the time production ramped up again, many customers had canceled their orders. Left with excess inventory and a heavy debt burden, the company found itself in a liquidity crisis that led to the Chapter 11 filing. In the meantime, competitors made significant inroads with the company's customers. Recapturing its earlier market share will prove extremely difficult.[17]

Clone the Leader—But Be Smart about It

The typical sequence in most industries is that #3 innovates, #1 copies (and thus validates), and #2 follows. When a market is growing rapidly and the incumbent #1 company is far ahead, the best strategy for a #2 company is be smart about how to clone the leader. This strategy works best when the #1 company is constrained by suppliers and unable to meet demand. In that case, the #2 company can simply ride the coattails of #1—in short, emulate and imitate. For years Burger King used this strategy against McDonald's internationally as well as domestically. As the market matured, however, its strategy had to change.

Lowe's, now the #2 building materials retailer, has cloned Home Depot's "big box" layout, the huge store that looks more like a warehouse than a retail space. The chain has embarked on an extremely ambitious plan to invest as much as $7 billion to build 80 megastores annually for several years, each occupying as much as 150,000 square feet. Lowe's, however, plans to change the genetic code by differentiating itself from Home Depot in three ways: (1) selling appliances as well as hardware (a move that Home Depot has copied); (2) providing products different from those offered by Home Depot, many under exclusive deals with well-known designers, and (3) offering major home renovation services under the same roof rather than in another store, as Home Depot is doing with its new independently located Expo Design Centers.

The examples of Burger King and Lowe's suggest that a #2 company should not simply clone the #1 company; rather it needs to undertake "smart cloning" by exceeding the leader's strengths, challenging and exploiting its weaknesses. As Bob Tillman, the CEO of Lowe's Companies, has said, "You can't just copy somebody; you've got to be better."[8] The challenge to both Burger King and Lowe's is huge, and probably neither one entertains the illusion that it can actually catch and surpass the industry leader. The sheer dominance of that leader in many markets, however, can work in the favor of both #2 players, given that many consumers prefer to have a choice in where they shop. Lowe's highly successful test markets in Home Depot's strongholds of Atlanta and Dallas bear this assumption out.

A #2 company can, of course, also try the fast-follower strategy recommended for #1 companies, but it will not gain as much by doing so because it lacks the massive market presence of #1. Moreover, the #2 company rarely has the ability to establish an industry standard; if it alone adopts an innovation, which the #1 company shuns, the market is much more likely to follow the leader. At best (or worst, depending on one's point of view), there might be two competing standards.

Topple the Leader

In a fast-growing market, market shares are very fluid. The #2 company (and even the #3) has an opportunity to forge ahead of #1 by better executing the full-line game plan. In the personal computer industry, Compaq surprisingly surpassed IBM and others to take the #1 market share position worldwide. Compaq was in turn challenged (unsuccessfully) by Packard Bell in the home market, then by Dell Computer Corporation in the broad market, with a business emphasis.

After almost a century of occupying the #1 position in its industry, Kellogg lost out to General Mills, maker of Wheaties, Cheerios, and Chex cereals, as well as Colombo yogurt and Pillsbury baking products. The Minneapolis-based General Mills recently acquired Pillsbury from Diageo, in effect doubling the company's size and helping it reach the #1 position. By building up its product offering, General Mills wrested market share away from the former industry leader and now claims a 32.2 percent share of the market. In contrast, Kellogg holds a 30.7 percent market share.

Challenge the Leader

In a slow-growing market, when the #2 company's market share differential with #1 is low and the #1 company is not behaving like a typical #1, then the #2 company can aggressively challenge #1 for market leadership. Creating the excitement of overtaking the #1 company can for a while drive the company. This has been true at Pepsi, Komatsu, Fuji, Airbus, and now Ford, each of which has set its sights on being #1. In these situations, the #2 company should create an emotional, passionate commitment to topple #1 from its berth.

Co-exist through Segmentation

If the market is mature and the #1 company has a dominant share, the best strategy for #2 is to coexist by segmenting the market and avoiding as much head-to-head competition as possible. Because the market leader can bring proportional resources to bear on defending its turf, such competition is expensive. If the market turns stagnant, the competitive struggle becomes more of a win-lose or zero-sum game.

In early 1999, the Miller Brewing Company made several acquisitions to fill out its product line. It acquired, for example, the Henry Weinhard and Mickey's brands from Stroh's and the Olde English 800 and Hamm's brands from Pabst, as well as a portion of that company's contract brewing business. Whether they could really help the company compete with Anheuser-Busch remained in doubt because Miller's core premium brands, Miller Lite and Miller Genuine Draft, were both struggling. Despite a 20 percent market share (compared with Anheuser-Busch's 50 percent), the absence of any strongly positioned brands put Miller in a highly vulnerable financial position. Margins on most of its products were extremely thin. Molson and Foster's are the only truly premium brands left in Miller's portfolio, but both are imports with very low volumes compared to the big domestic brands. Thus, Miller once again suffers from a brand proliferation problem: it has too many marginal brands and no strong core brands to drive the bottom line.[19]

If the #2 company segments the market in a new and compelling way, however, it can gain considerable market share over time. Kmart, for example, started in smaller markets, knowing well that it couldn't compete with Sears in the larger ones. The same strategy was later used against Kmart by Wal-Mart, which targeted even smaller towns.

While differentiating its offerings, the #2 company must adhere to industry norms but play a slightly different game than either the #1 or #3 company; otherwise, it risks getting stuck in the middle. In batteries, for example, Energizer is boxed in between #1 Duracell's premium image and #3 Rayovac's aggressive price cutting, giving customers no strong reason to purchase its products.

Strategies for #3 Companies

While the #1 and #2 companies can appear relatively secure in their positions, it is by no means inevitable that companies close to the ditch must eventually succumb to it. For the #3 player, the best defense from the ditch is to stay as far away as possible—that is, by increasing market share and building up the return on assets. Ironically one of the best means to this end is to go shopping in the ditch for an acquisition, partner, or alliance that can bring in new customers, new markets, and new products to help the #3 company mount a challenge to the market leaders. Barring that strategy, #3 companies can consider pairing up with a large specialist, especially one that is itself in danger of being pulled into the ditch. Switzerland's Nestlé S.A., for example, is an internationally leading maker of candy—among many other products including coffee, ice cream, and pet foods—but in terms of the U.S. candy industry it is the #3 player behind Hershey and Mars, Inc. Throughout its history it has grown by acquiring other companies such as U.K. confectioner Rowntree, maker of Kit Kat, in 1988, followed by purchases of Butterfinger and Baby Ruth in the 1990s.

In addition to bulking up, #3 companies can improve their position by following other strategies that fit with their goals and production, including but not limited to the following:

General Strategies for #3 Companies
- Innovate and differentiate
- Concentrate resources for best opportunities
- Use guerrilla marketing
- Take calculated risks
- Promote vertical partnerships
- Seek out horizontal partnerships

Innovate and Differentiate

By far the most important requirement for success for a #3 company is innovation, particularly in such a way that #1 cannot readily replicate. The competitor should never forget the rule that the #1 company is always looking to copy what the #3 company has invented. Even though it may take years for the #1 company to come up with a workable model, the #3 company should take no comfort in this time lag and should continue to innovate further on its products. For example, Chrysler sold 4 million minivans in a decade before GM, Ford, Toyota, and Honda were able to threaten its continued dominance in this market. As evident in practically any industry, neither the #3 company's product innovation nor its process innovation is safe from the market leaders.

In product innovation, successful #3 companies need to differentiate themselves quickly and visibly. Accordingly, they should count on outspending the #1 players on R&D as a percentage of total revenues. Their R&D efforts need to be highly productive. RC Cola looked for something it thought Coke could not easily duplicate or would have no interest in copying. Assuming that Coke would never change its recipe, RC invented Diet-Rite, the first low-calorie soft drink. Pepsi, the #2 player, countered very quickly, and Coke responded much later with Tab, which was not a big success.

Process innovation is also fair game for competitors, and #3 companies must be ready to steal or borrow innovative practices from members of other industries. They must also move quickly to embrace new and more efficient business processes. Again, the RC Cola case presents a good example in that company's decision to attack Coke in an area where presumably it had little flexibility: its bottling operations. For years Coke had used thick, recyclable glass bottles; thus, RC Cola introduced the aluminum can. Coke was forced to counter with a huge investment to change to the new process, and the delay cost the company a great deal.

In the long-distance telephone market, the #3 player Sprint has a long history of pioneering innovations, most of them related to its technology. It was the first company to invest heavily in fiber optics, creating the first fully digital phone network; the first to combine long-distance, local, and cellular services; the first to introduce ATM technology into its network; and the first to offer voice-activated calling. That is not a bad record, but its rivals have quickly copied each of these innovations.

In the early years of the personal computer market, Compaq was the #3 player behind IBM and Apple. In 1986, the company brought out the first computer to offer Intel's 386 microprocessor. In addition, Compaq created one of the industry's first portable computers and later pioneered the first PC-based server, the SystemPro. Its innovations, however, came with high price tags, which prevented the company from becoming a truly successful full-line generalist. Accordingly its market share fell steeply as the PC market matured. Changing its strategy in 1992, Compaq began designing products that were high on added value although no longer technology leaders. Coupled with highly efficient manufacturing and assembly methods, this strategy helped the company to an extraordinary turnaround and reemergence as a successful, globalized full-line player. Eventually Compaq overtook IBM to become the leading PC maker in the world.

Concentrate Resources for Best Opportunities

Having limited resources, the #3 company needs to use them effectively. While remaining a full-line player by virtue of being a generalist, the company must concentrate resources to take advantage of the best opportunities. Being "full-line" does not mean that one cannot be selective about the products one offers; in fact, a #3 player can take a page from the specialist's book. The #3 U.S. book publisher, Harper, has moved to a smaller but more focused roster of titles. The #3 battery maker, Rayovac, is #1 in high-margin categories such as hearing aid batteries. Companies can also be selective with customers and channels. Rayovac targeted channels such as auto parts stores, arts and craft stores, and retailers such as Sears, with which it has entered into an exclusive agreement.

Use Guerrilla Marketing

A #3 company can often gain market share by resorting to "guerrilla" tactics, looking for a competitor's Achilles' Heel, much as MCI did with its Friends and Family program. The #3 tries to turn the leader's size into a disadvantage, especially when that size prevents the #1 company from following the #3's lead. Just as RC Cola found the weak spot in Coke's production technology and introduced its aluminum can innovation, so the Coors Brewing Company, the third largest brewer in the United States behind Anheuser-Busch and Miller, has made a science of clever packaging. It too resorted to aluminum cans at a time in the 1950s when pressure was mounting from environmentalists and company managers to find a replacement for steel beverage cans. Other creative packaging promotions have included pigskin cans during football season, baseball bat-shaped bottles, wide-mouth can openings, John Wayne commemorative cans, holographic multi-packs, and the Killian "Irish pint" bottles to celebrate St. Patrick's Day.[20]

Another part of this strategy involves targeting the #2 company instead of the market leader. This approach works best if the #2 is perceived as weak. Rayovac introduced deep discounts, which have hurt #2 Energizer more than #1 Duracell, and much of Rayovac's market share gains—from 8 percent in 1996 to 16 percent in 1999—have come at Energizer's expense.

Take Calculated Risks

In general, #3 companies must take more risks than market leaders, given their more precarious position. Harper, for example, gambled heavily on the success of the movie *Titanic* and raised the print run for a companion book from 20,000 to 400,000 copies, all before the film was released. Sprint made an early and risky investment in fiber optics, then took yet another gamble when it became an early adopter of Qualcomm's CDMA technology for its nationwide PCS network.

Promote Vertical Partnerships

Some #3 companies can successfully insulate themselves from head-to-head competition with #1 and #2 players by forming alliances with their suppliers and customers. McDonnell Douglas and Lockheed, for example, survived for years by having a loyal customer in Delta. Rather than doing business with market leaders Boeing and Airbus, Delta used its leverage to obtain attractive terms from McDonnell Douglas and Lockheed.

The #3 player is usually the only one of the Big 3 small enough to create a level of genuine interdependence with its customers and suppliers. In the long-distance telecommunications market, the entry of local phone companies into the business gave Sprint, the #3 player, an opportunity to partner with them rather than view them as a threat. Sprint created a solid base of new revenues and utilized some of its spare network capacity.

Seek out Horizontal Partnerships

Sometimes the only route to survival is rapid gain of scale through the relatively straightforward mechanism of mergers and acquisitions. This approach has proved popular in the beer market and is happening with hospitals, HMOs, and pharmaceutical companies. Alternatively, smaller players can form a coalition to compete with larger players. The usual caveats of cultural compatibility and synergy apply; it is especially important that merged players be able to mesh their operations into an integrated whole without greatly increasing fixed costs. In the airline industry, companies are prevented from cross-border mergers, and many are turning instead to broad partnerships that include joint marketing, cross-selling, and code sharing.

Conclusion

Choosing a set of strategies for solidifying one's position in the inner circle of practically any industry, or for moving up (or down) in the pecking order, should make company leaders appreciate how useful it would be to have eyes not only in the front but in the back and sides of the head—just to keep track of what the rest of the industry is doing. Perhaps the single most important strategy is always to know what strategies are open to the competition. Needless to say, it is particularly important for the leaders of #1 companies to study what the #2 and #3 players might be cooking up next, and vice versa.

Strategies, of course, are not guarantees of success in warfare, athletics, love, or business. Many a great strategy has been devised, but the battle lost for failure to execute well or at all. Strategies are part rational, part irrational, part empirical, part intuitive. They thrive on past examples, which can never substitute for clear-headed assessments of present and future conditions. There is some science to this business, but also a lot of luck. It is a gift of great leaders to recognize an opportunity when like a crocus in early spring it lifts itself out of the half-frozen earth. As if it were not enough to observe the other members of the inner circle, leaders of the Big 3 companies must constantly be aware of where new life is springing up—in the niches and corners of the market, which are the fertile ground for specialists. After all, a specialist today may be a Big 3 player tomorrow, a truth we explore more fully in chapter 7.

7

Strategies for Specialists

How many ways can you improve a rearview mirror for a car or a truck? If you're the Gentex Corporation, a $300-million company based in Zeeland, Michigan, you do it by adding all sorts of valuable features—light-sensing technology that can darken or lighten the mirror for optimum visibility when another car's lights hit it, or special gauges to measure the outside temperature, tire pressure, mileage, or direction. Or how about adding OnStar communications capability?

Gentex is a super-nicher, a company that specializes in both a product (or group of products) and a targeted set of customers. While the company also manufactures smoke detectors and fire alarms, it is the rearview mirror business that gives Gentex its claim to fame. It controls 90 percent of the U.S. market for high-tech automotive electronic mirrors; its biggest customers are General Motors, Ford, and DaimlerChrysler, and it has international operations in Europe and Asia. For all practical purposes, it is a monopoly in its small corner of the automotive parts industry. Being a very big fish in a very small pond, Gentex escapes scrutiny as a monopolist; in fact, no one would ever think of raising any antitrust issues against the company.

Although Gentex is a highly specialized company in what would seem a microscopic niche, its strategies for success carry important lessons for any specialist looking to gain market share and raise profits. All businesses seek to grow, and specialists are no exception. Through its emphasis on cutting-edge technology, high-quality products, and innovation, Gentex follows the first rule in the strategist's handbook: it is holding firm to its market dominance and exclusivity. After all, that's what being a specialist means: focusing on a well-defined market, the company supplies products that its customers can find nowhere else, at least not easily. To keep up this promise, Gentex is always readying new innovations for its rearview mirrors, including automatic adjustments of air-conditioning based on the amount of measured sunlight, the ability to detect rain or fog before the human eye can see it, the automatic triggering of wipers and headlights, light-emitting diodes for cool-burning map lights, and voice recognition for e-mail access.[1]

As a super-nicher that supplies parts to big-name clients, Gentex has little interest in changing direction at this time and heading off in the direction of a full-line generalist. The company wants to break new ground primarily in product innovation, not dilute its specialty to reach a wider but less discriminating audience. Its strategies, in other words, are predicated on its intentions of remaining a specialist with a particular niche to fill.

Super-nichers such as Gentex do seem like monopolies. They control an enormous share of their specialty market. Although that population is certainly smaller than that served by the full-line generalists, it tends to be a group that is typically very loyal and knows exactly what it wants. The degree of monopoly power decreases somewhat for the regular specialists, those companies that either serve particular markets or deal in a set of products that customers can find at few other places. Although seemingly ubiquitous, full-line generalists such as IBM and General Motors have little monopoly power, despite the fact that they attract enormous numbers of customers. Their customers always have clear alternatives; the same cannot be said for the customers of a super-nicher.

The following chart presents these contrasts among generalists, specialists, and super-nichers. It is important to note, of course, that the populations served by the three types of players are not the same. That is, the 40 percent of the market that the typical generalist controls is in real numbers much larger than the 80 percent of the very different market that the super-nicher attracts. As we have seen, most generalists and specialists do not compete directly with one another; the two exist in a complementary relationship. Specialists can take a reasonably distanced view of the generalists; they are, broadly speaking, in the same industry, but are affected only peripherally by the actions of generalists. Should a sudden shift in conditions begin to undermine the uniqueness of their niches, specialists should rethink their strategies; perhaps they are not specialized enough.

	Generalist	Product or Market Specialist	Super-Nicher
Prevailing rule	Rule of Three: three players dominate	Rule of Two: Two players vie for lion's share	Rule of One: One player is a de facto monopoly

For example, the Rule of Two is evident in the women's lingerie market, where the two players are Victoria's Secret and Frederick's of Hollywood. Over the past several years, Victoria's Secret has come to dominate this specialty market. Its sales of $2.1 billion a year from 902 stores dwarfed those of Frederick's at only $140 million from 200 stores. Frederick's was forced into bankruptcy in June 2000 and reemerged in early 2001. The company is now trying to reposition itself to better appeal to the more mainstream clientele that Victoria's Secret has successfully targeted.

In this chapter, we examine conditions under which a Rule of Two or a Rule of One is more likely to play out—namely, in those parts of the market controlled by the specialists. We consider eight strategies for specialists, assuming that these niche companies, like Gentex, wish to remain specialists. Occasionally there can be disruptions or changes within an entire industry that turn a specialist toward becoming a full-line generalist. Such is happening now in the electronic manufacturing services (EMS) industry, which began as a group of niche players serving the needs of the OEM market. Today, that industry is global in scope and takes in revenues approaching $60 billion. Projections indicate that by 2003, the industry will grow to $200 billion. With the growing trend toward outsourcing and the ever-expanding capabilities of the leading companies, the EMS industry is growing rapidly and evolving into a Rule of Three structure.[2] Some specialists in this group, therefore, are likely to find new identities as full-line generalists.

The strategies for companies in the EMS industry differ somewhat from the strategies discussed in this chapter, which are intended primarily for companies that are content with being big fish in a small pond. The relative size of the pond, however, does not disguise the fact that there are dangers lurking in every corner and that even small fish can be predators. With this distinction in mind, the leaders of product or market specialists can select from the following discussion of eight strategies those that are most appropriate for their goals and market contexts:

Eight Strategies for Specialists
- Maintain exclusivity and product/market share
- Keep the specialty pure, but create subspecialties as needed
- Practice target marketing and avoid segment creep
- Offer sales expertise, great personal service, and superior experiences
- Shun fixed costs
- Create entry barriers
- Avoid the regional specialist's path
- Control growth

Maintain Exclusivity and Product/Market Dominance

Specialists will fail if they lose their uniqueness. They may succeed as something else; that is, they may become generalists, but they will no longer attract the same customers they once served. For supernichers especially, exclusivity is the key to their market dominance. Maintaining that posture should be the leading item in a portfolio of strategies for specialists of all sorts. Given that each offering needs to be distinctive, customers should not be able to make a head-to-head choice between a specialist and a competitor. Perfume makers and fashion designers, for instance, must offer unique attributes in their products that competitors cannot duplicate.

To achieve and maintain the degree of market dominance they need, product specialists have to keep channeling assets into productive R&D and proprietary technologies; market specialists, in contrast, need to deepen their understanding of their best customers through relationship marketing. Since there is a Rule of One for super-nichers, firms that are not in a leadership position within their defined market should consider either merging to achieve such a position or redefining the relevant market. For example, Zany Brainy and Noodle Kidoodle were both specialty toy retailers targeting the same niche, educational toys. Both followed similar strategies, providing excellent customer service, knowledgeable sales-people (usually former teachers and librarians), brightly colored stores, play areas for children to try out the toys, in-store activities such as readings by authors, and software demonstrations. The investment firm Goldsmith & Harris concluded from surveys that customers found "very few differences" between the two companies, and that their individual success depended predominantly on location.[3] Thus, rather than compete head-on with essentially identical strategies, the companies decided to merge and become the dominant leader in the category.[4]

The exclusivity advantage is the primary factor in the continued success of the "World's Best Bookstore"—Powell's City of Books in Portland, Oregon. Powell's is the largest independent bookstore anywhere—43,000 square feet of space, half a million volumes organized into 122 subject areas and some 1,000 periodicals. With six satellite stores in the Portland area, each devoted to a specialized subject such as travel, cooking, or computers, Powell's stocks about a million books. It buys as many as 4,000 used books every day.

In addition to its size and scope, the main innovation that Powell's offers is that it stocks new as well as used books, paperbacks as well as hardcovers. All the books are arranged together on the shelves, a clever way of displaying items that encourages many customers who come in looking for one item to buy others as well. The store can offer tremendous variety for every reading taste—for instance, multiple editions of *The Catcher in the Rye* from a used paperback costing $2 to a signed first edition for $1,200!

From its point of view, Powell's does not see itself competing with the superstores such as Barnes & Noble and Borders; nor does it compete with Internet specialist Amazon.com. As Powell's views the market, all these companies exist in a complementary relationship. Its strategy differs from those of the other firms in several respects: its primary niche is used books, not new; it lists only books on hand, not all books in print, to avoid unfillable orders; and it does no promotion, relying on word-of-mouth alone. Powell's has created something unique, which is the secret to competitive security.[5]

Keep the Specialty Pure, but Create Subspecialties as Needed

Specialists sometimes find that some of their customers demand a higher degree of specialization than they are able to offer under the umbrella definition of their specialty. The Sports Authority discovered that its more avid sports enthusiasts would rather do business with super-nichers; for example, serious bikers would rather go to a bicycle specialty store for greater expertise and selection than they can find in Sports Authority. Accordingly, the company has created specialty boutiques within its stores that focus on particular sports such as golf or soccer.

It stands to reason that any dilution by the specialist of its exclusive status is dangerous. When a company known for a product category reaches beyond that to embrace what it considers to be related businesses, it risks diluting its identity. La-Z-Boy, for example, was a successful product specialist controlling about 30 percent of the U.S. recliner business. Beginning in 1985, the company began diversifying into other furniture categories, acquiring five furniture makers. It now sells everything from dining room sets to entertainment centers, with brands such as Hammary and Kincaid. Revenues now exceed $1.2 billion. In other words, it is becoming "just another furniture company."

The danger is that the company will become unfocused and gradually lose its position within the chair category. Despite its 30 percent share of recliners, the company is far from achieving a safe hold on that portion. It is trying to grow its core business by creating products with greater appeal to women, as well as developing modern and retro styles for its chairs. Patrick Norton, the chairman of La-Z-Boy, is clearly worried about losing focus: "We sweat blood every time we advertise that we don't want to be a chair company."[6]

What options does the company have? It could try to trigger the Rule of Three in the furniture industry, which remains a highly fragmented one with little brand recognition. However, it is too small a player to do so credibly. Another option is break up into multiple product specialists, each with its own distinctive brand identity analogous to that of La-Z-Boy for chairs. If the company does neither, it will eventually find itself firmly seated in the ditch, which is even harder to get out of than one of its super-comfortable recliners!

Practice Target Marketing and Avoid Segment Creep

Startec Global Communications, a long-distance carrier that has grown rapidly by focusing on ethnic markets, spends only 5 percent of its revenues on marketing. The company, however, has a lot to show for that small outlay. Employing field research in 30 major metropolitan areas in the United States and Europe, Startec has had great success in reaching customers of various ethnic identities, including native Americans, Arabs (in the Anaheim, California market), Poles (in Chicago), Chinese (in New York), and Filipinos (in San Francisco). In areas closely identified with an ethnic population, the company sponsors cultural events and advertises in newspapers and on radio, achieving impressive results: Startec acquires ethnic customers at the rate of 20,000 a month.[7]

In the health care industry as well, product specialists are becoming more visible. They often target one medical condition (for example, heart disease) or a single service such as catheterization. The advantage they have over traditional full-service, non-profit hospitals is that they are focused, entrepreneurial, and better connected to capital and management expertise. They target their markets very carefully, looking for segments where the population is growing, where managed care has a high penetration, and where specialist incomes are declining. They specifically target hospitals' most profitable service lines, which typically subsidize the less profitable ones.[8]

An interesting case is that of product specialist Gatorade, the pioneer and leading player in the sports-drink category. Ten years after Coca-Cola and Pepsi entered the market, Gatorade still has an 81 percent share of the market, generating $1.5 billion in revenues in 1999, and growing at double-digit rates for five years running.

In 1965, Dr. Robert Cade, a specialist in kidney disease, created Gatorade for the University of Florida football team (the Gators, hence the name) to replenish the water and electrolytes that athletes lost when they sweated. Cade added sugar to increase the absorption of electrolytes and flavoring to make the drink palatable. Stokely Van-Camp, Inc. subsequently commercialized the product, then sold it to Quaker Oats in 1985, which initiated an aggressive marketing campaign to change prevailing attitudes about drinking fluids during athletic activities. The company even created the Gatorade Sports Sciences Institute to improve the product through research. It successfully placed coolers bearing the Gatorade logo on the sidelines of virtually every professional sports team and at some 60 major colleges. It also provided Gatorade for 5,000 races, including the best-known marathons.

In the early 1990s, the industry giants entered this fast-growing market. Coca-Cola introduced PowerAde; Pepsi came out with All-Sports. Meanwhile, Gatorade redoubled its marketing efforts, disguised as education; it created a bimonthly research review called Sports Science Exchange (which was sent to 25,000 coaches, educators, dieticians, and scientists), sponsored conferences, and published sports science text books. It even sponsored some 100 speakers, whose message was always the same: athletes need to drink a lot of fluid, and the best fluid is Gatorade. As a result of this aggressive marketing campaign, which included advertisements featuring Michael Jordan, Gatorade held on to its market share while growing the market. After 10 years, PowerAde's market share is only 12 percent, and AllSports has only 4 percent. Gatorade is one of the biggest single brands in the world.

Being the leader in its category, Gatorade is now trying to grow its market share through line extensions (such as Frost and Fierce) as well as new products. It is launching new products such as Propel, a "fitness water" with one-fifth the calories of Gatorade. Some new competitors such as SoBe, Red Bull, and Voo Doo Rain have entered the market with nutrient-enhanced isotonic drinks, but Gatorade is countering with its own "energy drink" called Torq.[9] One of the prices of success is the challenge of retaining one's independence, a lesson Gatorade learned all too well as Pepsi Cola and Coca-Cola tried to acquire the company and its popular line of products, with Pepsi emerging victorious.

Many specialists, especially those that have successfully targeted segments at the low end of the market, however, have a tendency to go through what might be called "segment creep." This is a process whereby the specialist gradually, almost imperceptibly, starts to raise its sights and competes in a more upscale market. In doing so, it runs smack into much better positioned incumbents in the new niche, while abandoning the segment where it achieved its success in the first place. The Ames retailing chain, for instance, aims at a target customer with a lower income than those that shop at Wal-Mart or Kmart. Setting their sights on Wal-Mart's and Kmart's customers, chains such as Zayre, Caldor, Hills, and Bradlees largely abandoned this segment. Ames, however, resolutely kept its focus on its segment, and as a result, it is still doing well, while Bradlees, Caldor, and Hills have perished.[10]

Segment creep can also happen in the other direction: a specialist that has been successful in a highly focused small segment starts to aim at a larger, more mainstream segment. In so doing, it is likely to run itself into the ditch—and into head-on competition with a generalist. For example, if telecommunications specialist Startec were to move beyond its focus on ethnic markets and target mainstream customers, it would be hopelessly out of its depth compared to the large incumbent carriers. The best way for the company to grow is to add other ethnic segments, and to sell these customers a wider array of telecommunication services.

Offer Sales Expertise, Great Personal Service, and Superior Experiences

As we have seen, full-line generalists such as Barnes & Noble and Borders present no threat to Powell's City of Books. For one thing, they stock only a fraction of the specialist's new book inventory, and they offer no used books at all. On its side, Powell's has never been tempted to clone itself or build a chain of stores. It understands all too well that it would be virtually impossible to recreate its "City of Books" anywhere else. Only the Internet has presented it with opportunities to expand its market scope and leverage its enormous inventory.

Amazon.com might have offered a competitive threat in 1994, but Powell's had launched its own Web site the year before, after computerizing its ever-changing catalog. By 1996, Powell's entire inventory was online, and sales grew by as much as 20 percent a month. Although it does not offer reviews, contests, customer comments, e-mail notifications, or customized recommendations, as Amazon.com does, Powell's site does give its customers a simple way to search the store's catalog. The logic is sound: since Powell's customers know exactly what they want, they are quite different from Amazon.com's clientele and require less hand-holding and advice. Whether online or in the store, Powell's customers have an experience equal to none they can get anywhere else except perhaps at one of the satellite stores.

The customer's "experience" is always the top item for the market specialist insurer USAA—formally, United States Automobile Association. The company targets military officers and their families. By focusing single-mindedly on service quality and on its three component parts—customers, work force, and technology—former CEO Gen. Robert McDermott revolutionized USAA's approach to its business and to its customers' financial needs. Now the fifth largest insurer of privately owned automobiles and homes, USAA has expanded rapidly into the field of financial services. In 1991, its 14,000 employees served more than 2 million customers and policy-holders and managed $20.7 billion in assets, up from $3.8 billion in 1983. By 1998, the company had 3 million customers and managed assets of $48 billion.

USAA uses technology not only to increase productivity but also to improve the quality of service. Its state-of-the-art electronic imaging system ensures that each day some 30,000 pieces of mail never leave the mailroom. Instead, an exact image of the relevant correspondence is placed electronically in a customer's file and is simultaneously accessible in an electronic "in-basket" to every service representative anywhere in the building. This high degree of personal service gives customers a strong sense of trust, which is reflected in a renewal rate of 98 percent, by far the highest in the insurance industry. USAA has achieved a stunning 95 percent penetration rate among military officers and a 52 percent rate on applications from policyholders for MasterCards (the industry average is only 10 percent).

USAA presents the essence of relationship marketing: hook the customer in various ways that cannot be duplicated and maintain the highest priority on customer satisfaction. Accordingly, the company considers service its highest objective, ahead of profits or growth. It uses no outside agents, but relies heavily on direct mail and personal telephone calls to customers. The insurer has no intention of moving outside its niche market, but it does seek to grow by providing new services to existing customers. In June 1995, for example, its banking facility, USAA Federal Savings, was named by *Money Magazine* as "the best bank in America."

Customers who would rather do business with small specialists than with huge generalists value highly the responsiveness and the individualized attention they receive. In the Internet Service Provider (ISP) market, which is dominated by large companies such as America Online and MSN, thousands of mom-and-pop ISPs continue to thrive and are in fact driving much of the growth in this industry by bringing non-mainstream customers online. Even as the dominance of the big providers has grown, the total number of ISPs has also increased from 1,500 in 1996 to more than 6,500 in 1999. In part, this growth came about because entry barriers are minimal: one company even sells a kit—"ISP in a Box"—for $4,000. The number of ISPs continues to grow primarily because they offer what the big companies cannot: friendly, personal service, and highly responsive individualized attention. Many even make house calls.[11]

Specialists have an opportunity to stand out from generalists and other specialists by creating unusual experiences for customers. While generalists can also create experiences, they have limited opportunities to create anything other than standardized, mass-produced experiences. In the fast food hamburger business, for example, numerous specialists continue to thrive in the face of competition from the Big 3—McDonald's, Burger King, and Wendy's. The specialists cannot compete on price or advertising; they can, however, compete on taste, ambience, and restaurant "personality." White Castle offers distinctive products such as its steam-cooked, square hamburgers known as Slyders. The Sonic Corporation, based in Oklahoma City, differentiates itself with a 1950s style of carhop service and creates a personal experience for every customer who drives in.[12]

Shun Fixed Costs

Specialists can slide into the ditch if their cost structure becomes too high. This often occurs with certain costs that follow a "step function" rather than increasing in proportion to volume. Examples include a move to a new manufacturing system or the creation of a new information technology platform. Such actions, especially if they are highly capital-intensive, often raise the break-even point beyond the reach of a specialist. The Spanish pizza maker Tele-Pizza SA has developed a "Pizza Magic" vending machine, which bakes a pizza for the consumer right at the point of service. The company plans to install 9,000 of these machines worldwide over the next several years, a strategy that will be costly and logistically challenging. TelePizza won't constitute a significant threat to industry incumbents Pizza Hut, Domino's, and Papa John's, but it could take some share from others that provide vending services. This scenario assumes, of course, that the vending machines work and consumers on the hoof are willing to wait for their pizzas to bake. The best strategy, obviously, is to avoid as many of these fixed costs as possible.

Create Entry Barriers

Because entry barriers are often low in the markets that specialists serve, these players are especially vulnerable to new entrants with superior technology or market access. It is therefore important for specialists to create entry barriers. For many specialists, a loyal, satisfied customer base might not be enough to ward off threats. Entry barriers could take the form of unique supplier relationships or exclusive distribution arrangements.

In the online travel booking industry, the largest players are Travelocity and Expedia (the Rule of Two in operation). Many smaller specialists exist, targeting particular niches such as packaged tours (for example, Maupintor.com) and cruises (Uniglobe.com). Since these segments are quite large, head-to-head competition with the Big 2 prevails. Other specialists are trying for a different kind of edge. For example, Lowestfare.com owns exclusive rights to purchase steeply discounted TWA tickets through 2003. Since 1986, CheapTickets has specialized in selling airlines' excess inventory originally by phone, now through its Internet site at CheapTickets.com. Several airlines give CheapTickets access to their surplus inventory.[13]

Avoid the Regional Specialist's Path

Some regional companies are successful as market specialists, essentially presenting a full-line generalist profile but within a specific geographic region. BellSouth, for instance, has positioned itself as a regional telecommunications company serving its nine-state home region in the southeastern part of the United States. If the company wishes to sustain this positioning, it must develop a truly regional identity, market in a way that links it culturally with the region, and develop specialized services and programs that are unique to its locales.

The regional specialist's strategy works only if two conditions are met: first, the region has to be truly distinctive from other regions, and second, the strategy must be specifically tailored to the distinctiveness of that region. If a regional specialist cannot meet one or both conditions, it is likely to be eventually acquired as its industry consolidates. Sooner or later, the full-line generalists will enter those markets and completely overwhelm the specialists.

Retailing, which has a high proportion of regionally focused players, offers numerous examples of this phenomenon. In the home improvement industry Hechinger, Home Quarters, and Builders Square are among the casualties. Now, the relentless growth of market leader Home Depot threatens another regional player, HomeBase, Inc. of Irvine, California. HomeBase once operated 88 stores in 10 western states, chiefly in California, where Home Depot had 125 stores and planned to add more. HomeBase has struggled as a result of the stiff competition: earnings fell 44 percent in 1999, and the chain announced it was closing 20 of its California stores and converting the remaining stores to a new name (House2Home). The company is futilely attempting to counter Home Depot's launch of upscale Expo Design Centers by announcing that it will launch five such stores of its own. The handwriting is on the wall, however, and the message is not one that HomeBase or its shareholders will find reassuring.[14]

Bradlees, Inc. fell into a similar predicament. A regional specialist with 104 stores in seven northeastern states, Bradlees has once again filed for Chapter 11 protection, having faced heavyweight competitors such as Kohl, Wal-Mart, and Target, all of which have accelerated their belated push into the region. Now valued primarily for its prime real estate locations, the retailer will most likely end up as an acquisition target by one of the Big 3 discount retailers.[15]

Control Growth

Like Icarus in the ancient Greek myth, People Express spread its wings and flew too near the sun. The discount airline that specialized in low-priced, short-haul flights destroyed all the advantages it had enjoyed as a specialist. The temptation to grow by trying to become a full-line generalist was just too strong. When it added international and cross-continental domestic flights, and started offering multiple classes of service, the company trespassed in markets controlled by the major airlines and invited their hostile reaction. In terms of its own operations, People Express was ill-equipped to handle the customers that it did get. Growing too fast, People Express found itself on the runway to oblivion, and in 1986, it was acquired by Continental Airlines, which was itself just emerging from Chapter 11 bankruptcy.

Contrast the demise of People Express with the steady growth and continued profitability of Southwest Airlines, which has resolutely stuck to its game plan of targeting short routes via secondary airports and using a single type of airplane and a single class of service. The typical market that Southwest enters grows dramatically as a direct result of its entry, thus enlarging the pie without directly threatening the major airlines.

Clothing retailer Benetton experienced stellar success in the U.S. market in the 1980s, but inadvertently cooled off its hot image by franchising itself into something ordinary and repeatable. In some extreme cases, competing franchises existed across the street or across the mall corridor from each other. Although it is not franchised, Starbucks could find itself in a similar predicament if it is not careful. In becoming so ubiquitous, the company risks diluting its "chic" image as a specialist.

Moreover, specialists must avoid lines of business that are scalable—that is, those that can be easily ramped up to serve thousands or millions of customers and can achieve significant economies of scale. Such businesses are the natural terrain of volume-based generalists, and specialists can achieve no better than short-term success in them. Venturing into scale-based business inevitably leads a specialist into the ditch. Specialist businesses, in fact, should exhibit *dis*economies of scale, penalizing companies that seek volume-based growth.

Growing through more precise market specialization is a much wiser strategy. Market specialists grow by first adding related products and services, and then by adding altogether new products and services. Successful growth through added products requires market strength, which is a function of numerous factors including business reputation (customers have to trust the company to be a one-stop shopping experience for them), access and infrastructure (logistics and geographical locations), distribution and sales, and customer support services. The McDonald's Corporation provides an excellent example of a company that began as a market specialist and grew in manageable ways by adding new products and services. The company started with hamburgers, then added French fries, milk shakes, salads, and various desserts. It expanded from being primarily a place where one ate lunch to being a full-scale restaurant that also serves breakfast and dinner. A major ingredient in its success was convincing the hamburger-hungry public that while they may not want a Big Mac for breakfast, McDonald's was the place where they should think about getting a quick Egg McMuffin or a Caesar salad with their dinner. In short, market specialists grow by first mastering their current product lines, then adding other product lines that their customers will find most valuable.

Software companies, for instance, often bundle their products with hardware. Telecommunications companies add services such as Internet access and voice mail. A company specializing in undercarriage rustproofing for cars can add protective products for other car parts such as the interior fabric or the exterior paint. Essentially, the company seeks to provide a version of one-stop shopping for as broad a range of products and services that it can offer efficiently and credibly.

Yet another area for growth lies in broadening a local or regional market focus, even to the point of extending to an international market if it conforms to the basic definition of the company's target market. As cultures and lifestyles worldwide become more homogeneous, this strategy begins to appear more feasible. The teen market today, for example, is seen as one in which differences across countries are fast vanishing.

Market specialists also need to consider ways to enhance the lifetime value of their customers by increasing their share of wallet over time. Sometimes they must change their product mix to adapt to customers' changing needs. A market specialist that defines its target market in terms of the demographic variable of age, for instance, faces a challenging dilemma. As its customers grow older, the company has three choices: (1) it can stay true to its original demographic definition, abandoning the aging customers in favor of new, younger ones; (2) it can "mature" with its customers and change its target market definition to reflect the fact of the demographics; or (3) it can launch a separate division to serve the aging customers while the original division continues to serve the traditional demographic. In the publishing world, *Playboy* matured with its original market, adding more nonfiction, interviews with famous people (for example, former President Jimmy Carter), and articles on serious themes. In doing so, the magazine has moved closer to publications such as the *New Yorker* and *Esquire*. Its original target market has been taken over by other magazines.

In contrast to the market specialist, the product specialist should grow by first dominating the market segments that find its products valuable. In other words, the company must remain a product specialist but search for new customers. Successful market growth requires product strength, which is a function of product versatility and innovation, value-added capabilities, and the ability to provide mass customization.

For example, DuPont grew its nylon business by adding new applications from apparel to tires to industrial machine gears to parachutes. As a result, its markets grew, as more customers realized they had need for such items. The market for baking soda has expanded many times over to include all sorts of cleaning and deodorizing applications beyond the original purpose for the product.

In some cases expansion to international markets may be an appropriate strategy for product specialists, despite the changes required in procurement and distribution. Many of them, however, will find more manageable growth in developing value-added services such as financing, installation, training, maintenance, and eventually outsourcing. Over time, product specialists tend to become more like service companies and develop greater market specialization.

Whether a company is a market or product specialist or a super-nicher, developing a strategy for controlled growth depends largely on the aspirations of its leaders and their realistic assessment of market conditions, including the condition of the Big 3. Although they are competitors in the sense that they are in the same industry or retail area, the Big 3 are likely to be interested in a different set of customers than those the specialists are serving. Where there is overlap, the specialists can expect to lose out to their bigger competitors, chiefly because they cannot match the generalists' prices or scope.

8

The Disruption of Markets

"What if someone offered you a Ferrari that got 100 miles to the gallon and cost $5,000?" That's how Blair McKendrick, an aviation enthusiast from Detroit, puts it when he ponders the next new thing in small jet planes, the Eclipse 500. In contrast to the current industry standard, the Cessna Citation, which seats eight passengers and costs a cool $3.6 million, the Eclipse 500 will seat only six but cost less than $850,000.[1] Thanks to an ultra-small engine that weighs only 85 pounds, the jet will be significantly cheaper to operate (the company claims it can fly for only 56 cents per mile). Even better, it will be able to fly almost as fast and as far as the Cessna.

No matter that the Eclipse 500 won't be ready for takeoff until the summer of 2003. People are lining up to place their orders; indeed, on the day that the Eclipse Aviation Corporation opened for business, it had already sold out its first 18 months of production—without spending a dime on advertising and marketing (except e-mail).[2] As an indication of the faith that others have in CEO Vern Raburn's commitment to meeting production deadlines, the company has been able to secure $125 million to fund the jet's development, testing, and launch.[3]

The Eclipse 500 innovation promises to disrupt the small jet aircraft industry by introducing a new technology, by expanding the market to include not only the super-rich but also the well-to-do

173

(who couldn't afford the multimillion-dollar Cessna), and by enlisting the support of new stakeholders and venture capitalists who are funding the project even before Eclipse Aviation satisfies all the regulatory requirements and tests. Here in this small, rather exclusive industry we find three major disruptions that can throw any industry into a tailspin: shifts in new technologies, markets, and investors. A fourth disruption—namely, governmental regulatory shifts—has not had an appreciable effect on this industry, although that is not to rule out some impact in the future. In this chapter we examine how these four forces—about which Joseph Schumpeter, the Harvard economist from 1932 until his death in 1950, theorized in his work on "creative destruction"—can rapidly destabilize any industry, no matter how stable and well established it appears.

As discussed earlier, all industries begin in a sort of controlled chaos: numerous entrants jostle for position, trying to establish themselves and find their niche. Eventually, competitive market forces begin to sort out the serious players and favor the rise of a small number of full-line generalists. If the Rule of Three is allowed to operate without government restrictions, the industry settles down into a state of relative calm and order. As in nature, so in business: systems move toward equilibrium and seek the path to greatest stability, which the Rule of Three bestows on an industry. Since this structure allows for the presence of any number of niche players, there is continual market entry, change, and growth even while a relative degree of stability is maintained. And because new niche players can readily enter, there are no contentious public policy issues to deal with: the market is open and anyone can come in. A harmonious government-industry relationship can, of course, enhance the state of equilibrium.

This state is likely to continue for some time, provided the companies inside a given industry are satisfying all of their stakeholders—employees, customers, and shareholders. To achieve that degree of satisfaction, they must deliver a high level of efficiency as well as continued growth. If an industry stops delivering on these essential dimensions, its equilibrium degenerates into stagnation. At that point—facing complete collapse—either the industry transforms itself, or somebody outside the industry transforms it, often painfully. Microsoft, for instance, transformed itself from MS-DOS to Windows and then to the Internet. After the PC and Internet revolutions, IBM remade itself into an e-business infrastructure supplier.

In *The Innovator's Dilemma,* Clayton Christensen argues that firms faced with disruptive technological change cannot succeed by following the usual management techniques. Managers must understand when it is appropriate to disregard their customers, and make "large and decisive" investments in new products and services.[4] We agree that with the right management mindset, incumbents not only can survive waves of disruption but can ride them to greater strength. Such companies are capable of anticipatory management, foreseeing and shaping the future and becoming their industry's change agent rather than the victim of the industry renewal process.

Many old economy industries that have stopped growing except at the demographic level—that is, at the rate of population growth—now look for a way to trigger growth. The electric utilities, whose growth rate is little more than 3 percent, are focusing less on better generation and transmission technologies and more on next-generation technologies such as fuel cells.

For many industries, it is not a matter of growth but survival. If an industry wants to survive—and which one doesn't?—it needs to create and participate in the changes. The steel industry, for example, has belatedly organized itself to fight off threats from aluminum as well as plastics. Members of other industries form consortia to align with the next wave of change or to fight an external threat. In the mid-1990s, for example, several cable companies formed Cable Labs to help them move into data applications and voice telephony, even as some telecommunications companies contemplated delivering video signals over their networks.

An industry can often grow by making obsolete what it has already profited from. Cellular networks evolved from analog (AMPS) to digital technology (TDMA or CDMA in the United States; GSM in Europe and most of the rest of the world) and will soon evolve to third-generation architecture. Meanwhile, camcorders are moving from analog to digital technology, while cameras are changing from chemical film to digital imaging. Reenergized by the human genome project, the pharmaceutical industry is now investing heavily in biogenetic research.

An active lobbying effort can also lead to an industry's growth, as the major airlines illustrated some years ago when they pushed strongly for deregulation. In this regard they anticipated their future and positioned themselves for the next evolution, even while other carriers, unprepared for the changes, became the victims of that disruptive force.

When one or more of these changes jolts an industry, the market structure can tilt and rock, demanding to be transformed from within. If the industry complies, the players have a chance to migrate to a new environment and survive. So it happened in the consumer electronics industry when the incumbents moved to digital technology without a major upheaval in the ranks. Now having evolved from VCRs to DVD players, the industry is moving from picture tubes to flat screens. If, however, an industry is unwilling to make the necessary adjustments, outside forces will gladly undertake the job. When nontraditional competitors enter an industry, as happened in the test and measurement industry, many of the incumbents will struggle or die.

These four forces for disruption are the lords of chaos that cannot abide the status quo. They ignite changes in the competitive landscape, regardless of the industry's size, population, power, or stability. They can cause once-secure players to contemplate life on the brink or something worse. They can shift the balance of power to an entirely different group of competitors.

Disruptive Technologies

Discontinuous technological change can dramatically alter the playing field, sometimes eliminating the market altogether or elevating a new set of Big 3 companies. Too focused on their own technologies, the incumbent leaders may fail to recognize emerging substitute technologies. Mechanical and electromechanical (even chemical) technologies can be supplanted by electronics, as typewriters were replaced by electronic word processors. On other fronts, radials revolutionized the tire industry, and digital switching transformed the telecommunications business, opening the way for Northern Telecom, an upstart player, to move into a position of global prominence. Later, another upstart, Cisco Systems, did it again to the telecommunications industry, enabling networks based on TCP/IP.

As Clayton Christensen points out, truly disruptive technology almost always comes from outside the industry, or at least from companies that are not industry leaders.[5] One classic and several current examples support this observation.

The Watch Industry

The watch industry presents a fascinating case study of an industry undergoing many upheavals over several decades, triggered by successive waves of technological innovation and dramatic market shifts.[6] The first agent of change was Timex, which started as the Waterbury Clock Company, a maker of clocks and pocket watches. During World War I, the U.S. Army asked the company to make the first wristwatches. After World War II, the renamed U.S. Time Company, with advanced mass production techniques, created the world's first inexpensive and highly reliable mechanical watch movement. The new wristwatch, called the Timex, debuted in 1950. It was both cheap and rugged, epitomized by its slogan "takes a licking and keeps on ticking," which became a household phrase.

By the end of the 1950s, Timex was selling a third of all watches in the United States. In the 1960s, the company moved up from its traditional focus on low-end watches and launched the concept of the watch as a fashion accessory. In 1961, the company challenged the Swiss dominance of the industry by developing a new watch movement technology—an unjeweled watch with pin-lever escapement. Timex decided to produce what essentially was a disposable watch, one so inexpensive that customers would never have it repaired, much as Kodak did with its "Instamatic" cameras. The watches would be sold in drug stores rather than jewelry stores, a strategy that Swiss watchmakers did not see as a threat. By the mid-1970s, however, Timex had sold more than 500 million watches and enjoyed a 50 percent market share in the United States. Its distribution channels included an astounding 250,000 different outlets.

Because of a disruptive technology, the watch industry subsequently underwent a major upheaval: a shift to electronics and the creation of solid-state digital watches. Durable and inexpensive, the new watches offered many features that traditional watches could not match. New competitors such as Texas Instruments and Casio suddenly entered the market, and U.S. companies controlled 75 percent of the fast-growing new category before yet another disruptive force made itself felt: watches became commoditized, as prices in Hong Kong, fast emerging as a major production center, fell to $1.50 each, while traditional watches cost at least ten times as much.

Still another new technology was ready to cause more havoc: quartz technology had been around since the late 1960s (the Swiss created but did not use it). In 1968, Seiko's earliest model, both bulky and inconvenient, cost more than $1,000. Bulova improved the technology with advances such as its tuning-fork controller used in the Accutron. By 1978, quartz-technology leader Seiko had made its manufacturer, K. Hattori & Company, the world's leader in the industry, with sales exceeding $1 billion, double those of its nearest competitor. Quartz watches, which combined mechanical and electronic parts, came to dominate the market, and the industry experienced a shakeout of small and mid-sized watchmakers. With over 50 percent of the huge Japanese market, Seiko stepped up its marketing in Europe and the United States, constantly improving the technology and adding special functions.

By 1980, quartz watches dominated the market, whereas digital watches were in steep decline. The fall of Swiss watchmakers was precipitous. From a world market share of 80 percent around 1971, Swiss companies declined to a 30 percent share, as competitors' lower prices and wider distribution left them stranded at the high end. The Swiss continued to play up the prestige and luxury factors, but the quartz revolution rendered their comparative advantage in skill and experience much less relevant. By 1984, the worldwide watch industry was chaotic; Japan and Hong Kong producers were dominant; the Swiss watch industry had dramatically consolidated, holding on to 85 percent of the shrinking high-end market, and only 17 percent of the market overall. All U.S. watchmakers except Timex disappeared in the brutal industry shakeout of the 1970s— the result of the two disruptive technologies (digital and quartz), coupled with fierce price competition from the Far East.

Timex and many Swiss companies embraced quartz technology, following the lead of Seiko and Citizen from Japan. Seiko, the global leader, decided to establish a position in the high-end market by acquiring the Swiss company Jean LaSalle, which combined Seiko's quartz movement with an ultra-thin Swiss-designed case.

Yet another disruption rocked this shaky industry in 1984. It came not from new technologies but from new marketing. In that year Nicolas Hayek launched the $30 Swatch, a bold, brightly colored plastic model designed to capture a broad share of the market. Using product teams of technicians, designers, and marketing specialists, Swatch managed to combine low prices with Swiss quality and outrageous designs, creating a fashion-based product that became a collector's item. By 1992, 100 million Swatches had been sold, and new limited collections were launched twice a year.

The Swiss had never before considered attacking the Japanese in the low end, but this strategy proved to be the savior of the Swiss watchmakers. By the late 1990s, the Swiss once again achieved worldwide market share leadership in watches while continuing to thrive at the high end. Brands such as Piaget, Rolex, Breguet, and Patek Philippe were at the top of the global luxury-watch business. Prices for select models approached $500,000, but even the economic recession of the early 1990s did not depress sales significantly.

The Imaging Industry

Kodak and Xerox, the two dominant leaders in the imaging industry, have existed primarily as chemical companies. Their R&D spending and technological know-how have been almost entirely based on understanding, controlling, and improving the chemistry behind image capture and display. Neither, however, has failed to recognize its vulnerability to competition from electronics-based companies.

Recently Kodak has moved aggressively into the digital imaging arena, becoming one of the global top three in digital cameras. After decades spent consolidating its global position in the film and photographic paper businesses, the company is trying hard to build up more of a hardware business. It is also investing in electronic display technology, recently announcing, for example, the first commercial full-color, active-matrix, organic light-emitting diode (OLED) display. This technology offers high-quality displays as thin as a dime, weighing less than half as much as comparably sized LCDs (liquid crystal displays) and consuming much less power.

Kodak clearly has no choice but to view digital imaging as an opportunity, not just as a threat to its core business of chemicals-based film, which still accounts for 90 percent of company profits. The prevailing argument has held that photo enthusiasts and professionals would continue to prefer chemical film since digital cameras could not achieve as high a resolution. That attitude, however, is changing. Kodak has developed a chip that can capture digital images with a resolution of 4,096 × 4,096 picture elements (pixels) per square inch. By some measures, this resolution is about twice that of 35mm film. Ironically this chip—another technological disruption—will hasten the decline of Kodak's film business. Kodak, however, understands it has no choice but to push ahead, regardless of the impact on its traditional business.

Two weeks after Kodak announced its breakthrough chip, a company called Foveon announced a rival image-sensing chip technology that may offer far superior price-performance. Based on a low-cost technology, the Foveon chip is expected to be far less expensive to produce. Kodak's new technology is basically the same as that used in most digital cameras and camcorders. It is a "better, faster, cheaper" solution, but even that cannot guarantee the company's market leadership, not when Foveon comes along with a "brave new world" approach. The imaging industry is experiencing rapid shifts in technology from chemistry to digital electronics and now to chips.[7]

Foveon has ambitious plans: when it launches its new sensor, the company plans to target the mass market rather than a small, upscale niche and to make the film camera completely obsolete. Disruptive technologies that attack "from below," as evident in both the film and the watch industries, usually have a much greater impact than those that are content to stay within a high-end niche.[8]

Linux and the Windows Empire

In 1998, the Linux operating system, with its open-source development model, was relatively unknown. A year later, its share of the market for server operating systems increased to 25 percent, more than that of all competitors except Windows NT, which had a 38 percent share. In the market for desktop computers, Linux trails far behind Windows, but is poised to overtake Apple's MacOS. By early 2000, Linux's market share for Web servers had increased to 31 percent.[9]

The Linux OS is truly a disruptive technology, a major headache for Microsoft and others in the industry. Linux could become the operating system standard for all kinds of computers and eventually move into corporate data centers. Its popularity is based on several factors: it can be downloaded for free, works on any computer, can be customized for an individual business, and is highly stable. A copy of Linux costs $80 and can be copied as often as needed, whereas a Microsoft Windows 2000 upgrade costs companies $970 to $1,640 per computer, according to Giga Information Group.

IBM has decided to make Linux available across every platform, including servers, mainframes, and desktop computers. Other prominent companies have joined the movement: Compaq is building Linux-based computers; Dell uses Linux in its servers and is building Linux laptops; Sun Microsystems distributes a version of Linux for use with its workstations and servers. Several companies, including Intel and Dell, have taken equity stakes in public and private Linux companies.

The Human Genome Project

According to Dr. Allen D. Roses, the worldwide director of genetics at Glaxo Wellcome Pharmaceuticals, genomics "will change the way medicine is practiced."[10] The revolution in genomics promises major upheavals in the pharmaceutical industry while bringing radically new therapies to the marketplace. By focusing on the root causes of illness, genomics will allow for the development of treatments customized to an individual's genetic makeup.[11]

The genome has been described as "the operating system for all of human biology."[12] In 1990, with $200 million a year in funding from the Department of Energy (DOE) and the National Institutes of Health, the U.S. Human Genome Project was undertaken. Its objective was to analyze the 30,000 gene sequences in the human genome. The mapping of the genome marks the beginning of a new competition to develop sophisticated drugs that can target thousands of elements in the body, in contrast to today's drugs that address some 500 disease-related proteins. Expected to last for 15 years, the project was completed in only 10, about the same time that a competing company, Celera Genomics Group, announced that it had also finished sequencing the entire human genome.

Big pharmaceutical companies are trying to modify their huge internal research programs to exploit the potential of genomics. However, the technology is so new and so different that small biotech firms and academic labs are seen as more likely to succeed in using genomics to achieve breakthroughs in identifying disease targets. To offset this disadvantage, many large companies are establishing alliances with small firms. Bristol-Myers Squibb is spending over 50 percent of its genomics research budget on collaborations with small companies. Pfizer has agreements both with Celera Genomics and with Incyte Genomics, a Celera competitor.

The new technology is expected to decrease the number of one-size-fits-all blockbuster drugs but to increase the number of drugs tailored to the genetic make-ups of different groups. A $1 billion drug could be replaced with five drugs, each generating $200 million but much more effective than the single panacea.

Millennium Pharmaceuticals, a genomics-centered company with the potential to become a major player in the pharmaceutical industry, hopes to cut the time and cost of developing new drugs in half. The company's market cap, as of September 2000, was $12 billion, even though its first products will not be out until 2003 or later. Having raised $800 million from equity investments and technology licensing agreements with Pfizer, Bristol-Myers Squibb, Bayer, and other big drug companies, Millennium stands to become a new leader in this industry, assuming that genomics shifts the balance of power from traditional drug companies to the biotech companies.

Disruptive Regulations

A regulatory shift can substantially restructure an industry. It can hasten the evolution to three full-line players, as occurred in a former monopoly like the long-distance telecommunications market, or it can lead to the rise of a new group of players, as we will see below in the case of the health care industry. The airline industry is still feeling the effects of its massive deregulation more than two decades ago, but it is now migrating toward a structure with three U.S. leaders and three major global alliances.

Major regulatory shifts are felt in two ways. First, as public policy changes encourage competition, industries with a history of heavy regulation may undergo successive waves of deregulation. The telecommunications and electric utility industries, both previously regarded as "natural monopolies" and regulated as such, have gone through such a process. The immediate impact on market structure is consolidation. Regulatory changes have triggered many mergers, for example, in the radio industry after the Telecommunications Act was passed in 1996. Second, regulatory change can trigger the creation of entirely new competitors. For example, a regulatory change in India in 1972 permitted domestic companies to produce generic versions of drugs patented in other countries, as long as they did not copy the process used to produce those drugs. This led to the emergence of a large number of new players in the industry.

Another example of regulatory change occurred in the 1999 repeal of the Glass-Steagall Act, which had been enacted after the Depression to separate investment and commercial banking. This led to $647 billion of consolidation in the financial services industry in the first half of 2000, including mergers between commercial banks and brokerages and investment banks. Chase Manhattan and J. P. Morgan, for example, merged to form J. P. Morgan Chase and Company, which now with some $670 billion in assets is the #2 bank in the United States (behind Bank of America). This merger comes on the heels of those of two global leaders: Switzerland's UBS with Paine Webber, and Credit Suisse First Boston with Donaldson, Lufkin & Jenrette.[13]

Regulation tends to follow the creation of an industry structure, particularly in those industries that are relatively new or that generate a high level of public hostility. Such industries typically organize around a new technology or product, and in the early years there is often no regulation. But as the industry matures, government can begin to regulate it, even when there might be self-regulation by trade associations. When the medical electronics industry began to form, the FDA believed that it had no jurisdiction. Its province was the food and drug business. Congress, however, soon expanded the FDA's charter to include oversight of this fast-growing new industry.

Industries can also become candidates for more stringent regulation when public sentiment—and thus political sentiment—turns sour. In fact, this phenomenon could be called re-regulation, after a deregulated industry disappoints the public. The U.S. health care industry, for example, faces more regulatory control, perhaps to rein in the power of health maintenance organizations (HMOs) or to limit pharmaceutical companies in their pricing policies. A government commission has recommended a patient's bill of rights, and more than 50 bills regarding alleged abuses in managed care were introduced in Congress in 1997 alone.[14] These changes, if enacted, will no doubt have a significant impact on the industry's structure. By the late 1990s, some 75 percent of Americans were in managed care plans, a huge increase from the 15 percent just ten years earlier. Many, however, were unhappy with their providers. A 1998 study by the Henry J. Kaiser Family Foundation found that a slight majority (52 percent) of Americans favored government regulation, even if costs should rise. Many HMOs also joined in the push for regulation, as a way of insulating themselves from too much competition and restoring public confidence.[15]

Likewise, a new round of regulation may await other industries. Good candidates include the electric utilities in California after the 2001 crisis in which customers endured rolling brownouts, and the natural gas industry in the U.S. Northeast, which suffered shortages and higher than normal prices during the winter of 2000–2001.

The Cable Industry

When it comes to regulation, the cable industry has long been on a roller-coaster ride. From its early years, when the industry had to fight the entrenched broadcasting industry and the FCC, to the freer markets after the 1984 Cable Act, followed by yet another round of strict controls established by the 1992 Cable Act, governmental policies have severely restricted this industry.

Long the whipping boy of regulators, legislators, the courts, and other institutions, the cable industry began to see its fortunes turn around in January 1974 when a White House committee recommended virtual deregulation of cable television, primarily on First Amendment grounds. In 1980, the FCC repealed its limit on distant-signal carriage and the syndicated exclusivity rules requiring cable to black out programming on distant signals that duplicated programming of local satellites.

In the Copyright Act of 1976, Congress affirmed the cable systems' right to import distant signals by paying semiannual royalties set by the statute and adjusted periodically by the newly formed Copyright Royalty Tribunal. The next year, the Supreme Court freed HBO to show movies still fresh from their theatrical release, and in the mid-1980s, the U.S. Court of Appeals struck down as unconstitutional the requirement that cable systems carry local broadcast signals. This ruling allowed systems to drop duplicative network signals and gave them greater flexibility in creating their channel lineups.

The industry's biggest victory was the Cable Communications Policy Act of 1984. Forged from a compromise between cable companies and municipalities, the act affirmed the cities' regulatory authority, but severely restricted it. Further, while it legalized the cities' entitlement to annual franchise fees of up to 5 percent of gross revenues, it also prohibited most cities from regulating cable rates as of December 29, 1986.

The prospect of uncapped prices generated a financial boom. As projected cash flow spiraled upward, so did the prices of cable systems. A period of rapid horizontal and vertical integration followed the Cable Act of 1984, led by Tele-Communications Inc. (TCI), the largest cable operator in the nation. Because of rate deregulation, cable operators had not only more cash, but also more borrowing power. This gave them greater liquidity, which they used to acquire other cable companies, upgrade infrastructure, and invest in programming.

After deregulation, TCI's history followed a familiar pattern of acquisitions and ultimately its being acquired by a larger player. The company began aggressively buying new systems, including United Artists Communications (later United Artists Entertainment) in 1986, the largest movie theater operator in the country. It next purchased Heritage Communications, including its Dallas system, in 1987 for $1.3 billion. In the late 1980s, it spent nearly $3 billion for more than 150 cable companies. During 1991, TCI acquired United Artists Cable in a deal that brought in a cable subscription base of 2.6 million U.S. households. By 1992, TCI served almost 20 percent of cable subscribers in the United States. Finally in 1998, AT&T acquired TCI to form AT&T Broadband.

The Telecommunications Industry

Ever since their separation from AT&T, the regional Bell companies chafed under the continuing restrictions on their operations. Long-distance companies clamored for access charge reductions and entry into the local market. Cable companies argued that the 1992 Cable Act handicapped them even as they were being threatened by direct broadcast satellites. Consumer groups wanted multiple players to compete for customers, lowering prices and raising service levels in the process. A hodgepodge of overlapping and conflicting jurisdictions frustrated those charged with regulating various communications industries. Congress had to do something to resolve the problems of national and state regulation of wireline and wireless telecommunications, municipal regulation of cable, and unresolved issues relating to broadcast satellites. Similar deregulations in Chile and the United Kingdom showed that a competitive "free-for-all," while disruptive to many industry players, is generally good for consumers, the economy, and eventually the industry. A new law was needed to reflect that fact.

In the first major overhaul of telecommunications law since the 1934 Communications Act, Congress passed the 1996 Telecommunications Act. Among its provisions four stand out as important examples of the disruptive power of regulation:

- An end to barriers between the operations of once-distinct companies such as cable operators, long-distance phone companies, and local phone companies. Each ultimately would be allowed to venture into the businesses of the others.
- The removal of price controls on telephone, cable television, and other services, assuming that new competitors such as satellite operators will keep consumer costs in check. Cable operators with fewer than 50,000 subscribers in a community, or fewer than 600,000 nationwide, were immediately freed of most rate caps. Larger operators were freed from regulation in March 1999.
- The permission for long-distance companies—already unregulated—to enter local service immediately. Local providers would be allowed to reach into the long-distance market once competition is established in the local market.
- Ownership restrictions on media companies to be eased. TV stations were allowed to reach up to 35 percent of the national audience, up from the previous limit of 25 percent. The limit on radio stations in a single market rose from five to eight, presenting an impetus to massive consolidation of the industry. A com-

pany could, for the first time, own a TV station and cable company in the same market.

After so many boundaries were removed, aggressive companies moved quickly to expand into new areas, particularly through alliances and mergers. The first year after the act saw the announcement of four major mergers: SBC and Pacific Telesis, Bell Atlantic and Nynex, British Telecom (BT) and MCI, and WorldCom and MFS; subsequently, WorldCom supplanted BT as MCI's prospective merger partner. Eventually other combinations included Ameritech's merging with SBC, and Bell Atlantic's with GTE to form Verizon. The net impact of these changes has been to create a Rule of Three among local exchange carriers as well as a Rule of Three in long distance.

The Global Airline Industry

The U.S. airline industry was deregulated in 1978. Since that time, the industry has undergone substantial consolidation, and now consists of six major airlines, many of which are the products of previous mergers (for example, in the 1980s, Frank Lorenzo folded five carriers into Continental Airlines). With the proposed mergers of United and US Airways, American and TWA, and perhaps Continental and Delta, the industry is well on its way to a domestic Rule of Three.

At the international level, however, things are quite different. In the mid-1990s, Europe emulated the U.S. liberalization of air travel, but it did not open intra-Europe traffic to outside airlines. The industry remains heavily regulated within most countries, and governed country by country rather than by global agreements. For the most part, foreign ownership of airlines has not been permitted, even in the United States. To get around this barrier, many airlines began forming alliances, entering into code sharing arrangements, and sharing airport lounges and frequent-flier programs. The trade journal *Airline Business* counted 579 bilateral partnerships involving the 220 main airlines in 2000.[16]

The U.S. Department of Transportation has aggressively pursued "open sky" agreements around the world and by 2000 had 45 such agreements in place.[17] The airlines of one country are allowed to fly anywhere they want in another country, as frequently as they want and at whatever fare they want to charge. However, in no cases have foreign airlines been allowed to offer service between two cities within another country. As a result of these agreements, U.S. airlines have done extremely well in Latin America. Because Latin American carriers are unable to connect their passengers to U.S. destinations other than the city they first land in, American carriers are winning a disproportionate share of travelers. In fact, several Latin American airlines have been driven into bankruptcy or into forced mergers with other domestic carriers. Brazil's four carriers, for example, may soon merge into just two.[18]

Given the advantage of its huge domestic market, which accounts for approximately 50 percent of worldwide air travel, the United States has refused to give the World Trade Organization the right to enforce global competition in aviation. This policy has been criticized as shortsighted and contrary to the interests of American and other consumers. If the industry could truly be deregulated at the global level, if "open skies" in the fullest sense of that term could be achieved, it would dramatically restructure the airlines industry once more.[19]

Since 1997, major airlines have created global alliances that feature code sharing, coordination of schedules, shared identity, and some degree of co-marketing. There are now three major global alliances: the Star Alliance, led by United Airlines, Lufthansa, and Air Canada; the OneWorld Alliance led by American Airlines, British Airways, and Cathay Pacific Airways; and SkyTeam, whose members are Delta, Air France, Aeromexico, and Korean Air. Some smaller alliances have also been formed.

Disruptive Market Shifts

The disruptions that come from regulatory changes and new technologies can be on the order of earthquakes whose effects are deeply staged and immediately felt. Both can rock an industry and lead to almost immediate shakeouts of those players with weak foundations. This is not always the case, however, with the third kind of disruptive force, the shifts in markets, which can take sometimes years to evolve and manifest themselves. Nevertheless, their cumulative effect over time can be just as dramatic as that of the other forces.

Consider how markets gradually change. A new enterprise enters a market long dominated by the pioneers, which may have lost touch with the customers they have served for so long. Companies that once organized themselves to cater to preexisting preferences can find themselves with the wrong business model, or worse, when those preferences change. Timex came into a market dominated for decades by the makers of pocket watches. The company offered a new product, something quite innovative, and practically no one since then knows a fob pocket from a doublet. Gillette came out with safety razors, and the barber's leather strap was consigned to the museum. L'eggs (now a division of the Sara Lee Corporation) did it in women's hosiery, rendering garters obsolete. All of them achieved market leadership by overtaking the established rivals.

And all of these players redefined the markets in a gradual fashion rather than in some abrupt shift in customer values and preferences. It takes a while to educate people to new ways of thinking, dressing, eating, shaving, or telling time. In this section, we illustrate this process by looking at three major kinds of market shifts:

1. In a **channel shift** a newcomer, often with a new product, introduces some innovation in distribution and packaging. L'eggs transformed the pantyhose business largely through new packaging, new advertising, and new distribution channels. In an analogous way, Dell Computer Corporation managed the same feat with its "Dell Direct" model for distribution. The company changed the way that personal computers, especially in the United States, are distributed.
2. In a **demographic shift** a major change occurs in the makeup of the people who buy a company's products. The graying of the U.S. population, as the first Baby Boomers begin to retire, is causing radical changes in numerous consumer goods industries. Strapped for time and concerned about health issues, people may be ready for a menu prepared by Healthy Choice.
3. In a **cultural shift** people begin changing their attitudes toward long-held rituals and ideas. Many social critics have observed

how informal we have become—in dress, in work habits, in social etiquette, in what is allowed in the media. Nowhere are such changes more evident than in the U.S. apparel industry.

Channel Shifts

In 1959, at Glen Raven Mills near Burlington, North Carolina, a remarkable symbol of women's liberation was created: panty hose was invented, and no woman has dressed the same since. The product was typically stretched over leg-shaped cardboard inserts, packaged, and sold only at department stores. In 1971, the Hanes Hosiery Company of Winston-Salem launched the "L'eggs" brand panty hose with several major marketing innovations. Robert E. Elberson, Hanes's CEO, asked his advertising agency to create an image for a product with consistent quality and a memorable brand name. He also wanted it to be easy to keep in stock and to be displayed in a unique way that kept competitors out. L'eggs hosiery was wrapped into a ball and packaged in a plastic oversized egg. Most significantly, it was sold in supermarkets and drug stores, using consignment marketing, a then-novel approach. The product was an instant smash hit, with sales exceeding expectations fifteenfold. The key factors behind its success were its unique packaging and the enormous convenience to consumers, who could purchase the product in neighborhood stores, rather than making a trip to a pricey downtown department store. Through consignment selling, Hanes largely solved the out-of-stock problem common to hosiery displays. The "direct-to-store" delivery model was also key to L'eggs' success.

The L'eggs brand benefited immensely from the clever advertising slogan "Nothing beats a great pair of L'eggs," which became one of the best-known tag lines of all time. The company was such a part of Americana that one of its display units is now exhibited at the Whitney Museum of American Art.[20] The company's strong brand and loyal customer base have made L'eggs a big success in direct marketing as well. A large proportion of its sales are now made through direct mail and the Internet.

On a larger order of magnitude, the Internet economy led many people to speculate, rather wildly as we now know, on the viability of pure dot.coms. The electronic component will surely rise over time, but will remain smaller than the physical one. Pure online players are unlikely to challenge the full-line generalists within their industry in terms of overall market share, since at least for the immediate future virtually every sector of retailing will continue to rely predominantly on the physical distribution channel (see sidebar "Pure vs. Hybrid Dot.coms").

Pure vs. Hybrid Dot.coms

PURE dot.coms can be viable, provided they see themselves as either product or market specialists rather than full-line generalists. For example, Cars.com is a clear example of a company that will be a product specialist. On the other hand, Amazon.com started out as a product specialist focused only on books, but has evolved into a market specialist that offers a range of products for customers who respond well to its online commerce model. Although that model does not work for all consumers, the technologically savvy ones like the reviews by other customers, the personalized recommendations, and the use of "one-click" ordering and "purchase circles" (the practice of identifying popular items with groups the customer chooses to track).

To continue to dominate their markets, traditional full-line generalists must evolve into hybrid players that actively leverage the Internet as one of their key distribution channels. Rather than treat it as a stand-alone channel serving a distinct market segment, they must extract as much synergy between the Internet channel and their brick-and-mortar channels as possible. The principle of "integrated operations" is essential to the long-term success of generalists, and they must strive for as much integration and as many customer options as possible. The degree of integration needed is analogous to that of the restaurant offering "dine-in," "deliver," and "take-out" as three customer options.

That said, some Internet-based players have such overwhelming advantages over their traditional counterparts that they are in a position to evolve into true full-line generalists themselves. Their success will depend on how the market values the on-line entity. For example, America Online leveraged its enormous price-earnings multiple to purchase Time-Warner. Likewise, eBay could become a major force in all kinds of auctions by using its highly valued stock to make acquisitions of traditional auction houses such as Christie's or Sotheby's (the latter might look especially inviting, given its recent strategic partnership with Amazon.com). Already eBay has purchased the upscale auctioneer Butterfields.

Demographic Shifts

As a consequence of the long economic boom in the United States beginning in the 1990s, an exceptionally large and robust premium segment has been created in many industries. This change has occurred at the same time that the middle class in the United States and elsewhere has been in a relative decline. Society has moved closer to a three-part configuration, with a more even distribution between the upper, middle, and lower ends of the scale (though the middle is still clearly the largest segment). What remains of the middle class is now wealthier, more upwardly mobile, and more interested in premium brands.

This shift in social conditions and ambitions has had an enormous impact on generalists and specialists, as illustrated by the luxury car market. Until the late 1980s, this segment of the automobile market was quite small. Only a handful of brands competed in the space, which was controlled chiefly by the specialists such as Mercedes-Benz and BMW. Then the Acura came along, followed by Lexus and Infiniti, and suddenly Japanese automakers had created an upsurge of growth in that segment (a "dematuring," if you will) by building high-quality luxury cars and pricing them aggressively against what the incumbents were producing. The impact on the market was immediate and long lasting. Both Mercedes-Benz and BMW eventually responded by improving their products while lowering prices. The total size of the luxury market grew dramatically, to the point that it has become a key part of the overall business for every full-line generalist. According to J. D. Power analyst Jeff Schuster, sales of near-luxury cars were up 22 percent in 1999, whereas overall auto sales rose only 7 percent.[21]

The same phenomenon can be seen in many other industries. In the small appliance industry, for instance, Cuisinart and Braun had the same impact as Acura did, whereas JennAir and SubZero did the same for large appliances. This market change helped inspire Whirlpool's acquisition of KitchenAid and may lead to the potential acquisition of Maytag by Electrolux.

If the premium market grows into a mainstream market, the scale advantage outweighs specialty advantage. Leaving aside the super-premium segment (which is still the domain of specialists such as Rolls Royce and Lamborghini), the premium segment has become so mainstream that full-line generalists have to participate in it. However, there are important marketing considerations that must be kept in mind. We recommend that full-line generalists pursue a dual branding strategy, maintaining a clear and separate identity for the premium segment. Beyond branding, it may make sense to treat the premium segment as a separate and distinct part of the organization. Ford has created a separate division to house all of its luxury brands. In power tools, Black & Decker serves the large professional market using the DeWalt brand.

On a larger scale, dramatic shifts are occurring in consumption patterns in most developed countries, especially as a result of the graying of the population. Responsive to appeals based on health and nutrition, older consumers expect not to have to choose between taste and nutritional value, or quality and convenience. Companies able to deliver all these seemingly incompatible attributes will thrive. In the United States, Healthy Choice, for example, is well positioned to become a full-line player in prepared foods. Kellogg and Nestlé have created new business units devoted to the development of nutraceuticals, or functional foods. The upheavals from such demographic changes present opportunities for new companies to stake out competitive positions in previously mature industries.[22]

The aging of society holds many implications for personal services. Demand for home-based health services, home-based assisted living, assistance with cooking, cleaning, and yard work, for instance, is soaring. Home-improvement superstores, which have prospered by riding the do-it-yourself wave—a market now in decline, according to Harvard's Joint Center for Housing Studies,[23] as customers think more about "buying" it themselves as opposed to "doing" it themselves—will need to reinvent themselves. Home Depot, Lowe's, and Sears are all looking to boost growth in their services businesses. Other companies that manufacture home-oriented products—from Campbell's Soup to Procter & Gamble—will have to consider similar shifts.[24]

The concern for health and wellness has led consumers to demand radical changes in product offerings and business models.

Many major American cities have enacted laws against smoking in public places, including restaurants, and the consumption of hard liquor has fallen significantly among some demographic groups. These changes present a significant challenge to food and beverage producers, and even the dominant player in the inner circle of three is not guaranteed success if the market is eroding.

Moreover, in working longer hours and keeping up with family responsibilities, consumers of all ages are now more pressed for time. People who used to cook at home and rarely ate out now find a home-cooked meal something of a special occasion. Take-out food now surpasses the amount of food consumed in restaurants. What's more, supermarket sales in the new category of prepared foods called "home meal replacements" are growing rapidly and expected to reach $176 billion a year in 2001. All told, take-out, home-delivered, and "grab-and-go" foods account for yearly sales of $460 billion.

Age and health concerns are merely two items in the long list of demographic factors that can disrupt traditional markets and supplant the Rule of Three players. It cannot be overemphasized that making it into that inner circle, while a mark of great accomplishment, is no guarantee that one will stay there for long. No competitive market is static, even if some appear to resist change longer than others.

Cultural Shifts

The trend toward informal office apparel, particularly in the United States, has recently become a fact of culture. Whatever its causes, this informality in dress and demeanor has changed the look of the American workplace. Even in the United Kingdom, conservative companies such as Merrill Lynch, Arthur Andersen, and Credit Suisse First Boston have relaxed their dress codes. Designers such as Ralph Lauren, Bill Blass, and Hugo Boss Burton have seen revenues from the sale of suits and ties drop sharply as the new dress codes—variously referred to as Corporate Casual, Fridaywear, Dress-Down Friday, and Work at Ease—redefine the clothes people wear.[25]

Eighty-seven percent of U.S. employers reported in 1999 having a casual dress policy at least one day a week (down slightly from 95 percent in 1998), according to the Society of Human Resource Management.[26] The impact of this trend on U.S. manufacturers of business suits is enormous. According to the NPD Group in New York, figures from 1988 show that companies sold $4.2 billion of suits, suit separates, and sports coats, representing over 14 percent of total men's apparel sales. Those numbers dropped to $3.8 billion and just under 11 percent in 1992, and $3.3 billion and less than 8 percent in 1993. By 1998, sales dropped to $2.7 billion, representing just 5 percent of the men's apparel market.[27] Responding to this trend, retail chain Men's Wearhouse created a seven-minute video entitled "How to Dress Casually and Still Mean Business." Over the last eight years, casual clothing has gone from zero to 35 percent of its business.

As a disruptive force in competitive markets, a shift in cultural values is typically a rather slow-moving event, a gradual evolution that may have its origins in a sudden explosion of change in a geographically localized area before it spreads nationwide or across the globe. In his recent book *The Tipping Point,* for instance, Malcolm Gladwell traces the Hush Puppies revival to the hip bars and clubs of downtown Manhattan in late 1994, a fad that later caught fire and spread widely, much to the delight of Wolverine, the company that makes the shoes. In 1995, the brand soared unexpectedly to sales of 430,000 pairs.[28] Trends and fads may be here one day and gone the next, but like category 5 tornadoes they can leave a path of destruction in their wakes. The turmoil may be just enough to upset the balance of any seemingly stable industry and shift the order at the top.

Disruptive Investing

Historically, savvy investors have both benefited from and accelerated major transformations in the economy. At the beginning of the industrial period, big landowners began shifting their investments from land and agriculture to trade and industry. The European nobility invested in emerging industries such as metals and chemicals, giving a major boost to social and economic changes already underway. Without the financial backing of this class, both the pace and the direction of change would have been very different.

In the United States, those individuals who had the wherewithal and foresight to invest in the economic engines of the future and capture their gains from those of the past before they became dramatically devalued prospered enormously. The Rockefellers, the Carnegies, the Vanderbilts, the Dukes, for instance, had enormous impacts on the industries they were involved in.

Today there are still plenty of wealthy individuals willing to take the covers off their deep wells of capital. For instance, Carl Icahn, Michael Milken, and Warren Buffett have influenced the pecking order within old industries as well as financed the growth of new ones. But the institutional investors, not the single individuals, have become the primary source of investment. Many of them, especially those charged with investing pension funds, are very cautious and put money into low-risk traditional investments rather than funding upstart challengers. As mutual funds have emerged as major players in capital markets, however, the competition for funding has changed. Differing widely in their investment philosophies and tolerances for risk, mutual funds still offer a wider range of business opportunities to be funded. Elsewhere, a much less dynamic investment culture exists. Financial institutions and corporate partners—for example, the members of a keiretsu in Japan—continue to hold a much larger proportion of shares of companies than they do in the United States.

In the past, new companies with bold ideas about challenging the status quo in an industry with new technology or a new business model found little institutional support; they had to engage in guerrilla warfare to establish a new front. The more radical their ideas, the less likely it was that they could attract financial support. The situation today is reversed. The more radical the idea, the more likely, it seems, that it will attract financial backing.

As for creating a disruption in existing markets, the biggest explosion has been the growth in venture capital investments. In recent years, billions of dollars have poured into disruptive new technologies and business models, fueling and being fueled by the increase in initial public offerings (IPOs). In 1999, venture capital investments reached a record $48.3 billion, up 151.6 percent over the previous year's amount, according to the National Venture Capital Association.[29]

Finally, there are very few remaining global barriers to capital flow. Good ideas can attract capital regardless of where they originate. Venture capital firms have increasingly gone global, and disruptive, well-funded challengers can now emerge from places that few incumbents would have considered likely sources in the past.

A good example of how investor enthusiasm for the "next big thing" can have a big impact on the incumbent players in an industry is the optical networking phenomenon. The demand for communication bandwidth has grown rapidly, doubling every nine months (double the rate for computing power). The three major players in the networking business—Nortel Networks, Lucent Technologies, and Cisco Systems—suddenly found themselves confronting a host of new competitors with new approaches to boosting bandwidth. Many of these companies attracted investors' interest and garnered the support of blue-chip venture capital firms. Many went public early, in most cases before they had any revenue at all.

Armed with their extremely valuable stock as currency, the companies grew rapidly, attracting employees and making acquisitions of their own. Within an amazingly short time, these upstarts threatened even a stalwart company such as Lucent. Among the incumbent players, the contrast between Nortel and Lucent was striking. Nortel recognized and acted on the shift to optical technology much earlier than Lucent did. As a result, Nortel stock rose almost five-fold from the beginning of 1999 until 2001, whereas Lucent's stock fell 40 percent from its 1999 high.[30] While the market correction of 2000–2001 lowered the financial power of new entrants, it did not spare the incumbents in the networking business, whose life is clearly not going to get easier any time soon.[31]

Whatever twists and turns lie ahead for investment firms, whether market conditions persuade them to become more conservative or take greater risks, the dramatic effects they have on Rule of Three markets will continue to be felt for a long time. No player is safe, or its position assured. The forces of creative destruction that Joseph Schumpeter wrote about in 1934 are alive and well today, exemplified by the four lords of chaos we have discussed in this chapter: new technologies, new regulations, new markets, and new investors. All market players need to take appropriate steps to anticipate their futures and chart their courses.

Conclusion

The Rule of Three is much more than an interesting theoretical construct; it is a powerful empirical reality that must be factored into corporate strategizing. Understanding the likely end points of market evolution is critical to the ability of executives to develop strategies that result in success.

As examples from a multitude of industries show, the Rule of Three is a nearly universal phenomenon, which business leaders, managers, entrepreneurs, and students of business can use to gain valuable insights into the nature of competitive markets. "Natural" market structures do indeed exist: most industries, left to develop without artificial constraints, reveal a complementarity of generalists and specialists, two groups that typically do not compete with each other; rather each finds customers whose needs and desires it can satisfy. Furthermore, in nearly all industries, three strong generalists emerge, along with numerous specialists. All can survive and do well, relatively speaking, until the market is destabilized and a shakeout or several successive shakeouts leads to further consolidation and repositioning.

The key lesson is the market evolution theory at the heart of the Rule of Three: most markets are cyclical in their evolution, and strategizing must therefore be done with time horizons spanning decades or more, far exceeding normal planning norms. In particular, managers must be on the lookout for the major drivers of market restructuring: new technologies, regulatory shifts, and market shifts. Failure to understand and appreciate these events can cause business people to engage in "unnatural" marketplace behavior, perhaps ultimately dooming their companies.

Our analysis of both local and global industries has led us to formulate a number of axiomatic generalizations or rules:

1. Mature markets are characterized by the existence of three major players along with numerous product or market specialists.

2. The financial performance of the large players improves with increased market share—but only up to a point, typically around 40 percent. Beyond that point, diseconomies of scale set in, along with political problems related to heightened regulatory scrutiny.

3. The Big 3 companies are valued at a premium (price/earnings ratio) compared with smaller companies. The oil industry is a recent example.

4. The performance of specialist companies deteriorates as they grow market share within the overall market, but improves as they grow their share of a specialty niche.

5. Successful super-niche players are, in essence, monopolists in their niches, commanding as much as an 80 or 90 percent of the niche market.

6. If the market leader commands a 70 percent market share or more as a result of patents or proprietary standards—for example, IBM in the heyday of mainframes—there is no room for a second full-line generalist. However, such dominance usually cannot last, and new generalists eventually emerge.

7. If the leader commands between 50 and 70 percent of the market, there is no room for a third full-line generalist. We have seen, for example, how Boeing and Airbus pushed McDonnell-Douglas into the ditch and eventually into a merger with Boeing.

8. A new #3 generalist usually reappears in the long run, despite the leaders' command of the market.

9. If the market leader enjoys much less than a 40 percent share, there may temporarily be room for a #4 generalist.

10. If a generalist sinks below a 10 percent share, it falls into the "ditch" and must either find a way to win back market share or become a specialist.

11. If the market is suffering a downturn, the fight between #1 and #2 often sends #3 into the ditch. Thus, the battles between Coca-Cola and Pepsi drove RC Cola into the ditch, just as the battle between GM and Ford drove Chrysler into the ditch in the 1970s.

12. The dogfight between #1 and #2 tends not to hurt the specialists.

13. Generalists who try to operate specialists' businesses generally fail. Kmart, for example, had to shed its specialty retail businesses, such as Walden Books.

14. Global leaders have to be strong in at least two of the triad markets—North America, Europe, and Asia. Toyota has a sizable presence in Asia as well as North America, whereas Ford is strong in North America and Europe.

15. The #1 company is usually the *least* innovative, although it may have the largest R&D budget.

16. Such companies should adopt a "fast-follower" strategic posture when it comes to innovation.

17. The #3 company is usually the *most* innovative. Its innovations are usually "stolen," however, by the #1 or #2 companies.

18. Such companies should try to protect their innovations through patents; however, such protection is becoming more difficult to sustain over time, as the large pharmaceuticals companies can testify. Alternatively, they should try to develop strategies that the #1 company cannot match, as MCI did with its "Friends and Family" program.

19. The extent to which the #3 player enjoys a comfortable or precarious existence depends on how far away that player is from the ditch.

20. Companies in the ditch exhibit the worst financial performance and have a difficult time surviving.

21. The ditch can be thought of as the bankruptcy court's waiting room.

22. Ditch companies can emerge as big players only if there is no viable third-ranked player to block them. They can emerge as specialists only if they are able to identify a defensible niche in

which they have a sustainable competitive advantage through unique resource endowments.

Armed with these rules, corporate executives and managers should be better able to apply their understanding of the Rule of Three to specific points relevant to their company, market, and industry. For example, they can more readily grasp the nature of market competition and confrontation. They can more accurately assess their company's current position within its industry and set objectives that the company has reasonable hopes of achieving. Given the company's position and the shape of the competitive market, is it a better strategy to roll up a fragmented industry, consolidate an industry with many majors, change the game by redefining the industry at a higher level, or seek to achieve a leadership position within a current or future industry definition? A broad view of Rule of Three principles will assist leaders in identifying external candidates for mergers as well as internal ones for demergers or spin-offs. Accordingly they should be better able to assess the resources and strategic assets needed to implement an acquisition or demerger strategy.

Company leaders can also use the Rule of Three principles to determine a set of critical factors to measure the success of any strategy, whether for branding, distribution, investments in fixed assets, outsourcing, R&D management, or a host of other issues. Moreover, they can refine their business models to optimize financial performance vis-à-vis the company's position within its industry or the evolution that the industry is currently undergoing. This understanding is fundamental in deciding whether to pursue market share or to shorten the company's reach, whether to seek a leadership position within the industry or to act as a fast-follower as others take the lead. In short, the Rule of Three is a valuable guide to managers who ask whether it makes sense for their company to be driven by the market or whether the company should take the active role in driving the market, or whether there should be some give-and-take between those two extremes.

Since no company can absolutely guarantee its position within an industry, especially when markets are globalizing and are subject to the four major forces of disruption described in chapter 8, it is important that business managers learn to recognize the early warning signals of an upcoming industry shakeout. Forewarned, they can then set strategies to take maximum advantage of any opportunities that become available. Most important, they can better see ways of staying out of the ditch.

Specialists who understand the Rule of Three will recognize the games being played by the big players in an industry. They will keep a keen eye for new opportunities available to smaller players. Having observed the dangers of being lured into the ditch by the desire to grow "too much, too fast," as detailed in chapter 4, specialists will be in a better position to understand the right and wrong ways to pursue market share growth. If they wish to take the path toward acquisition, they can use Rule of Three principles to develop strategies to make their companies more attractive takeover candidates. On the other side, they can determine how best to keep themselves free and independent.

Although the field can become crowded, specialization offers myriad opportunities for slow, organic, and profitable growth. While they may be less affected by what the Big 3 within a given industry are doing, specialists need to recognize the early warning signs of too rapid growth. Although they may feel pressure to respond to demands set by directors, employees, stockholders, and customers, they are well advised to listen carefully to the voices of experience offered by companies that have been lured into the ditch.

The lure of greater market share is a powerful one, which has caused many successful specialist companies to sacrifice their distinguishing characteristics and dilute their competencies in a headlong pursuit of growth, only to end up in the ditch. As we have pointed out, such strategies are viable only if a clear, unblocked opportunity to occupy a generalist position exists. If not, firms would be far better off deploying the same resources into a geographic expansion within existing niches or creating new niches.

In addition to being valuable for corporate leaders, the Rule of Three will prove essential for those in investment banking, consulting, and venture capital who must make decisions on funding acquisitions, spin-offs, and other industry reconfigurations. Specifically, with an understanding of the Rule of Three, investment bankers and funding sources can better evaluate a company's financial performance relative to that of appropriate peer groups, weighing comparable aspects using the most appropriate measures. The broad view afforded by the Rule of Three can sharpen their acumen for identifying and recommending the best prospects for mergers and acquisitions, based on companies' market positions and strategic fit.

In general, the Rule of Three has deep implications for companies large and small on how best to generate and control growth, increase shareholder value, and drive efficiency. Above all, the Rule of Three can be used to pinpoint a company's position in the evolution of the industry in which it competes. This perspective is essential to those whose decisions affect the company's steady progress even in a destabilized market, whether that disruption comes from naturally occurring forces or whether it originates in artificial constraints such as imposed government regulations. In a constantly changing market—especially one evolving from the local to the national, multinational, or global level—it is critical to know how and when to act or when it is best to sit still.

The greatest impact and potential dislocations arising from the Rule of Three occur when an industry makes a major geographic transition—from regional to national, or even more dramatically, from national to global. The impact of this transition on a number of industries, including tires, appliances, automobiles, telecommunications, and hotels has been the emergence of a new core of inner circle companies, with, at times, surprising winners and losers.

As more markets become globalized or get transformed through technology in coming years, managers everywhere will have to reassess their corporate positioning and strategic goals. For some, this will spell a once-in-a-lifetime opportunity to seize the initiative and firmly establish their companies on a larger stage. For many others, it will require hard thinking about strategic choices, and the courage to make painful but necessary decisions about markets not served and products not offered.

A Brief History of Mergers in the United States

Industry consolidation is heavily affected by regulatory changes that encourage or prevent mergers and acquisitions. In the United States five primary merger waves occurred in the twentieth century, most of them taking place during stock market booms when stocks became a cheaper currency than money. Although a naturally occurring process, each one involved one or more "artificial" drivers such as a fundamental regulatory change that dramatically altered the face of many industries. This was certainly the case with the first three merger waves.[1] In some instances the regulation prevented mergers and acquisitions, whereas in others it encouraged them.

1. The first major wave of mergers occurred near the beginning of the twentieth century. Even though the Sherman Antitrust Act had been passed in 1890, mergers that created near monopolies with as much as 90 percent of the market were permitted. Although it forbade collusive agreements between firms, the law was silent on mergers. Buoyed by a booming stock market, firms in many industries merged rapidly to create near monopolies. U.S. Steel, for example, was formed with 65 percent of steel-making capacity; American Tobacco cornered 90 percent of the market. This merger wave was intense but relatively short, ending in 1904 when the Supreme Court expanded the

interpretation of the Sherman Act. In 1914, Congress passed the Clayton Antitrust Act, which explicitly prohibited monopolization through mergers.

2. In the economic boom times of the late 1920s, the stock market was especially receptive to new securities issued to finance the creation of oligopolies—concentrated industries dominated by a few firms. Companies such as Allied Chemical and Bethlehem Steel rode the top of this merger wave. Not surprisingly, the Great Depression and the stock market collapse put an abrupt end to mergers.

3. Public policy, embodied in the passage of the Celler-Kefauver Act of 1950, turned fiercely against the mergers of firms within the same industry. This atmosphere dampened merger activity until the late 1960s, when another stock market boom and a favorable market for new equities pressured corporate leaders to grow their companies again. Precluded from within-industry mergers, they opted for "conglomerate" mergers, acquiring firms from completely different industries.

Corporations justified these forays into unknown waters by pushing the concept of "business portfolios." By diversifying and investing in other industries, they argued, they could ride out the cyclical swings in one industry. ITT, Teledyne, and Beatrice Foods exemplify the unwieldy corporate creatures spawned in this era. While some of these combinations did well, most were failures. All the major oil companies, for example, acquired businesses far removed from their own: Exxon Corporation acquired Reliance Electric; Mobil Corporation bought Montgomery Ward; Atlantic Richfield Company merged with Anaconda. The prognosis for them was never good, and the reality was even worse.

This era also gave rise to the development of new tools for managers struggling to make sense of these ungainly creations and extract some synergy out of operating them as unified corporate entities. The most prominent of these was the Boston Consulting Group's portfolio planning approach, which introduced the concept of strategic business units (SBUs) and recommended that companies manage cash flow across them based on their position with a portfolio-planning matrix. Units that had a high market share in a slow growth market ("cash cows") would spin off cash flow that could be deployed to nurture other units with a low share of a fast-growing business ("question marks" or "problem children").

4. The fourth wave wiped out much of what had taken place in the third wave. In the late 1970s, companies started to sell off unrelated businesses to other willing buyers. On a scale never before seen, sell-offs occurred through management and leveraged buyouts. New financial instruments—the high-yield but risky bonds known as junk bonds—financed the rationalization of many industries.

   In the early 1980s, antitrust enforcement was relaxed under the Reagan administration, and mergers took off anew, especially in industries that had been deregulated under the Carter administration, such as airlines and trucking. The greater emphasis on shareholder value also triggered many acquisitions as well as sell-offs. By the end of the 1980s and into the early 1990s, few true conglomerates remained; even diversified companies such as General Electric could point to a host of commonalities and sources of synergy across their seemingly diverse businesses.

5. The most recent merger wave began in the mid-1990s, again in concert with a sustained boom in the stock market. The factors that distinguished this merger wave were: the rapid pace of technological change in many, if not most, industries (especially with the creation of the World Wide Web); the end of the Cold War and the subsequent opening up of markets worldwide; related to those developments, the demise of economic and political ideologies around the world, replaced by pragmatists; the lowering of trade barriers globally as well as within expanding regional trade alliances; and continued deregulation (on a global basis) in such key industries as telecommunications, media, financial services (especially banking), health care, and airlines.

The record-shattering pace of national as well as cross-border mergers in recent years has been matched by an almost equally intense trend toward demergers. The result: an almost wholesale rationalization of business ownership structures—who does what for whom—around two principles: a sharper focus on core businesses and an insistence on extremely high levels of efficiency. Not coincidentally most of the industries affected by these developments have already reached or are well on their way toward the market structure described by the Rule of Three.

Market Snapshots

The U.S. Burger Market

The fast-food market is the fastest growing segment of the restaurant business in the United States, encompassing all types of limited service restaurants offering ready-to-eat dining.[1] In the burger segment McDonald's Corporation is the largest operator with 2000 worldwide system sales of $40.2 billion.[2] The #2 player is Burger King, with worldwide system sales of $11.4 billion, followed by Wendy's in the #3 position with sales of $7.1 billion.[3] High buyer power, low barriers to entry, intense rivalry among competitors, and ease of substitution characterize this market. These factors have made this a very competitive low-price, high-volume market.

McDonald's

In 1999, McDonald's had a 43.1 percent share of the burger market. It is estimated that nearly 7 percent of the American population eats at McDonald's on any given day.[4] The company has become the world's largest and most profitable food services operation, and one of the world's most widely recognized brands.[5] As of early 2001, McDonald's operated over 29,000 restaurants, 14,400 of which are franchised in 118 countries.[6]

The first McDonald's restaurant opened on April 15, 1955.[7] In the early years the company was characterized by rapid expansion in an embryonic market. In order to benefit fully from its first-mover advantage, the company opened itself to franchising. Following this strategy, the company reduced the financial burden of swift expansion and spurred rapid growth. In order to ensure consistency in the brand, the company initially chose to set up restaurants itself and then to franchise them as soon as they were running smoothly.[8] As a result, McDonald's controlled the uniformity of its restaurants and continues even today to own most of the real estate for its restaurants.

Advertising heavily in order to build up brand recognition, the company established its golden arches trademark in 1962. McDonald's went public in 1965, a move that helped the company implement an aggressive growth strategy and develop a comprehensive sales and marketing platform. During the 1970s production efficiency and product consistency became the company's focus. In response to customer demand for convenience and fast service, the company added a drive-through lane in 1975. It added new items to its product lines—for instance, a full breakfast line in 1978—and focused on product consistency as one of its competitive advantages.

In the "burger wars" of the 1970s, most competitors resorted to cutting prices. McDonald's, however, continued to advertise extensively and focus on new product development. The company's growth through the 1970s and 1980s can be attributed to its successful promotion of product differentiation. Furthermore, McDonald's ability to meet and exceed consumer expectations by adapting its product offering to social and demographic trends kept it ahead of its competition.

In the mid-1980s, when consumers became more conscious about their eating habits, McDonald's introduced its Chicken McNuggets and ready-to-eat salads. In the late 1980s, the market started showing signs of maturing. Competition in the domestic market slowed U.S. operations growth to about 5 percent a year.[9] Accordingly, the company began looking at new market possibilities, emphasizing international expansion. In the last several years, McDonald's has significantly increased the number of countries in which it operates, from 79 countries in 1995 to 118 in 2000.[10] Today, while only one-third of the company's restaurants are situated outside the United

States, around 60 percent of its revenues and profits come from international sales, over double the foreign contribution of a decade ago.[11]

In its attempts to develop alternate channels, the company set out to develop nontraditional sites. The program identified a $47 billion market of special locations for the company's satellite concept store, the low-overhead mini-McDonald's, first "invented" in Singapore and deemed to be a perfect medium.[12] These new locations included retail, institutional, recreational, and niche opportunities.

In a stagnant domestic market, McDonald's has found new ways to grow, most notably by embarking on a new pricing and menu strategy. In 1994, the company offered the Extra Value Meal, a discounted package of a sandwich, fries, and drink, which was expected to offset their lower margins with increased volumes.[13] It also made many attempts to cut costs and improve efficiency.

McDonald's has always been looking for ways to expand. Recently, it bought Ohio-based Donatos Pizza and the Boston Market (formerly Boston Chicken) restaurant chain, and invested in Food.com. It also plans to form eMac Digital, a revolutionary business-to-business exchange for the food service market.[14] In sum, McDonald's success over the years has been based upon three factors: operating efficiency, product consistency, and marketing power.

Burger King

Burger King is the #2 player with a 19.6 percent market share in 1999 and 11,333 stores by early 2001. Its strategy has largely been reactive and rarely cohesive since its inception in 1954. This inconsistency stems from the historically loose affiliation between the company and its franchisees, the high turnover rate of management, and its inability to define its target market and core competencies. In order to differentiate itself from the competition, Burger King was the first to install plastic dining areas.[15] In 1957, the company expanded its menu and added its signature sandwich, the Whopper.

In order to expand more rapidly, Burger King also resorted to franchising. Problems arose, however, when exclusive rights began to be sold to franchisees. Apart from the lack of consistency within the brand, some franchisees expanded faster than the parent company. Two large Louisiana franchisees, for instance, took control of the Chicago market. By 1971, they owned 351 stores and even attempted to buy Burger King from Pillsbury.

In 1977, under new management Burger King began to exert control over its powerful franchisees. New agreements prevented single franchises from becoming too big and established inspections and unscheduled visits by management.

As is typical of the #2 player, Burger King imitated the innovations of its competitors. It responded to McDonald's breakfast menu, although it took the company almost five years to develop successfully competitive menus. It responded to Wendy's chicken sandwiches by offering a line of its own specialty sandwiches. It also improved its menu by adding a salad bar and other light items, in imitation of Wendy's.

In 1995, in an attempt to develop a strategic focus, Burger King loosely defined its target market as anyone who ate fast food. The company tried to become "all things to all people," adding new items such as pizzas, weight-watchers' meals, and 33 other menu programs that were eventually discontinued. It also attempted to compete with restaurants in the casual dining segment by implementing a limited service called the dinner-basket program, which was eventually discontinued.

Ultimately, these initiatives deteriorated the brand and spread the company profits thin. Realizing that the lack of strategy was proving expensive, the company decided to return to its core competency—making burgers and selling them at a low price. Because its franchisees opposed lowering prices, Burger King was the last chain to switch to value pricing.[16]

Burger King has also implemented an asset redeployment strategy, in which the company builds and maintains sites where it makes the most economic sense, given its core business.[17] In 1990, it successfully joined with Walt Disney Studios in its promotional efforts and formed the Burger King Kids Club. Until the partnership with Disney ended in 1997, the company offered special meals, toys, and character glasses that featured themes from the latest Walt Disney cartoon releases. Currently, Burger King is in 58 countries and continues to look overseas for further expansion, but only 10 percent of its income is derived from overseas as opposed to 60 percent for McDonald's.

Wendy's

Company founder and CEO Dave Thomas opened the first Wendy's Old-Fashioned Hamburger restaurant in 1969, naming it after his eight-year-old daughter. With 5,500 restaurants, Wendy's has held the #3 position in the burger segment since 1992, with just over 12 percent market share in 1999. It has focused on value and good quality to differentiate itself and to compete on different terms than its competitors do.

As the #3 player, Wendy's has indeed been innovative in its industry. It was the first to start using fresh beef (a practice competitors ridiculed) and to introduce a pick-up window with a separate grill. Wendy's innovates and caters to "special tastes" through its specialty products. Its innovations are creative dressings added to the basic hamburgers and chicken sandwiches. It was the first fast-food restaurant to introduce salad bars (1979) and baked potatoes (1983) nationwide.

Wendy's caters to both the price-conscious consumer and quality seeker by offering a 99-cent value and moderately priced combo meals that include commodity and specialty items. Wendy has also explored nontraditional sites and in 1994 even briefly tested sites inside Wal-Mart stores. It is, however, cautious in its approach and maintains that it will enter nontraditional sites only where it makes sense and the company can be assured that its high quality will be maintained.[18]

Ditch Dweller: Hardee's

Hardee's briefly ousted Wendy's from the #3 position in the 1980s through its innovative advertising campaigns. In 1994, it held a 9.5 percent market share. Its problems resemble those of Burger King's, including unclear marketing campaigns, too many product lines to manage, upper management turmoil, and dissatisfied franchisees. When Hardee's acquired Roy Rogers' in 1990, the company's strengths began to erode.[19] Integrating the two was an expensive process with minimal returns. Although it has a 70-item menu that covers breakfast, lunch, and dinner, no one item stands out.[20]

Hardee's former parent Imasco offered little support to the struggling fast-food company and in 1997 sold Hardee's to CKE for

---

$327 million. The chain comprised 788 company-owned Hardee's restaurants and 2,364 franchised outlets. Hardee's has continued to perform poorly, and CKE has been trying to lower its debt by selling more restaurants to franchisees.[21]

Specialists

The leaders in drive-throughs—Rally's, Checker's, and Hot n' Now—claim to be filling the niche for fast, convenient service and inexpensive food. In the late 1980s and early 1990s, this segment saw explosive growth. Rally's and Checker's were recognized among the fastest growing restaurants and darlings of Wall Street. However, as McDonald's and Burger King began appearing in gas stations, department stores, and other nontraditional sites, these niche players have lost some of their advantage.

The Pizza Market

The U.S. pizza market comprises two different types of players: the small entrepreneurs and the large national chains.[22] Validating the Rule of Three, the large national chains are dominated by three companies: Pizza Hut, Domino's, and Papa John's. The market shares of these three organizations are: 21 percent, 12 percent, and 7 percent respectively.[23] Because of recent paltry growth rates, the market has experienced advertising and price wars. In better times, major players maintained separate focuses and concentrated on specific markets. For example, Pizza Hut maintained a strong focus on providing a variety of products at its dine-in locations. Domino's strength lay in its delivery of products. Papa John's focused on high-quality products and customer satisfaction.

Pizza Hut

With more than 10,000 restaurants, Dallas-based Pizza Hut is the largest pizza chain in the world. Its U.S. sales totaled some $5 billion in 1999.[24] Having lagged behind under PepsiCo management, the company was spun off along with Taco Bell and KFC to form Tricon, the world's largest restaurant company.

Pizza Hut sustains growth by driving volume through a variety of distribution channels, providing superior customer value, and promoting a single corporate identity while offering a range of products to different customer segments. The company's greatest strength, its size, allows it to extend its reach to many customers through multiple distribution channels and to enjoy economies of scale in advertising, purchasing, and overall operating efficiencies. As a result of its dine-in restaurants and stand-alone delivery units, the company has high costs in labor, real estate, and other fixed assets. Under Tricon, however, its focus has been to keep costs down by forming a single unified purchasing cooperative for the three restaurants, leveraging more than $4 billion in purchasing power.[25] The company offers a wide range of products and has recently included items such as chicken wings, bread sticks, sandwiches, and salads. In addition, Tricon has recently tested a new concept of teaming Pizza Hut with Taco Bell and KFC within a single location, enabling the company to sell more items to more consumers.[26]

Pizza Hut has successfully maintained a common corporate identity while developing strong subbrands to differentiate itself from the competition. It spends heavily on brand positioning and advertising, as much as $95 million on measured media in 1998.[27] It is a fast-follower in that it designed its New York style pizza to imitate that of local pizzerias and attract a new customer segment.[28] During the 1999 Super Bowl, Pizza Hut launched the Big New Yorker Pizza, the most successful pizza in recent history. It also started delivering pizza in 1986 only after Domino's proved that service offering could be successful. In addition, it launched a total quality campaign after its competitors announced similar initiatives.

The company has reduced inefficiencies and emphasized improving financial results at the restaurant level, closing more than 800 underperforming restaurants in 1997. Pizza Hut has also invested heavily in quality during the past few years, including $35 million in improving its toppings and another $15 million in fine-tuning its ovens. In addition, the company hopes to reduce annual employee turnover to 100 percent from the current 140 percent, while not compromising on store cleanliness and service standards.[29] Other strategies include leveraging its many distribution channels to drive volume and reach more customers, differentiating its products through branding, and growing the total pizza market through heavy advertising. As an indication of its success, Pizza Hut has enjoyed ten straight quarters of growth.[30]

Domino's Pizza

Founded in 1960, Domino's Pizza is currently the largest privately held restaurant chain, with worldwide sales of $3.54 billion in 2000, and 6,600 owned and franchised stores in the United States and 64 international markets. In 2000, Domino's enjoyed an increase of 5.3 percent in sales over 1999.[31] From its inception the company has concentrated on operations more than marketing: to be the leader in pizza delivery throughout the world as is expressed in the company's mission statement.

In December 1998, Bain Capital, a Boston-based private equity firm, bought a 93 percent stake in the company. Domino's is investing extensively in fixed assets, mainly software and technology systems aiming to increase efficiency and productivity. These include inventory management equipment to ensure JIT delivery of materials and mapping programs that assist in predicting delivery time and graphing locations.[32] Additionally, in 1998, management initiated a cost-reduction initiative to improve the overall profitability of operations.[33] Even though the company spends $40 million to $50 million on advertising annually, it realizes that it cannot take Pizza Hut head on. It therefore wisely follows a different focus and coexists with Pizza Hut through segmentation (by concentrating solely on delivery, not in-store eating). Domino's advantage also rests in its extensive, international presence. With three types of pizzas and three side items, Domino's scope of offering is as expansive as those of most players in the market.

Unlike its competition, Domino's uses only one channel: home delivery. It is not an innovator in products, although it was the first in the industry to improve its delivery cartons by using corrugated cardboard boxes with air holes to prevent steam from destroying the box and the pizza, and in 1998 it added its "Heat Wave" bag delivery, which helps keep pizzas hot and crispy while en route. Aiming to deliver pizzas fast, hot, and right, Domino's provides a service to its customers as much as a product.

Papa John's International, Inc.

Louisville-based Papa John's is the fastest growing pizza company in America. The company started as a regional player, but has expanded both nationally and internationally. In 1999, it overtook Little Caesar's for the #3 spot and reported sales of over $1.4 billion. Papa John's has over 2,500 restaurants throughout the United States and ten international markets.[34] It emphasizes quality, a hallmark of its marketing strategy.

The company's advantage arises from its high quality and carefully selected markets. Papa John's success can be attributed to sourcing the best possible ingredients, stringent quality control, and dedication to customer satisfaction. Its motto—"better ingredients, better pizza"—emphasizes its high quality; however, the negative advertising war with Pizza Hut over the freshness of its ingredients has led it into an ugly court battle as it violated U.S. advertising laws and disparaged the Pizza Hut name.[35] It has focused solely on delivery as its distribution channel. Papa John's has vertically integrated its dough production with twelve dough commissaries across the United States.[36] Another strategy used by Papa John's to transform from a specialist to generalist is the implementation of technology. By partnering with Cybermeals, the chain can offer its customers the convenience of ordering pizza online.

Ditch Dweller: Little Caesar's

Once the nation's third largest pizza chain, Little Caesar's has been on shaky grounds because of the aggressive Papa John's. Founded in 1959, Little Caesar's is known not only for its humorous TV spots but also for its introduction of a two-for-one deal, later coined "Pizza! Pizza! Two great pizzas. One low price." One of the company's main strengths has been its national brand awareness and extensive advertising. However, that strategy has been in question, given that the company is in deep financial trouble and has experienced three years of declining sales, market share, and store locations.[37] Since the company has always maintained a low-price position, it is constantly looking to cut costs related to infrastructure and product ingredients. It has achieved infrastructure cost cuts through a use of alternate locations. In addition, it has a strategic alliance with Kmart, which has added 1,500 Little Caesar's Pizza outlets to its stores, the outlets being dubbed as K-café.[38] Other cost cutting has come through the use of inferior, less expensive products. By mid-1999, the company closed more than 300 of its U.S. restaurants.[39]

In 1997, Little Caesar's rolled out two new products: an oversized line of pizzas and three-foot rectangular pizzas. These launches, however, were flawed. Franchisees complained that they were not given time to implement the program before the advertising campaign began.

Other Players

Sbarro, a nondelivery competitor, started as a deli, but expanded widely. Generating revenues of $400 million, it expanded at a rate of about 80 per year in malls and travel plazas beginning in 1991.

California Pizza Kitchen (CPK) is another competitor picking up its growth in alternative formats such as ASAP in malls, airports, and concert facilities. Founded in 1985, CPK currently operates over 100 restaurants in 21 states, generating sales of about $211 million in 2000. It also boasts a unique menu offering pizza toppings such as barbecued chicken, roasted duck, and pineapple.

The Cold Cereal Market

The cold cereal market is dominated by two major competitors who control a combined 63 percent of the market.[40] The long-time market leader Kellogg has recently slipped to the #2 position with a 30.7 percent share, while General Mills has risen to #1 with a 32.2 percent share.[41] The #3 position with a 16.3 percent share is held by Post, a division of Kraft Foods, which is part of the Philip Morris Companies, Inc. Smaller players such as Quaker, Ralcorp, Malt-O-Meal, and private labels control the remainder of the market. In addition, numerous specialty producers hold niches in the natural and organic categories.

After more than 20 years of steady growth, cereal sales began to drop in the period 1994–1997. After declining by 4.8 percent in 1997, sales were flat in 1998. The market has seen gradual price increases by 2 to 3 percent in recent years. It experiences severe competition and has high barriers to entry.[42]

General Mills, Inc.

General Mills ranks among the largest consumer foods companies in the United States, with a #1 or #2 market position in virtually every category in which it competes. Its worldwide sales total $6.7 billion. The company's largest business is Big G cereals, which represent 35 percent of its sales and include some of the most popular cereal brands in America, such as Wheaties, Cheerios, Chex, Total, Lucky Charms, Trix, Cocoa Puffs, Fiber One, Oatmeal Crisp, and Golden Grahams.[43]

The fact that General Mills has overtaken Kellogg is a testament to the success of its strategy in recent years. Earlier, Kellogg used to be at least 10 share points ahead. In 1989, General Mills formed a strategic alliance with Nestlé in hopes of dramatically expanding its international cereal business. Cereal Partners Worldwide (CPW) now boasts more than 40 cereal brands and has operations in over 70 international markets. Nestlé brands include Chocapic and Nesquik. CPW has quickly become the second largest cereal company outside North America.

In 1994, the company cut promotion costs and lowered prices 11 percent on many cereals. Post followed suit and reduced cereal prices by 20 percent, ultimately sending category profitability into a tailspin. In the resulting price wars, General Mills won market share from both Post and Kellogg. However, since that time, total category volume has recorded annual growth of only 1 percent compared with 3 percent five years ago.

In 1997, General Mills spent $570 million acquiring the Chex snack and cereal lines from Ralcorp Holdings. Because of reduced earnings in 1997, General Mills raised cereal prices by 2.6 percent and announced restructuring plans that would close some of its oldest and least efficient plants.[44] Since 1995, General Mills' strategy has been rebuilding market share through line extensions and acquisitions. It has also focused on highlighting the nutritional benefits of its cereals. In March 1998, General Mills announced the launch of organic cereal, the first certified organic cereal from a major manufacturer. Additionally, the company is a big proponent of event marketing. For example, Honey Nut Cheerios awards more than $50,000 in music scholarships to youths annually as well as sponsoring a 30-day music tour called "Honey Nut Cheerios Sound of Soul." A sports enthusiast, General Mills sponsors NASCAR races and spends big on promotions, signing Mark McGwire of the St. Louis Cardinals to promote its Wheaties cereal product.

Appendix 2

Kellogg Company

Originally designed as a special diet for patients, the cold cereal concept evolved into something much larger, ultimately resulting in creation of the Kellogg Company in 1922. The company relied on its heritage as well as an imaginative advertising and new product introduction to spur growth. It promoted its products using a broad mix of devices, including in-store coupons, premiums, cross-brand offers, sweepstakes, and contests. Kellogg sustained its position in the marketing-intensive, heavily advertised cereal category by repeatedly raising prices. Competitors followed suit. Faced with a declining market and price pressures from low-priced competitors, however, Kellogg was forced to cut marketing expenses to maintain market share.

The cold cereal market has come to depend on discounting and repricing.[45] With 80 percent of its worldwide sales derived from cereal, Kellogg is more susceptible to fluctuations in the market than its competition. In an attempt to recapture its market share, the company developed a growth strategy based on a five-point plan: building leadership in product innovation, strengthening the company's seven largest cereal markets, accelerating the growth of its convenience foods business, developing a more focused organization, and continuing to reduce costs.

Post

Post began in 1895 with its first brand of cereal called Postum. Throughout the late 1920s, Post acquired over a dozen companies and expanded its product line to include 60 items. As expected of the #3 company, Post has shown remarkable innovation. Company founder C. W. Post introduced marketing techniques such as extensive advertising, coupons, free samples, product demonstrations, plant tours, and recipe books that are now market standards. Later the company initiated a coupon strategy unlike any the industry had seen: it issued a single coupon redeemable across its entire line of cereals. The maneuver was estimated to save Post $200 million in marketing and promotional costs. Moreover, the company reduced prices in 1996 across its product lines by 20 percent in an attempt to take away market share from Kellogg and General Mills. Today the Post line includes more than 24 well-known brands. The Rule of

Three continues to play out in this industry, and as typical of many #3 companies, Post has lost market share as a result of the fierce battle between Kellogg and General Mills for the top position.

Niche Players

Smaller players such as Quaker Oats, Malt-O-Meal, and Ralcorp offer less expensive alternatives to major brands and fill market gaps. Well known for its hot cereals, Quaker Oats, the fourth largest cold cereal company, is building its cold cereal business with brands such as Cap'n Crunch. Among the few cold cereal companies that have experienced growth in the last few years, Quaker Oats offers innovative packaging and a low-priced option to consumers.

Adopting roughly the same strategy as Quaker Oats, Minnesota-based Malt-O-Meal, Inc., sells discounted hot and cold cereals. Over the last several years, numerous specialty players have performed well because they capitalized on changing social values and the growing demand for "natural and organic" products, for which they charge a premium. Focusing on concerns for health and wellness, small firms such as Hain Foods Group, Whole Food Market, New Energy Naturals, and Natural Nutrition Group have experienced combined market share growth. The largest private label cereal maker, the St. Louis-based Ralcorp Holdings, Inc., however, has recently experienced decreases in sales.

The Soft Contact Lens Market

Competition is intense in the soft contact lens market as companies engage in extensive price cutting, especially among branded products.[46] Innovation and technological advances are considered as the key enablers of competitiveness in this fragmented but consolidating market. The three full-line generalists—Johnson & Johnson, CIBA Vision, and Bausch and Lomb—have a combined market share of 60 percent. Further growth and consolidation are expected in this market.

Vistakon

Vistakon, the vision care subsidiary owned by Johnson & Johnson (J&J), is the leader in the U.S. soft contact lens market, with a 24 percent market share.[47] The company is unique in that its support from a massive health care provider allows it to take advantage of bundling and cross-selling opportunities. In addition, Vistakon has been able to drive volume as the low-cost producer. When Vistakon trailed CIBA Vision and Bausch and Lomb, it became the innovator in the market, introducing in 1987 the weekly disposable lenses Acuvue. It followed with the daily disposable lens in May 1995.[48] J&J took full advantage of its first-to-market strategy by flooding its distribution channels with free samples and undertaking a major TV advertising campaign.

As typical of the #1 player, however, Vistakon has recently played more the role of the fast-follower than innovator—a wise strategy given its new market position. Its core competency is producing disposable lenses; accordingly it has not yet ventured into the production of daily-wear contact lenses. Relying on the size and advertising might of J&J, the company continues to use the Acuvue brand for its bifocal disposable lenses and to take advantage of its dual brand positioning with the Surevue line. It does not hesitate to use discounting when necessary to drive volume. The firm distributes its lenses only in the United States—a major weakness in a globalizing market.

CIBA Vision

CIBA Vision is the #2 player with a 20 percent market share. It entered the contact lens manufacturing business in 1980 when its parent company, Ciba-Geigy, established this line of business as a part of its U.S. pharmaceutical division. Much more innovative than the #1 player, CIBA introduced eye-color-enhancing lenses, soft contact lenses designed exclusively for planned replacement, soft lenses for both farsighted and nearsighted patients, and disposable tinted soft contact lenses.[49]

CIBA Vision's main sources of advantage are its size, scope, and assets turnover efficiency. It derives these from its shared operations with other ophthalmic businesses under the parent company, Ciba-Geigy, which in December 1996 merged with Sandoz Ltd., a major Swiss pharmaceutical company, to form Novartis, one of the world's largest life sciences companies. All CIBA products are marketed under the CIBA Vision umbrella.

CIBA is clearly a volume-driven player that depends on economies of scale and selective cross-subsidization among its various ophthalmic pharmaceutical businesses. The company recently introduced "Lightstream," a breakthrough technology that significantly lowers the cost of product of single-day-use lenses. It recently acquired the former niche player Wesley Jessen VisionCare, Inc., which specialized in cosmetic lenses that change or enhance the wearer's eye color appearance, toric (convex) lenses that correct vision for people with astigmatism, and premium lenses that offer value-added features such as protection from ultraviolet light.[50] CIBA Vision seeks to cut manufacturing costs while producing high volume, especially for its planned replacement and disposable lenses. Its U.S. sales constitute 50 percent of its worldwide totals. CIBA Vision is already available in about 90 countries. The company has a powerful distribution network, both domestically and internationally.

Bausch and Lomb

Bausch and Lomb is the #3 player with a 16 percent share of the U.S. market for soft contact lenses.[51] The first to enter this market with the release of its Softlens contacts in 1971, the company held its first-mover advantage for a while, capitalizing on its three-year head start, name recognition, and marketing strategies. When competitors introduced extended-wear contact lenses and bifocal lenses, Bausch and Lomb was caught off guard and toppled from its #1 position by Johnson & Johnson, which introduced disposable contact lenses. Bausch and Lomb responded to the threat by rapidly expanding its product line to encompass a broader spectrum of lenses.

As a volume-driven player, the company is currently undergoing restructuring efforts to reduce costs and take advantage of economies of scale. It continues to increase its advertising spending and has repackaged some of its products to feature the B&L name more prominently. It offers a diverse array of contact lenses and ancillary products under a common marketing identity; moreover, it has a strong distribution network and good relationships with distributors. Known for its innovation, Bausch and Lomb expanded its presence in eye care through acquisitions in the ophthalmic surgery market and recently announced the latest breakthrough in contact lenses. PureVision is a soft contact lens that is "truly safe to wear to bed."[52] Recent product extensions include a lens that corrects presbyopia and a disposable contact lens for consumers with astigmatism.

Niche Players

Ocular Sciences differentiates itself by focusing on product quality, technological innovation, and channel branding. In the disposable contact lens market, the company's brands include Hydron, Edge, Ultraflex, SmartChoice, Echelon, and Ultra T, but the company also produces private-label lenses. It sells to eye care professionals and about 90 retailers worldwide.[53] Having recently won approval from the Ministry of Health in Japan, the company now markets its products through its selling partner Seiko.

CooperVision is a specialist in high-end premium-priced lenses. Its major line is its Toric lenses that correct astigmatism. Other products include Preference spherical lenses and Natural Touch cosmetic lenses. CooperVision's uniqueness lies in its special material and manufacturing ability to provide high-quality lenses. In 1997, it had margins of approximately 70 percent.[54] The company recently acquired the European firm Aspect Vision, a local leader in disposable, frequent replacement spherical lenses, which come at lower prices but also with fewer features.

Niche player UltraVision is dedicated to the development, manufacturing, and marketing of state-of-the-art specialty contact lens products. Its products—UltraCon and EpiCon—are revolutionary contact lenses developed from the company's proprietary material. The former is for patients with astigmatism; the latter for patients with pathological eye conditions.[55] UltraVision recently acquired several firms to facilitate global growth. These include Igel Companies in the United Kingdom and the contact lens subsidiaries of Alliance Technology and Development Limited in the United Kingdom and Australia.

The Athletic Footwear Market

In the $16 billion global market for athletic footwear, the top three companies—Nike, Adidas, and Reebok—control as much as a 60 percent share.[56] The U.S. market, where the Big 3 claim a 70 percent share, represents almost half of that prize, estimated at $7.5 billion. Nike is, by far, the industry leader, commanding over twice the share of the #2 player Adidas, while Reebok is a distant third.

Nike

In the late 1990s Nike experienced a small drop in its market share, down 2 percent, perhaps as a result of unfavorable press regarding its overseas manufacturing plants, or perhaps attributable to the exit of superstar Michael Jordan from the ranks of professional basketball. Whatever the causes, Nike enjoys an almost universally recognized logo, the "Swoosh," and is able to capitalize on its brand popularity by manufacturing and marketing an entire line of athletic clothing and gear, including skates, hockey sticks, watches, and hats. The company operates its own Niketown stores and channels its products to major retailers, some 19,000 accounts in over 140 countries. In an attempt to grow this market even more, Nike has embarked on a "World Shoe" initiative in developing countries where it can price its shoes in the range of $15 to $40.

Adidas

Adidas has chosen to expand its market share through acquisition and marketing. The company's 1997 acquisition of the French sports equipment company Salomon S.A. added three new brands: Salomon (winter sports equipment), Taylor Made (golf equipment), and Mavic (bicycle components). In addition, Adidas-Salomon AG sponsored the 1998 World Cup in France, calling the industry's attention to this increasingly popular sport. The company now controls approximately 16 percent of the market, a tremendous improvement over the company's condition in 1993 when it was ready to declare bankruptcy.

Reebok

At 11 percent market share, Reebok International, Ltd. is not the most innovative company, as one might expect of the #3 player, but it is diversifying its product lines. In addition to offering the Greg Norman line of clothing and equipment for golfers, Reebok makes the Rockport line of casual and dress shoes, as well as athletic shoes bearing the names of Ralph Lauren and Polo. No match for Nike's deep pockets, Reebok spends only about a third of what its larger competitor allocates to worldwide advertising campaigns.

Niche Players

The specialists claim the remaining 40 percent of this market, each competing in an appropriate niche where it can enjoy strong margins. Based in Westlake, California, K-Swiss manufactures tennis shoes almost exclusively. It has very few models, the "Classic" being by far the most popular. That shoe is made from only three pieces of leather stitched together, sporting five stripes on the side and D-rings for the laces. The company sells to approximately 3,000 accounts, as opposed to most other major athletic footwear companies that have as many as 15,000 clients.

Saucony is a super-nicher with an innovative line of products and a devoted following of satisfied customers, most of them runners. The company's technologically advanced shoes use the "GRID system," a multipatented and innovative mid-sole system with molded strings engineered to ensure the runner's comfort. Its latest model, the 4D Grid, retails for $140.

The athletic footwear industry, for the most part, is growing slowly. Designer brands from Tommy Hilfiger, Ralph Lauren, and DKNY offer some threat to the major players. Fashion trends are largely unpredictable, as exemplified by the recent popularity of retro shoes, such as the Nike Cortez, the Reebok Princess, and the Converse canvas Chuck Taylor All Star model. The remarkable rise of interest in soccer, particularly in the United States, signals an opening for more specialists as well as a possible field for the Big 3 to grow their markets.

The Candy Market

The Big 3 in the candy market in North America include Hershey, Mars, and Nestlé.[57] Together they control 60 percent of the market. Several specialized companies such as LifeSavers, Tootsie Roll, Russell Stover, Brach & Brock, and Favorite Brands have been profitable in serving small niches.[58]

Hershey

Hershey is the #1 player in the North American candy market with a share of approximately 30 percent.[59] For the most part, the company has followed strategies considered optimal for a market leader in the Rule of Three framework: volume focus, market growth emphasis, low costs, and multiple distribution channels.

While remaining focused on its core confectionery businesses, Hershey has increased volume through strategic acquisitions and timely divestitures. It has recently made three major purchases, acquiring in 1988 the Peter Paul Company, thereby surpassing M&M Mars for the lead in the domestic market. This move proved pivotal, as it gave Hershey ten of the top 20 brands in the United States. In 1996, Hershey's made two other acquisitions: Henry Heide, Inc., which allowed Hershey to expand into nonchocolate candies, and Leaf North America, one of Hershey's top competitors. These major acquisitions have been balanced with divestiture of low-volume brands and the sale of noncore pasta and grocery groups.

The company has long-term agreements to manufacture major brands such as Cadbury and Caramello (Cadbury Schweppes plc) and Kit Kat and Rolo (Nestlé SA) in the United States. It has also stimulated market growth by developing new products in both existing and new markets. Some examples include reduced fat (or nofat) candy bars such as Sweet Escapes.[60]

The company has maintained prices in the face of rising raw material costs, but only by reducing the amount of product per package and hedging in the foreign markets. In addition, forward purchasing minimizes the effect of price fluctuations.

Hershey sells its products through numerous distribution channels, including grocery wholesalers, chain grocery stores, candy distributors, mass merchandisers, wholesale clubs and chain drug stores. In 1998, Wal-Mart accounted for approximately 14 percent of Hershey's total net sales.[61]

Mars, Inc.

Mars is the second largest candy maker in the United States, holding approximately a 20 percent share of the market.[62] Its strategy is to challenge the leader by increasing volume and market growth, taking a fast-follower approach to innovation, and reducing costs.

The Mars Company is quite conservative. Unlike Hershey, it does not grow through acquisition because of a company policy to finance all capital expenditures using cash rather than debt. Its main strategy has been the multinational expansion of current brands, quality, and manufacturing efficiency. Most of the product innovation at Mars has come through line extension and a follower strategy. By introducing Promises, for example, Mars followed Hershey and Nestlé into the single-serve chocolates, competing against Kisses and Treasures. The company also introduced a dark chocolate Dove bar in response to Hershey's Symphony.

Though Mars has not always been the leader in product innovations, it has often led the way in the adoption of new manufacturing technologies and techniques. Almost all of the company's 41 worldwide factories run 24 hours a day, seven days a week "at speeds that few competitors could even imagine."[63] Moreover, it operates with 30 percent fewer employees than its closest competitor, producing more candy per employer than any other company. In 1990, Mars' average revenue per employee was $429,000, whereas Hershey averaged only $228,000. Mars' conservatism regarding new products continues to be an obstacle to its challenge-the-leader strategy.

Nestlé

Nestlé currently holds the #1 position in the world in the soluble coffee, soup, and chocolates markets.[64] As the company's fourth largest category, chocolates and confections bring in 15 percent of revenues. A world leader among candy producers, Nestlé is the #3 player in the United States. As such and in keeping with Rule of Three principles, it has established itself as an innovator in the candy market.

With its White Crunch, Nestlé was one of the first companies to introduce white chocolate in a bar form. Such novelties as its Magic Ball (a chocolate covered ball with a Disney toy inside) have helped Nestlé become the leader in that specialty market with a 24.4 percent share.[65] Children's candy and novelty products are branded under the Willie Wonka Candy Company, a division of its subsidiary Sunmark, Inc.[66] The company has pursued many co-branding ventures with the likes of Disney and the National Basketball Association.[67] The firm also has been innovative in product line extensions and packaging—for example, the Treasures brand of bite-size chocolate nuggets and the "Bigger Bag," which weighs 28 ounces.

Specialists

Life Savers, the king of hard candies, is a subsidiary of RJR Nabisco and is the fifth leading marketer and fourth leading advertiser of candy in the United States. It owns Delites, a top brand of diet candy, and GummiSavers, a nonchocolate chewy candy brand.[68]

Brach & Brock, the sixth largest candy marketer in the United States, came about through the acquisition of Brock Candy Company of Chattanooga, Tennessee by the E. J. Brach Corporation of Chicago. The company has become significantly more innovative by transforming itself from a commodity, price-driven business into a branded candy company.

Favorite Brands International Inc. entered the market in 1995. It was originally formed by a group of investors to acquire the caramel and marshmallow businesses from Kraft Foods. It continued to grow in the nonchocolate candy market by acquiring five other candy companies, helping to make the company the seventh largest candy maker in the United States.[69]

With a 76 percent market share, the Russell Stover Company is a leader in the boxed chocolate segment of the candy market. The company acquired Whitman's Chocolate Company in 1993 and has since enjoyed an annual growth of 18 percent. Boxed chocolates, both seasonal and nonseasonal, account for 8 percent of Russell Stover's sales. For years the company has been well known for its licensing agreements for the images of Superman, Snoopy, Bugs Bunny, Elvis, and Barbie, among others. In addition, Russell Stover is credited with creating the heart-shaped box for Valentine's Day candies.

Tootsie Rolls account for 50 percent of the total sales for the company of the same name. The other half comes from a variety of products such as Dots and Junior Ants (which Tootsie Roll acquired from Warner Lambert in 1993).[70] In addition, during the 1980s, the company acquired a number of other firms and was noted for adding "pizzazz" to those companies, primarily through changing the packaging.

The Prepared Baby Food Market

In the United States, the baby food category accounts for about 7 percent of the total $58.7 billion prepared food category.[71] "Baby" food is defined as that for children from infancy to three years, and of all the food included in this category, the "prepared" type accounts for 37 percent. The three major players in the U.S. prepared baby food market are Gerber, Beech-Nut, and Heinz.

Gerber

On the advice of a pediatrician in 1927, Dorothy Gerber and her husband Dan developed the Gerber baby food line at the family's Fremont Canning Company. Having access to the resources of her husband's company, Dorothy was able to establish a national distribution network, which helped put her products in first place in this market. Gerber has held this position for over 70 years.

As befits the #1 company, Gerber has been primarily a follower rather than an innovator, but once it does enter a field, it innovates through brand extension. Gerber has a virtual lock on the wholesale market through which most small and mid-size retailers make their purchases. However, the emphasis on supermarkets has delayed Gerber in moving to other channels as its competitors have done. Approximately 88 percent of all prepared baby food sales are through supermarkets and grocers. Mass merchandisers and wholesale clubs account for a distant 4 percent of total retail sales.

Gerber's pricing strategy seeks to maximize profits in the face of competition from smaller players. There is no competition from private labels, presumably because parents are willing to pay for the peace of mind they get when they buy a nationally recognized product. In the late 1980s, Gerber raised prices an average of 8 percent a year, in contrast to the food price index, which rose only 4.5 percent annually over the same period.[72] Gerber maintains a price premium over Beech-Nut and Heinz in an estimated 72 percent of the products where there is direct competition. For the remaining 28 percent of directly comparable products, Gerber charges the second highest price.

To counter market stagnation, Gerber targets various demographic segments. Introducing Graduates in 1992, Gerber grew the entire baby food market as it cornered a segment in which competition was less fierce in the short term. The company is now targeting specific ethnic segments and senior adults with variations of its traditional Gerber brand. Thus, while the company is not a true product innovator, it can be seen as a segmentation innovator given the manner in which it develops new niches.

Beech-Nut

In 1994, Ralston Purina, Inc. spun off its RalCorp Holdings, the product lines of which included dry cereals and the Beech-Nut line of prepared baby foods (which accounted for 14.5 percent of RalCorp's revenue).[73] This line includes the Special Harvest line of organic baby foods and "Table Time" prepared products, single servings that can be microwaved.

Beech-Nut remains primarily a regional player, with 11 coastal markets accounting for 75 percent of its sales.[74] Under RalCorp, marketing, distribution, and sales have been integrated and manufacturing consolidated to streamline this regionally concentrated supplier. The company is using more targeted print advertising and direct mail programs, having abandoned most of its mass media communications. Recent distribution agreements with ten new retail accounts will help expand Beech-Nut's presence. Exports, particularly to eastern Europe, are also on the rise.[75]

Given the premium pricing strategy followed by Gerber, and the localized profile of Beech-Nut, a period of price stability is advantageous to both players. Beech-Nut has tried to coexist with Gerber by turning to a geographically focused segmentation approach.

Heinz

In 1991, Heinz narrowly edged out Beech-Nut for the #2 position in market share. At that point, Anthony O'Reilly, Heinz's CEO, decided to focus on other endeavors. He cut the advertising and promotion budget by 60 percent, but the company lost over 3 percent of its market share over three years and dropped to the #3 position. Thereafter, the company increased its promotional budget, pumped additional resources into new product development, and acquired a niche player to expand its market share.

Heinz once had the narrowest product line of the Big 3. The

company addressed this problem by launching two new products under the umbrella branding strategy to compete directly with Gerber. Both products were focused on winning loyalty from customers who value low price. Heinz introduced new packaging designed to convey the image of value and quality, and items were priced several cents lower than the comparable Gerber products.

Heinz enjoys strong brand recognition in the United States as a result of its other products such as ketchup. While this national scope provides an advantage over the regional Beech-Nut brand, Heinz has been unable to leverage its distribution breadth against Gerber's virtual lock on the wholesale channel. Wholesalers still tend to favor Gerber products, choosing between Beech-Nut or Heinz as a second line.

Heinz's recovery strategy includes the acquisition of Earth's Best, an organic producer of baby food. While buying market share is not necessarily an innovative solution, the approach does utilize a preferred strategy for a #3 player—namely, horizontal mergers. The acquisition was finalized in 1996, and Heinz continues to narrow the gap between its market position and that of #2 Beech-Nut.[76]

The strategies of Gerber and Heinz are a poor fit with their relative position in the market. Gerber should be a fast-follower rather than an innovator, whereas Heinz exhibits far more market leader tendencies than its #3 position dictates. Only Beech-Nut maintains strategies consistent with its market share, although the company shifts from strategies predicated on its being #2 as it seeks on the one hand to clone Gerber and on the other to challenge it.

Specialists

With Heinz's recent acquisition of Earth's Best, there remains only one significant specialist in this market, Ross Pediatrics. Innovation and segmentation best describe the product development approach of this niche player. Known for its Pedialyte supplement, Ross Pediatrics has entered the baby food drink marketplace with a premium-priced line of 8-ounce, soy-based drinks called Toddler's Best.

The Big Three

The Big Three in U.S. Industries

Accounting/consulting companies
PricewaterhouseCoopers
Arthur Andersen
Ernst & Young

Agriculture equipment makers
John Deere
CNH Global
AGCO

Aircraft engine makers
General Electric
Pratt & Whitney
Rolls-Royce

Airlines
United Airlines
American Airlines
Delta Air Lines

Apparel companies
Levi Strauss
VF Corp.
Jones Apparel Group Inc.

Athletic shoe companies
Nike
Adidas
Reebok

Automation Telematics
OnStar
TeleAid
Wingcast

Baby foods companies
Gerber
Beech-Nut
Heinz

Banks
Citigroup
Bank of America
J.P. Morgan Chase

Battery makers
Duracell
Energizer
Rayovac

Beer companies
Anheuser-Busch
Miller
Coors/Stroh

Brokerage firms
Merrill Lynch
Morgan Stanley Dean Witter
Goldman Sachs Group

Booksellers
Barnes & Noble
Borders
Book-A-Million

Burger chains
McDonald's Corp.
Burger King
Wendy's

Business magazines
Fortune
Forbes
Business Week

Candy makers
Hershey
Mars, Inc.
Nestlé

Car rental agencies
Enterprise
Hertz
ANC

Carpet manufacturers
Shaw Industries
Mohawk
Beaulieu

Cereal companies
General Mills
Kellogg
Post

Chemical companies
E. I. Du Pont de Nemours
Dow Chemical
Monsanto

**Communications equipment
  companies**
Nortel Networks
Cisco
Lucent Technologies

Computer peripherals
Seagate Technologies
EMC Corporation
Quantum

Computer services outsourcing companies
IBM
EDS
CSC

Consumer reporting agencies
Equifax
TransUnion
Experian

Contact lens makers
Vistakon
CibaVision
Bausch & Lomb

Credit card networks
Visa
Mastercard
American Express

Database software companies
Oracle
Informix
Sybase

Discount brokers
Charles Schwab
Fidelity Brokerage Services
Quick & Reilly

Discount Merchandisers
Wal-Mart
Kmart
Target

Disk drive makers
Seagate Technologies
Quantum
Western Digital Corp.

Drugstore chains
Walgreen
CVS
Rite-Aid

Electric shaver companies
Norelco
Remington
Braun

Electronic design automation companies
Cadence Design Systems
Synopsys
Avant!

Fiberglass insulation manufacturers
Owens Corning
Schuller International
CertainTeed

Forest and paper products companies
International Paper
Georgia-Pacific
Weyerhauser

Grain companies
Cargill
ConAgra
AE Staley

Healthcare distribution
McKesson HBOC
Cardinal Health
AmeriSource

Insurance companies
Allstate
State Farm
Farmers' Group

Jeans makers
Levi Strauss
Lee
Wrangler

Learning Centers
Sylvan Learning Centers
Huntington Learning Center
Kumon Math and Reading
  Centers

Logging companies
Mitsubishi
MacMillan-Bloedel
Georgia-Pacific

Long distance carriers
AT&T
MCI/Worldcom
Sprint

Movie theatre chains
United Artists
Loews Cineplex
AMC Entertainment

Office furniture manufacturers
Steelcase
Haworth
Herman Miller

Online travel agencies
Travelocity
Expedia
Preview Travel

Outdoor media companies
Outdoor Systems
Eller
Lamar

Overnight couriers
Federal Express
United Parcel Service
Airborne

PC software makers
Microsoft
Novell/WordPerfect
Lotus

PDAs
Palm
Handspring
Compaq

Petroleum producers
Exxon/Mobil
Texaco
Chevron

Pharmaceutical companies
Merck
Johnson & Johnson
Bristol-Myers Squibb

Pizza chains
Pizza Hut
Domino's
Papa John's

Publishing companies
Time Warner
Hearst Magazines
Conde Nast

Radio station chains
Clear Channel
Hicks/Muse
CBS

Rail freight companies
Union Pacific
CSX
Southern Pacific

Resort operators
Carnival
RCCL
Princess

Securities firms
Morgan Stanley Dean Witter
Merrill Lynch
Goldman Sachs

Security systems makers
Sensormatic
Knowgo
Checkpoint

Soft contact lens makers
Johnson & Johnson
CIBA Vision
Bausch and Lomb

Talent agencies
Creative Artists Agency
International Creative Management
William Morris Agency

Television networks
NBC
ABC
CBS

Textile manufacturing firms
Shaw Industries
Mohawk Industries
Spring Industries

Tobacco companies
Philip Morris
R. J. Reynolds
Universal

Trucking companies
Consolidated Freightways
Yellow Freight System
Roadway Express

Warehouse clubs
Price/Costco
Sam's Club
BJ's Wholesale Club

Web portal companies
Yahoo
AOL
MSN

Waste management companies
Waste Management
Allied Waste Industries
Republic Industries

Wireless carriers
Verizon Wireless
Cingular
AT&T Wireless

The Big Three in Europe and Asia

Australian banks
Westpac
National Australia Bank
St. George Bank

European consumer electronics manufacturers
Philips (Netherlands)
Thomson (France)
Nokia (Finland)

Australian tobacco companies
Philip Morris
WD & HO Wills
Rothmans

European food companies
Unilever (UK. Netherlands)
Nestlé (Switzerland)
BSN Groupe (France)

Australian supermarket chains
Woolworth's
Coles Myer's
Franklins

European power generating equipment manufacturers
Marconi plc (United Kingdom)
Siemens (Germany)
Asea Brown Boveri, Ltd. (Switzerland)

European airlines
British Airways (United Kingdom)
Lufthansa (Germany)
Air France (France)

European semiconductor makers
Philips (Netherlands)
SGS-Thomson (France)
Siemens (Germany)

European appliance makers
Electrolux AB (Sweden)
Bosch-Siemens (Germany)
Whirlpool (United States)

French automakers
Renault
Peugeot
Citroen

French banks
Banque Nationale de Paris
Societe Generale
Credit Lyonnais

French publishing houses
Le Seuil
Grasset
Gallimard

German banks
Deutsche Bank AG
Dresdner Bank AG
Commerzbank AG

German chemical companies
Bayer
BASF
Hoechst

Indian software companies
Wipro
Infosys
Satyam

Japanese automakers
Toyota
Honda
Nissan

Japanese brewers
Kirin
Asahi
Sapporo

Japanese cosmetic companies
Shiseido
Kao
Kanebo

Japanese electronic manufacturers
Matsushita
Sony
Toshiba

Japanese elevator/escalator manufacturers
Toshiba
Hitachi
Mitsubishi

Japanese securities houses
Nomura Securities
Nikko Securities
Daiwa Securities

Japanese shipping companies
Nippon Yusen K.K.
Kawasaki Kisen Kaisha
Mitsui O.S.K. Lines

South Korean automakers
Hyundai
Daewoo
Kia

South Korean chipmakers
Samsung
Hyundai
Goldstar

South Korean consumer electronics companies
Samsung Electronics
Daewoo Electronics
LG Electronics

South Korean shipbuilders
Hyundai Heavy Industries
Daewoo Heavy Industries
Samsung Heavy Industries

Swiss banks
Union Bank
Swiss Bank Corporation
Credit Suisse

Swiss pharmaceutical companies
Ciba-Geigy
Hoffman-La Roche
Sandoz

Truck manufacturers
Iveco
Mercedes-Benz
Renault-Volvo

U.K. banks
HSBC
Barclays
Lloyd's TSB

U.K. bookmakers and betting parlors
Coral
Ladbrokes
William Hill

U.K. candy producers
Mars
Nestle
Cadbury

U.K. cement companies
Circle
Portland
Castle

U.K. grocery retailers
Sainsbury
Tesco
Argyll (owns Safeway in U.S)

U.K. local bus companies
Stagecoach
Aniva
First Group

U.K. travel groups
Thomson
Airtours
Owners Abroad

The Global Big Three

Advertising agencies
Publicis Groupe SA ADS
Omnicom Group Inc.
Interpublic GR OF COS

Aerospace companies
Boeing Co
United Technologies Corp.
Lockheed Martin Corp

Airline alliances
Star Alliance
One World Alliance
Sky Team

Aluminum producers
Alcoa Inc
Pechiney S.A. ADR
Alcan Inc.

Appliance makers
GE
Whirlpool
Electrolux

Athletic footwear makers
Nike
Adidas
Reebok

Beverage companies
Coca-Cola
Pepsi
Diageo

Biotechnology companies
Monsanto Co.
Amgen Inc.
Quest Diagnostics Inc.

Coal companies
Massey Energy Co.
Consol Energy Inc.
Arch Coal Inc.

Cosmetics companies
Procter & Gamble Co.
L'Oreal
Unilever

Consumer electronics manufac-turers
Matsushita Electric Ind. Co.
Sony Corp.
Koninklijke Philips Elec.

Cruise lines
Carnival
Royal Caribbean
Princess

Custodial banks
Bank of New York
Chase Manhattan
State Street

Defense contractors
Lockheed Martin Corp.
Boeing Co.
BAE Systems

Engineering & construction companies
Bechtel
Raytheon
Stone and Webster

Entertainment producers
Viacom Inc.
Fox Entertainment Group
Metro-Goldwyn-Mayer Inc.

Food producers
Unilever N.V.
ConAgra Foods
IBP Inc.

Forest products companies
Georgia-Pacific CP
Weyerhaeuser Co.
Willamette Industries

Health care insurers
Aetna Inc.
United Health Group Inc.
Cigna Corp.

Hotel chains
Marriott
Hilton
Sheraton

Household products companies, durable
Newell Rubbermaid Inc.
Fortune Brands Inc.
Spring Industries Inc.

Household products companies, non-durable
Procter & Gamble Co.
Kimberly Clark Corp.
Colgate-Palmolive Co.

Insurance companies, full line
AXA ADS
American International Group
Aegon NV

Insurance companies, property & casualty
Allstate Corp.
Loews Corp.
CAN Financial Corp.

Investment banks
Morgan Stanley
Merrill Lynch
Goldman Sachs

Medical supply companies
Abbott Laboratories
Baxter International Inc.
Becton, Dickinson & Co.

Mining companies
BHP LTD
Rio Tinto plc ADR
Cameco Corp.

Mobile phone manufacturers
Ericsson
Nokia
Motorola

Music publishers
Warner EMI
Sony
BMG

Office equipment companies
Cannon Inc.
Xerox Corp.
Ikon Office Solutions

PBX equipment manufacturers
Lucent
Northern Telecom
Siemens/Rolm

Personal computer companies
Compaq
Dell
HP

Power plant companies
ABB Alstom
General Electric
Siemens

Railroads
Union Pacific Corp.
Canadian Pacific Ltd.
Burlington & Santa Fe

Semiconductor manufacturers
Intel Corp.
Texas Instruments Inc.
Applied Materials Inc.

Shipbuilders
Todd Shipyards Corp.
Anangel-Amer Shipbuilding
Conrad Industries Inc.

Steel companies
Corus Group plc
Pohang Iron & Steel ADS
USX-U.S. Steel Group

Tire manufacturers
Goodyear
Michelin
Bridgestone

Tobacco companies
Philip Morris
Japan Tobacco
British American Tobacco

Toy makers
Mattel Inc.
Hasbro Inc.
Electronic Arts Inc.

Notes

Introduction. The Rule of Three:
What It Is and How It Works

1. See, for example, Robert D. Buzzell, "Are There Natural Market Structures?" *Journal of Marketing*, 1981; and Michael E. Porter, *Competitive Strategy: Techniques for Analyzing Industries and Competitors* (New York: Free Press, 1980).

1. Four Mechanisms for Increasing Efficiency

1. United States v. Von's Grocery Co. 384 U.S. 270 no. 303, March 22, 1966.
2. "Socket to Them," *Economist,* November 7, 1992, p. 74.
3. Ralinda Young Lurie, "The World VCR Industry," Harvard Business School Case 9-387-098, January 23, 1990.
4. http://ccnga.uwaterloo.ca/~jscouria/GSM/gsmreport.html
5. www.gsmworld.com/about/history_page16.html
6. http://www.gsmworld.com/membership/ass_sub_stats.html
7. Universal Wireless Communications at www.uwcc.org. See also CDMA Worldwide at cdg.org.
8. http://fbox.vt.edu.10021/J/jorice/summary.htm
9. This observation was made by Robert Kahn in his presentation entitled "Building Information Highways" at the Business Week-sponsored conference "Information Highways: Linking America for Interactive Communications," September 11–12, 1991 (transcript available from *Journal Graphics*).

10. John Naughton, *A Brief History of the Future: From Radio Days to Internet Years in a Lifetime* (Woodstock, N.Y.: Overlook Press, 2000).

11. "Railroads in the Age of Regulation, 1900–1980," *Encyclopedia of American Business History and Biography,* ed. Keith L. Bryant, Jr. (New York: Facts On File Publications, 1998).

12. Fay Hansen, "Global Mergers & Acquisitions Explode," *Business Credit,* June 2000, pp. 22–25.

13. Ibid.

14. Michael Porter, who cites the profusion of competitors as a contributing force in the heightened competitive intensity of the Japanese market. See *The Competitive Advantage of Nations* (New York: Free Press, 1990).

15. Till Vestring, "Japan's New Wave of M&A," *Asian Wall Street Journal,* May 18, 2000, p. 8.

16. "Cross-Border Mergers," *The Economist,* October 5, 2000.

17. David Wessel, "Cross-Border Mergers Soared in 1999; Most Deals Were Struck by Western Europeans; Asia Has Started to Catch Up," *Asian Wall Street Journal,* July 20, 2000, p. 24.

18. Data for all three tables are taken from www.mergerstat.com.

19. G. Pascal Zachary, "Big Bundles: Consolidation Sweeps the Software Industry," *Wall Street Journal,* March 23, 1994, p. A1.

20. "Airline Industry," *The Columbia Encyclopedia,* ed. Paul Lagassé, 6th ed. (New York: Columbia University Press, 2000), p. 43.

21. Ibid.

22. "Civil Aeronautics Board," Microsoft® Encarta® Online Encyclopedia 2000. http://encarta.msn.com © 1997–2000 Microsoft Corporation. All rights reserved.

23. "Airline Industry," *Columbia Encyclopedia,* p. 43.

24. William M. Leary, ed., "The Airline Industry: Introduction," *Encyclopedia of American Business History and Biography* (New York: Facts on File, 1992).

25. Cynthia Johnson, "Airline Industry," Hoover's Online.

26. Wendy Zellner et al., "How Many Airlines Will Stay Aloft?" *Business Week,* June 19, 2000, p. 50.

27. Information in this section is based on Maryellen Brown, "The Pharmaceutical Industry—An Exception No More?" unpub-

lished paper presented for course requirements for MBA degree at Bentley College, Waltham, Mass. Other sources include: "Pharmaceuticals: Manufacturing Industry Trade Outlook for 2000," *Biomedical Market Newsletter,* May 31, 2000 (an edited version of U.S. Dept. of Commerce version from May 2000 study); Fortune 500 Global 500 list, available at www.fortune.com; Pfizer Web site, available at www.pfizer.com; David Noonan, "Why Drugs Cost So Much," *Newsweek,* September 25, 2000; Adam Marcus, "Drug Ad Spending Surging," *Health-SCOUT,* September 21, 2000; Pharmaceutical Research and Manufacturers of America, Publications, available at www.nhrma.org; George M. Taber, "Remaking an Industry: Drugmakers Have an Urge to Merge as They Try to Get Their Profits Back Up," *Time,* September 4, 1995; Farah Kostreski, "Drug Company Megamerger," *Family Practice News,* March 1, 2000; Diane Hamilton, "Glaxo, SmithKline Share Plunge after Merger Fails," *Naples News,* February 24, 1998; "How Increased Competition from Generic Drugs Has Affected Prices and Returns in the Pharmaceutical Industry," Congressional Budget Office, Washington, D.C., July 1998, available at www.cbo.gov; "Pricing and Competition in the Pharmaceutical Market," Congressional Budget Office, Washington, D.C., July 1998, available at www.cbo.gov.

28. "Concentrating on the Core," *Med Ad News,* September 1, 2000.
29. This section is extracted from Shaker A. Zahra and Rajendra S. Sisodia, "Surviving Industry Shakeouts," *Handbook of Business Strategy* (New York: Faulkner & Gray, 1997).
30. This process has been referred to as "informationalizing" the business. See Stan Davis and Bill Davidson, *2020 Vision* (New York: Simon & Schuster, 1992). Also, many firms have achieved breakthrough improvements in efficiency and thus competitiveness by "reengineering" their core business processes. Such firms often raise the performance plateau in their industry by an order of magnitude, forcing competitors either to emulate them or to exit the industry. See Michael Hammer and James Champy, *Reengineering the Corporation* (New York: Harper Business Press, 1993).
31. This is a general tendency: multiple shakeouts eventually leave

an industry with a small number of main players and a cast of supporting, specialized companies—the classic Rule of Three structure.

2. Where Three Is Not a Crowd

1. Cited in "Face Value: Putting America on Wheels," *Economist,* December 25, 1999, p. 82.
2. This section is based on the following sources: "The Automobile Industry," *Encyclopedia of American Business History and Biography* (New York: Facts on File Publications, 1998); Alan K. Binder, "The GM Story: From Near Bankruptcy to Global Powerhouse," *Ward's Auto World*, May 2000, p. 154; David C. Smith, "Bumpy Ride into the 21st Century," *Ward's Auto World,* January 2000, p. 92; "1914: Putting America on Wheels," *The Economist,* December 31, 1999, p. 82; Meryl Davids, "Henry Ford (1863–1947): Loving the Line," *The Journal of Business Strategy,* September/October 1999, p. 29.
3. David A. Hounshell, *From the American System to Mass Production 1800–1932: The Development of Manufacturing Technology in the United States* (Baltimore: Johns Hopkins University Press, 1984).
4. *Hoover's Handbook of American Business 1995* (Austin: Hoover's Business Press, 1996).
5. Charles Burck, "Ford's Mr. Turnaround: We Have More To Do," *Fortune*, March 4, 1985, p. 83.
6. Steven Klepper and Elizabeth Graddy, "The Evolution of New Industries and the Determinants of Market Structure," *The Rand Journal of Economics,* 21 (Spring 1990), p. 1.
7. Rob Ericson, MBA candidate at George Mason University, unpublished course paper. See also Office of the Secretary of Defense, Department of Defense Procurement, The Top 100 Home Page (web1.whs.osd.mil/peidhome/protrend/prochist/actions.htm), 1996; Office of the Assistant Secretary of Defense (Public Affairs), "DoD Completes Review of Raytheon-Hughes," October 2, 1997; *Electronic News* (1991), 43.2160, March 24, 1997; Department of Justice, Statement of L. Klein Joel, assistant attorney general, antitrust division, U.S. Senate,

July 24, 1997; Charles V. Bagli, "Two Giants Join a Merger Parade in Arms Industry," *New York Times,* July 4, 1997.

8. CNH Global, B.V., corporate press release, November 24, 1999.

9. CNH Global, B.V., "About CNH," "Multiple Brand," and "Multiple Distribution Strategy," available from http://www.cnh.com/about/brands.html.

10. Douglas Frantz, "Secret Partners: The Unraveling of a Conspiracy," *New York Times,* October 8, 2000, p. 1.

11. Cathy Anterasian, John L. Graham, and R. Bruce Money, "Are U.S. Managers Superstitious about Market Share?" *Sloan Management Review* 37:4 (June 22, 1996): 67.

12. David M. Szymanski, Sundar G. Bharadwaj, and P. Rajan Varadarajan, "An Analysis of the Market Share-Profitability Relationship," *Journal of Marketing* 57:3 (1993): 1.

13. Ibid.

14. Ibid.

15. John A. Howard and Jagdish N. Sheth, *The Theory of Buyer Behavior* (New York: John Wiley and Sons, 1969).

3. Specialists and Generalists

1. Jacques Chevron, "Do You Know How Flexible Your Brand Is?" *Brandweek*, July 17, 2000, p. 28.

2. Ming-Jer Chen and Donald C. Hambrick, "Speed, Stealth, and Selective Attack: How Small Firms Differ from Large Firms in Competitive Behavior," *Academy of Management Journal,* 38:2 (April 1995): 453.

3. Shlomo Maital, "Tales of Scale and Scope," *Barron's,* February 13, 1995, p. 54.

4. "CE Suppliers Get Report Cards," *Dealerscope,* March 2000.

5. The original divisions of General Motors were Chevrolet, Pontiac, Oldsmobile, Buick, Cadillac, and, later, GMC. Saturn, Saab, Vauxhall, Hummer, and Opel were added through new business ventures and acquisitions. GM has other affiliations with Isuzu and Suzuki, as well as numerous nonautomotive ventures. In December 2000, GM decided to close down its famed Oldsmobile line, an announcement that for many market watchers is another sign of trouble at the world's largest

automaker. At the same time the company announced that it would lay off some 15,000 workers.

6. This argument is based on "Tough as Nails: Home Depot Raises the Ante, Targets Mom-and-Pop Rivals," *Wall Street Journal,* January 25, 1999, p. A1.

7. Cynthia Bates, "The Black & Decker Corporation: Household Products Group (A)," Harvard Business School case no. 9-587-057.

8. George Pitcher, "Consumer Brands Cull Makes Room for Global Brands," *Marketing Week,* November 4, 1999, p. 23.

9. Jagdish N. Sheth and Rajendra S. Sisodia, "Feeling the Heat: Making Marketing More Productive," *Marketing Management,* American Management Association, pt. 1, vol. 4, no. 2 (Fall 1995): 8–23.

10. David C. Court and Mark G. Leiter, "Brand Leverage," *The McKinsey Quarterly,* no. 2 (1999): 100.

11. "Automotive Megamergers Augur Changing Role for Suppliers," *Manufacturing Engineering,* March 1999, p. 20.

4. The Ditch

1. Steve Cocheo, "Midsize Squeeze," *ABA Banking Journal,* June 1998, pp. 36–45.

2. Robert La Franco, "Loudspeaker Envy: Sidney Harman Would Be Enjoying His 80s More Were It Not for Amar Bose," *Forbes,* August 9, 1999, p. 68.

3. Melinda Fulmer, "Noah's Bagel Seeks Bankruptcy Protection; 74 Stores Closed," *Los Angeles Times,* April 28, 2000, p. C2.

4. Roxanna Guilford, "Retail Failure and Its Far-Reaching Fallout," *Apparel Industry Magazine,* January 2000, pp. 52–56.

5. James A. White, "London Fog Industries Seeks Protection Under Chapter 11 of Bankruptcy Code," *Wall Street Journal,* September 28, 1999, p. A6.

6. David Ignatius, "J. Peterman's Shattered Dreams," *Washington Post,* September 12, 1999, p. B7.

7. Amy Gilroy, "Whistler Files Chap. 11, Will Focus on Radar," *Twice,* June 21, 1999, pp. 46–47.

8. Bruce Orwall, "Carmike Cinemas Files for Chapter 11 In Wake of Growth of 'Megaplex' Theaters," *Wall Street Journal,* August 9, 2000, p. B7.

9. Jim Milliot, "Scaled-down Crown Books Emerges From Bankruptcy," *Publishers Weekly,* November 22, 1999, p. 9.

10. Martin Sikora, "Scouring for Pearls in Bankruptcies," *Mergers & Acquisitions,* 35:4 (April 2000): 6–9.

11. Ibid.

12. Emily Thornton, "Can This Carmaker Stop Its Skid?" *Business Week,* March 23, 1998, p. 23; "Mitsubishi Runs Out of Gas," *Economist,* March 25, 2000, p. 68; Alisa Priddle, "A Marriage of Convenience," *Ward's Auto World,* May 2000, pp. 73–74.

13. Michael Chazin, "In the Shadow of Industry Giants," *Upholstery Design and Manufacturing,* September 1997, pp. 12–16.

14. David Kirkpatrick, "The Second Coming of Apple," *Fortune,* November 9, 1998, pp. 86–92.

15. Hillary Rosner, "Acer America: Trying Desperately to Get Off 'Tier Two'," *MC Technology Marketing Intelligence,* April 1998, pp. 42–45.

16. Ibid.

17. Tobi Elkin, "Acer Sets Doubled Budget to Support Internet Push," *Advertising Age,* January 10, 2000, p. 44.

18. "Kodak Develops a Battery Strategy," *Discount Merchandiser,* August 1999, p. 64.

19. William M. Bulkeley, "Unisys, Back from the Edge, Stresses Service, Comfort," *Wall Street Journal,* April 22, 1999, p. B4.

20. "The Car Man Who Says No," *Economist,* August 5, 2000, p. 64.

21. Emily Thornton and Kathleen Kerwin, "Honda: Can the Company Go It Alone?" *Business Week,* July 5, 1999, p. 42.

22. Julie Candler, "Woman Car Buyer—Don't Call Her a Niche Anymore," *Advertising Age,* January 21, 1991, p. S8.

5. Globalization and the Rule of Three

1. Thomas A. Stewart, "Getting Real about Going Global: What's Fizz? What's Fizzle?" *Fortune,* February 15, 1999, pp. 170–72.

2. Kenichi Ohmae, *Triad Power: The Coming Shape of Global Competition* (New York: Free Press, 1985).

3. "Foreign Investment in Latin America Up 32%," *Los Angeles Times,* February 2, 2000, p. C4.

4. Brendan M. Case, "Mexico Airlines a Potential Prize: Privati-

zation Expected to Catch Interest of American Carriers," *Dallas Morning News,* October 8, 1999, p. 1D.

5. Stewart, p. 170.

6. Daniel Yergin and Joseph Stanislaw, *The Commanding Heights: The Battle Between Government and the Marketplace That Is Remaking the Modern World* (New York: Simon & Schuster, 1998).

7. Janet Guyon, "Europe's New Capitalists," *Fortune,* February 15, 1999, p. 104.

8. Craig Karmin, "The Global Shareholder: In the '90s, the World Discovered the Stock Market—and Capitalism Was Redefined," *Wall Street Journal,* May 8, 2000, p. R4. Karmin cites the following statistics from Morgan Stanley Capital International:

Market	*2/28/90*	*4/28/00*
United States	$2,839	$17,006
Japan	3,525	4,431
United Kingdom	784	2,776
Germany	353	1,506
France	316	1,442
Canada	239	817
Italy	165	801
Hong Kong	81	341
All-Country World Index	$16,088*	$35,249

*Figure is for 9/29/95, the earliest available.
Note: The World Index, which focuses on the largest, liquid, and open markets, included 45 countries on 9/29/95 and 48 countries on 4/28/00.

9. Gregg Easterbrook, "Who's Afraid of Globalization?" *Wall Street Journal,* April 14, 2000, p. A18.

10. Gail Edmondson, "See the World, Erase Its Borders," *Business Week,* August 28, 2000, pp. 113–14.

11. Ibid. Edmondson cites data from Standard & Poor's.

12. Anthony Bianco, "The Enduring Corporation," *Business Week,* August 28, 2000, pp. 198–204.

13. Stephen D. Moore, "Germany's Once-Mighty Drug Industry

Becomes an Also-Ran on Global Market," *Wall Street Journal,* January 10, 2000, p. A18.

14. Ibid.

15. Media General Financial Services.

16. "Electrolux Faces Battle in Tough Appliance Market," *Los Angeles Times,* March 12, 1986, p. 2.

17. Zachary Schiller, "Turning Up the Heat in the Kitchen—Mergers Have Given Four Companies 80% of the Major Appliance Business—and the Competition is Scorching," *Business Week,* August 4, 1986, p. 76.

18. Lois Therrien, "Raytheon May Find Itself on the Defensive," *Business Week,* May 26, 1986, p. 72; Subrata N. Chakravarty, "The Limits of Synergy," *Forbes,* October 15, 1990, p. 38; Michael E. Knell, "Raytheon Buys Appliance Maker," *Boston Herald,* October 1, 1994, p. 1; Chris Reidy, "Raytheon's Amana Unveils 'Status Symbol' Refrigerator," *Boston Globe,* May 16, 1996, p. 67; Joann Muller, "Raytheon Completes Deal for Appliance Unit," *Boston Globe,* September 11, 1997, p. D3.

19. Robert Johnson and Matthew Winkler, "Venture Is Set by Whirlpool and N.V. Philips—Firms' Accord Will Create Major Appliance Seller With $6 Billion Volume," *Wall Street Journal,* August 19, 1988.

20. Joe Jancsurak, "Holistic Strategy Pays Off," *Appliance Manufacturer* 43:2 (February 1995): 17.

21. Joe Jancsurak, "Big Plans for Europe's Big Three," *Appliance Manufacturer,* 43:4 (April 1995): 26.

22. Greg Steinmetz and Carl Quintanilla, "Tough Target: Whirlpool Expected Easy Going in Europe, and It Got a Big Shock—It Found Competition Harsh As Local Appliance Firms Raised Their Efficiency—A Problem with Its Name," *Wall Street Journal,* April 10, 1998, p. A1.

23. Patricia Callahan and Kara Scannell, "Maytag Discusses Acquisition with Three Firms—No Takeover Deals Are on the Table Yet after String of Weak Quarters," *Wall Street Journal,* August 25, 2000, p. B4.

24. Likewise, other French companies such as Groupe Schneider (now Schneider Electric SA) and Alcatel were the first to trigger globalization in their industries.

25. Robert Ball, "The Michelin Man Rolls into Akron's Backyard," *Fortune,* December 1974, p. 138.
26. Richard Sandomir, "A Turn in Tires?" *Financial World,* March 1, 1981, p. 22.
27. Lad Kuzela, "The Rise of the Mega Managers," *Industry Week,* November 24, 1986, p. 37.
28. Zachary Schiller, "Goodyear Feels the Heat," *Business Week,* March 7, 1988, p. 26; "Wheels within Wheels," *Economist,* March 12, 1988, p. 62.
29. "The Tire Industry's Costly Obsession with Size," *Economist,* June 8, 1991, pp. 65–66.
30. Ibid., p. 65.

6. Strategies for Generalists

1. "Discount Stores Marked by Dominance, Growth," *Chain Store Age,* August 2000.
2. Robert H. Hayes and David M. Upton, "Operations-Based Strategy," *California Management Review,* 40:4 (Summer 1998), pp. 8–25.
3. Laura Liebeck, "Déjà Vu: Kmart to Remake Itself," *Discount Store News*, September 5, 1994, p. 1.
4. Mark Cecil, "Troubled Kmart Should Emulate Its Peers, Analysts Say," *Mergers & Acquisitions Report,* August 7, 2000, p. 6.
5. Hillary Chura, "Marketers of the Century: Anheuser-Busch," *Advertising Age,* December 13, 1999.
6. Anheuser-Busch Company press release, www.anheuser-busch.com/news/volume2000.html.
7. Theodore Levitt, "Innovative Imitation," *Harvard Business Review,* September–October, 1966, pp. 63–70.
8. Peter F. Drucker, "Entrepreneurial Strategies," *California Management Review,* 27:2 (Winter 1985): 9–26.
9. Venkatesh Shankar, Gregory S. Carpenter, and Lakshman Krishnamurthi, "The Advantages of Entry in the Growth Stage of the Product Life Cycle: An Empirical Analysis," *Journal of Marketing Research,* 36:2 (May 1999): pp. 269–76.
10. Peter N. Golder and Gerard J. Tellis, "Pioneer Advantage: Marketing Logic or Marketing Legend?" *Journal of Marketing Research,* May 1993, pp. 158–70.

11. Robert D. Buzzell and Bradley T. Gale, *The PIMS Principles: Linking Strategy to Performance* (New York: Free Press, 1987). See especially chapter 9, "Strategies for Market Leaders and Followers."

12. Lisa Gibbs, "Carnival vs. Royal Caribbean," *Money,* 29:4 (April 2000): 56A-B.

13. Dean Foust, "Now, Coke Is No Longer 'It'," *Business Week,* February 28, 2000.

14. Peter Drucker, as quoted in R. Lenzner & S. S. Johnson, "Seeing Things as They Really Are," *Forbes,* March 10, 1997, 159:5, pp. 122–128.

15. Roy S. Johnson, "Lowe's Borrows the Blueprint," *Fortune,* November 23, 1998, pp. 212–19.

16. Brett C. Smith, "Ford's Consumer-Based Strategy," *Automotive Manufacturing & Production,* August 1999, p. 18.

17. James P. Miller, "Venerable, Popular Fruit of the Loom Seeks Chapter 11; Bankruptcy-Court Filing Tied To Operational Foul-Ups and a Heavy Debt Load," *Wall Street Journal,* December 30, 1999, pp. A3, A4; Suzette Hill, "Fruit of the Loom: So Fruit Isn't That Healthy After All," *Apparel Industry Magazine,* 61:6 (June 2000): 54.

18. Johnson, "Lowe's Borrows the Blueprint," pp. 212–19.

19. Gerry Khermouch, "New Brands Help, but Miller Needs to Fix Its Core Brands, Execs Say," *Brandweek,* February 15, 1999.

20. Laura Liebeck, "Vendors Brew Up Holiday Batch," *Discount Store News,* November 23, 1998, 37:22, pp 23–24.

7. Strategies for Specialists

1. Norihiko Shirouzu, "High-Tech Hotbed for Car Makers: Lowly Mirror," *Wall Street Journal,* August 25, 2000, p. B1.

2. Robert McGarvey, "Making Out," *Upside,* 12:2 (February 2000): 134–142.

3. JoAnn Greco, "Retailing's Rule Breakers," *Journal of Business Strategy,* 18:2 (March/April 1997): 28–33.

4. Ibid.

5. Charles Mann, "Volume Business," *Inc.,* June 17, 1997, pp. 54–61.

6. Kelly Barron, "Company at a Crossroads: Does Reclining

Mean Declining? La-Z-Boy Hopes Not," *Forbes,* January 25, 1999, p. 60.

7. Chandrani Ghosh, "Plugged In: What's Different about a Phone Service Pitched to Immigrants? Just the Pitching," *Forbes,* April 5, 1999, p. 70.

8. Kate Berry, "Niche Players: Your Next Challenge," *Trustee,* July/August 1998, pp. 27–28.

9. Jonathan Eig, "Science and Sweat: Gatorade's Formula for Staying on Top," *Wall Street Journal,* May 5, 2000, p. A1; Debbie Howell, "Gatorade vs. the Beverage Giants: Going Head to Head in Sports Drinks," *Discount Store News,* February 7, 2000, p. 58; Gerry Khermouch, "Quaker Sets Gatorade Energy Drink," *Brandweek,* November 15, 1999, p. 6.

10. Debby Stankevich, "Writing Its Own History," *Discount Merchandiser,* March 1999, p. 30.

11. Seth Lubove and Anne Linsmayer, "Mom and POPs Thrive . . . : A Shakeout Was Supposed to Thin the Ranks of Internet Providers. So How Come Thousands of Little Ones Are Proliferating?" *Forbes*, February 22, 1999, p. 120.

12. Carol Casper, "In the Shadow of the Giants," *Restaurant Business,* December 1, 1997, pp. 41–48.

13. Robert McGarvey, "Profiting in the Niches," *Upside,* May 2000, p. 237.

14. Leslie Earnets, "Struggling HomeBase Taps New CEO in Bid for Turnaround," *Los Angeles Times,* March 4, 2000, p. C1.

15. "Bradlees Braces for Battle," *Chain Store Age,* 76:4 (April 2000): 39–41.

8. The Disruption of Markets

1. Erick Schonfeld, "The Little (Jet) Engine That Could," *Fortune,* July 24, 2000, pp. 132–42.

2. Ibid.

3. "Eclipse Aviation Corporation Secures an Additional $65 Million to Fund Continued Development of Next-Generation Jet," Business Wire, December 4, 2000.

4. Clayton M. Christensen, *The Innovator's Dilemma: When New Technologies Cause Great Firms to Fail* (Boston: Harvard Business School Publishing, 1997), p. xii.

5. Ibid., pp. xvii–xxiv.

6. This discussion is based on the following sources: "Digital Watches—Bringing Watchmaking Back to the U.S.," *Business Week,* October 27, 1975, p. 78; "Seiko's Smash—The Quartz Watch Overwhelms the Industry," *Business Week,* June 5, 1978, p. 86; "Japanese Heat on the Watch Industry: Why Consumer Products Lag at Texas Instruments," *Business Week,* May 5, 1980, p. 92; "Japan: Taking on the Swiss in Luxury Watches/Switzerland: The Top Watchmakers May Be Synchronizing," *Business Week,* June 15, 1981, p. 49; "Watches: What Are the Swiss Doing Wrong?" *Financial Times* (London), August 31, 1981, p. 23; "Price Wars and a Glut Have the World's Watchmakers in Chaos: 'Can Timex Take a Licking and Keep on Ticking'?" *Business Week,* February 20, 1984, p. 5; David S. Landes, "Time Runs Out for the Swiss," *Across the Board,* January 1984, p. 46; Laura Pilarski and Andrea Gabor, "A Last-Minute Comeback for Swiss Watchmakers," *Business Week,* November 26, 1984, p. 139; "Swatch: Ambitious," *The Economist,* April 18, 1992, p. 74; Margaret Studer, "Switzerland's Luxury-Watch Industry Continues to Defy Economic Downturn, *Wall Street Journal,* August 10, 1992, p. A5F; Ann Williams, "A Brief History of Time," *Asian Business,* December 1, 1998, p. 62.

7. Charged Coupled Device (CCD) cameras had a maximum resolution of 6 million pixels per square inch. The new Foveon and Kodak sensors are both capable of a resolution of 16.8 million pixels a square inch—double that of conventional film. The big difference is the simplicity and potentially huge cost advantage of CMOS (complementary metal-oxide semiconductor) technology.

8. John Teresko, "Kodak's New Image," *Industry Week,* July 17, 2000, pp. 38–44; John Markoff, "Low-Price, Highly Ambitious Digital Chip," *New York Times,* September 11, 2000.

9. "Shades of Hype," *Economist,* June 17, 2000, p. 62; Deborah Solomon, "Could Linux Outdo Windows? Web Sites, Manufacturers Turn to Low-Cost Upstart," *USA Today,* March 9, 2000, p. 1B.

10. John Carey, "The Genome Gold Rush," *Business Week,* June 12, 2000.

11. Ibid.

12. Ellen Licking, "A Pharma Star Is Born?" *Business Week,* September 25, 2000.

13. Heather Timmons, "The Chase to Become a Financial Supermarket," *Business Week,* September 25, 2000, p. 42.

14. Lou Pavia, "The Top Ten Trends in Managed Care," *Trustee,* June 1998, pp. 24–26.

15. Jamie Budzick, "The Race for Regulation," *Managed Healthcare,* September 1998, pp. 20–23.

16. "Dangerous Liaisons," *Economist,* July 8, 2000, pp. 61–62.

17. Mark Mitchell, "Nothing But Air," *Far Eastern Economic Review,* May 4, 2000, p. 21.

18. Ian Katz, "Shakeout in the Latin Skies," *Business Week,* February 28, 2000; p. 42.

19. Michael K. Evans, "It's Time for Real Airline Deregulation," *Industry Week,* May 17, 1999, p. 84.

20. Angela Shannon, "Panty Hose Maker Hatches Plan to Revive L'eggs," *Star-Ledger* (Newark), January 12, 1997; Linda Petersen, "Shed the Egg, Spare the Image," *Brandweek,* July 7, 1991, p. 9; Carol E. Curtis, "Nothing Beats a Great Pair of L'eggs," *Forbes,* September 29, 1980, p. 72.

21. Jerry Edgerton, "Pay Less for Luxury," *Money,* September 2000, pp. 143–44.

22. Steve Dwyer, "The Right Prescription for Maturing Boomers," *Prepared Foods,* February 1, 1997, p. 12.

23. Eugenie Allen, "Pardon Our Appearance," *New York Times,* April 21, 1999, p. 23.

24. Jagdish N. Sheth and Rajendra S. Sisodia, "Outsourcing Comes Home," *Wall Street Journal,* June 28, 1999, p. A26.

25. Alexander Garrett, "Work: Dress (Down) for Success: The Office Suit Has Had Its Day," *Observer,* May 7, 2000, p. 16; Davan Maharaj, "More Firms Giving Workers a Dressing-Down They Like," *Los Angeles Times,* April 30, 2000, p. C-1; Dominic Rushe, "Death of Suit Leaves Retailers in Mourning Again," *Sunday London Times,* October 10, 1999, p. 12; Janet Adamy, "Rental Suits Some to a T-shirt: Formal Business Attire May Be Going the Way of the Tuxedo," *News & Observer* (Raleigh, N.C.), March 29, 2000, p. D1; Louise Chunn, "Real Lives: When Mr Suit Becomes Mr Corporate Casual," *The Independent,* October 6, 1996, p. 3.

26. Patricia Wen, "The Right Fit Casual Dress Doesn't Suit All Workers," *Boston Globe,* July 31, 2000, p. B6.

27. Mike Duff, "Men's Wearhouse Adds Additional Layers with Expanded Casual Line, New Formalwear," *Discount Store News,* April 3, 2000, pp. 3, 45.

28. Malcolm Gladwell, *The Tipping Point: How Little Things Can make a Big Difference* (Boston: Little, Brown, 2000), pp. 3–5.

29. www.vcapital.com.

30. Steven Syre and Charles Stein, "As Nortel Networks Races On, Lucent Struggles to Catch Up," *Boston Globe,* July 28, 2000, p. C1.

31. Alec Appelbaum, "How Sycamore Aims to Stay Hot," *SmartMoney.com,* June 7, 2000.

Appendix 1. A Brief History of Mergers in the United States

1. Andrei Shleifer and Robert W. Vishny, "The Takeover Wave of the 1980s," *Science,* August 17, 1990, p. 745.

Appendix 2. Market Snapshots

1. This discussion is based on a course project by Emory University MBA students Joel DeRoy, Melissa Campbell, Lisa Millar, Stephen Autera, Valrie VinCola, Andreas Skyers, and Saline Hovey.

2. McDonald's Corporation 2000 annual report.

3 www.burgerking.com; www.wendys.com.

4. *Restaurants and Institutions,* July 15, 1995.

5. Hoover's database, 1996.

6. www.mcdonalds.com

7. Ibid.

8. Lisa Mirabile, *International Directory of Company Histories* (Chicago: St. James Press, 1990).

9. InvesText Company Report # 4164093, January 26, 1996.

10. Ibid.

11. Harlan Byrne, "Welcome to McWorld," *Barron's,* August 29, 1994.

12. Richard Papiernik, "Now Meet Mac-ettes," *Financial World,* April 12, 1994.

13. Jim Kirk, "McDonald's Value," *Adweek,* January 1, 1994.

14. Dow Jones Interactive.

15. *International Directory of Company Histories,* ed. Thomas Derdak.
16. Charles Bernestein, "Burger Chains Focus on Menu Quality," *Restaurants and Institutions,* July 15, 1995.
17. "Burger King Acquires 57 Restaurants: Acquisition Underscores Company's Commitment to Growth," Business Wire, January 31, 1996.
18. Wendy's 1994 annual report.
19. Marilyn Alva, "Reversal of Fortune?" *Restaurant Business,* December 10, 1995.
20. Karen Benezra, "Heavy on Beef, Lean on Identity," *Brandweek,* December 11, 1995.
21. "Struggling CKE Restaurants Posts 2d-Quarter Loss, Issues Warning," *Dow Jones Business News,* September 14, 2000.
22. This discussion is based on a course project by Emory University MBA students George Barkley, Alison Cowan, Michael Espenshade, Malou Hughes, Doris Mitterhuber, Andy Prinz, Kattia Sanchez, Erik Sjogren, and Carrie Weinberg.
23. Pizza Hut 1999 annual report.
24. Hoover's online.
25. Pizza Hut press release, February 11, 1999.
26. Mark Hamstra, "Operators See Potential in Tricon's Newest Prototype," *Nation's Restaurant News,* October 5, 1998, p. 3, 170.
27. Louise Kramer, "Papa John's blasts Rival Pizza Hut's Ad Imagery," *Advertising Age,* January 25, 1998.
28. PR Newswire, January 28, 1999.
29. "Tricon Trio Turnaround," *Food Institute Report,* January 22, 1999.
30. Tricon 1999 annual report.
31. Domino's Pizza Web site, www.dominos.com.
32. "Slice of Pizza Niche," *Nation's Restaurant News,* February 9, 1998, pp. 49–50.
33. PR Newswire, March 25, 1995.
34. Hoover's online.
35. "What's Hot," *Brunico Communications,* December 1999.
36. John Greenwald, "Slice, Dice and Devour," *Time,* October 26, 1998, pp. 64–66.

37. "Has Little Caesar's Lost the Recipe for Pizza Success?" *Houston Chronicle,* October 25, 1998, p. 3.

38. "Kmart Corporation," *Nation's Restaurant Business,* January 1998.

39. "Pizza! Pizza! Little Caesar Expands into Japan," *Nation's Restaurant Business,* January 1998.

40. This section is based on a course project by Emory University MBA students George Buckley, Patrick Dodson, Hugh Garber, Andrea N. Lauer, Robin Mohlenrich, Michael Saunders, and Miriam Taylor.

41. Alejandro Bodipo-Memba, "General Mills Now Cereal King," *Des Moines Register,* February 22, 2001, p. 6.

42. "Foods—Processed: Cold Cereal Category Monitor," *Merrill Lynch Analyst Report,* January 26, 1999.

43. Corporate Web site, www.generalmills.com.

44 *Hoover's Handbook of American Business* (Austin: Reference Press, 1998), p. 652.

45 *Commercial Appeal* (Memphis), January 26, 1999.

46. This section is based on a course project by Emory University MBA students Elissa Booth, Tom Finnegan, Derek Kittel, John Mittleman, Laura Jones, Shveta Randeria, Melinda Rogers, Matt Smith, and Lynne White.

47 *Wall Street Journal,* March 18, 1999, p. B14.

48 *Financial World,* January 18, 1994, pp. 30–32.

49. http://www.cibavision.com/home.asp

50. "Wesley Jessen VisionCare Expands Disposable Lens Manufacturing," *Chemical Business Newsbase,* March 17, 1998.

51. Laura Johannes, "Bausch & Lomb Calls Contacts Safe for Sleeping," *Wall Street Journal,* March 18, 1999, p. B14.

52. Ibid.

53. Hoover's online.

54. Cooper Companies annual report 1997.

55. "UltraVision Introduces New Aberration-Blocking Soft Disposable Contact Lenses across Canada," *Canada News Wire,* January 6, 1998.

56. This section is based on Salah Mouhawil, "Athletic Footwear Companies and the 'Rule of Three'," unpublished paper prepared for Marketing 612, Bentley College, Fall 2000.

57. This discussion is based on a course project by Emory University MBA students Pete Ballard, Roger Colson, J. P. Eggers, Sezi Giray, Julie Holter, Kerry McArdie, Don Pollock, Frank Sieper, and Enhong Wang.

58. "U.S. Market for Candy (1998)," Packaged Facts, Find/SVP database, August 1998.

59. Ibid.

60. "The Top 100 Food Companies Worldwide," *Food Engineering,* 1996 international edition.

61. "Hershey Engineers Drive Innovation," *Food Engineering,* May 1998.

62. "U.S. Market for Candy (1998)," Packaged Facts.

63. Joel Glenn Brenner, "Planet of the M&M's," *Washington Post Magazine,* April 12, 1992, p. 11

64. www.nestle.jp.

65. "U.S. Market for Candy (1998)," Packaged Facts.

66. "Nestlé Streamlines Sunmark Candy Brands," *Brandweek,* February 8, 1999.

67. "Novelty Hasn't Worn Off for Candy Manufacturer," *Discount Store News,* July 13, 1998.

68. "U.S. Market for Candy (1998)," Packaged Facts.

69. Ibid.

70. Ibid.

71. This discussion is based on a course project by Emory University MBA students Yolanda Bennett, Felix Contreras, Rebecca Gilbert, David King, Dan Michaels, and Jonathan Stelling.

72. Leah Rickard, "Gerber Trots Out New Ads," *Advertising Age,* April 11, 1994, p. 1.

73. "Baby Food," *Euromonitor,* September 1996.

74. Julie Liesse, "Ralston Spin-off Happy to be Small," *Advertising Age,* December 12, 1994.

75. "Baby Food," *Euromonitor,* September 1996.

76. Ibid.

Acknowledgments

The Rule of Three framework for the evolution of competitive markets and the creation of the "shopping mall" analogy for the hybrid of oligopolistic (full line generalists) and monopolistic competition (product and market specialists) have evolved over more than twenty years of research and consulting work. Starting in the early 1980s, we conducted industry analyses and provided strategic consulting for competitors in the appliances, automobiles, passenger tires, retailing, consumer electronics and packaged goods industries. These experiences were further enhanced when we started to work in deregulating service industries such as airlines, telecommunications, electric utilities and financial services.

We would like to, therefore, thank the many senior executives in these industries who have used the Rule of Three framework in their companies and have helped us to refine it over the years.

We would also like to acknowledge the valuable contributions, over the years, of numerous academic colleagues as well as MBA and Executive MBA students at the University of Southern California (USC), Emory University, George Mason University, and Bentley College. Their enthusiastic reception of the Rule of Three framework encouraged us to write this book.

We would like to thank Tassu Shervani, Todd Esplin, Himani Goel, Daniel Russo, Arushi Sood, and Tenzin Lama for their research assistance; and we would especially like to thank Beth Robinson and Sonya Owens for their cheerful and unfailingly efficient administrative help.

We thank G. Patton Wright for his superb support in shaping the manuscript for publication. We also thank Rafe Sagalyn, our agent, and Fred Hills, our editor at The Free Press, for their support and enthusiasm.

Finally, we would like to acknowledge the debt that we—and indeed all—thinkers about business strategy owe to the late Bruce Henderson, founder of the Boston Consulting Group (BCG). While our ideas and insights developed independently of his, it was Bruce Henderson who first noted a phenomenon similar to the one we describe here, in a BCG Perspectives piece titled "The Rule of Three and Four," issued in 1976.

Jagdish (Jag) N. Sheth
Emory University
Rajendra (Raj) S. Sisodia
Bentley College

Index

Index